CAN UNIONS SURVIVE?

CAN UNIONS SURVIVE?

The Rejuvenation of the American Labor Movement

Charles B. Craver

New York University Press
New York and London

NEW YORK UNIVERSITY PRESS
New York and London

Library of Congress Cataloging-in-Publication Data
Craver, Charles B.
Can unions survive? : the rejuvenation of the American labor
movement / Charles B. Craver.
p.   cm.
Includes bibliographical references and index.
ISBN 0-8147-1498-6
1. Trade-unions—United States—History.   2. Labor movement—
United States—History.   3. Industrial relations—United States—
History.   4. Labor laws and legislation—United States—History.
I. Title.
HD6508.C739   1993   92-40980
331.88'0973—dc20   CIP

New York University Press books are printed on acid-free paper,
and their binding materials are chosen for strength and durability.

Manufactured in the United States of America

c   10   9   8   7   6   5   4   3   2   1

Dedicated to American Workers,
Many of Whom Need a Collective Voice
to Counter the Economic Power
of Their Corporate Employers.

CONTENTS

ACKNOWLEDGMENTS

The foundation for this project began to develop while I was a graduate student at the New York State School of Industrial and Labor Relations at Cornell University. The outstanding professors at that institution introduced me to the historical, economic, and sociological concepts that are relevant to an understanding of the current plight of labor unions. I must particularly acknowledge my indebtedness to Professor Jean McKelvey, who established a learning environment that inspired each student to strive for academic excellence.

I am greatly indebted to Niko Pfund, my New York University Press editor, who initially encouraged me to write this book and who provided many suggestions that significantly improved the final product. An unnamed external reviewer also made many beneficial suggestions. Dina Gold, my research assistant, provided exemplary editorial assistance that transcended anything I had the right to expect. Marion Crain, Paul Weiler, and David Silberman reviewed the entire manuscript and made helpful comments. David Foss conscientiously made the editorial changes in the final manuscript.

I must finally thank my wife, Katey, who not only provided crucial encouragement, but also read each chapter and suggested important editorial changes.

PART ONE

I. OVERVIEW

THE INDUSTRIAL SYSTEM, it seems clear, is unfavorable to the union. Power passes to the technostructure and this lessens the conflict of interest between employer and employee which gave the union much of its reason for existence.... The union belongs to a particular stage in the development of the industrial system. When that stage passes so does the union in anything like its original position of power.[1]

[I]f there were no unions, workers would merely reinvent them. Without some kind of strong institutional voice to represent them, millions of individual workers would be completely at the mercy of giant corporate bureaucracies whose only interest is to maximize profits by minimizing the cost of labor. With all their shortcomings, the unions are the only organized voice in America that working people have.[2]

Every year, several hundred thousand unrepresented American employees are discharged without good cause. Millions more are laid off by companies that transfer their production jobs to lower wage facilities in the South or in Mexico and other developing countries. When employees at firms like Greyhound and Eastern Airlines walk out to protest wage and benefit reductions, they are permanently replaced and their representative labor organizations are destroyed. Senior personnel who participate in strikes against firms like Trans World Airlines have their hard-earned positions filled by new workers and less senior co-workers who cross the picket line during the labor dispute. Employees who strike technologically advanced corporations like AT&T discover that their employers can continue to maintain basic operations without the assistance of their regular workers. The waning economic power of organized labor makes it increasingly difficult for unionized employees to maintain beneficial compensation levels and to preserve long-term employment security.

Most unorganized workers exercise no meaningful control over these critical areas.

During the past decade, deregulation and government budget problems have led to a decrease in enforcement of health and safety laws. As a result, thousands of American workers are seriously injured each year in industrial accidents that could have been prevented through mandated periodic safety inspections. In September 1991, twenty-five workers perished during a fire at a chicken processing plant in Hamlet, North Carolina.[3] Their nonunion facility had not been inspected by safety and health officials for more than a decade. The locked fire exits that would have been easily discovered during a walk-through inspection prevented the escape of the persons trapped in the burning building. Conscientious shop stewards would not have permitted those safety law violations to continue.

Although the Employee Retirement Income Security Act[4] requires private corporations to fund their pension plans in an actuarily sound manner, millions of workers are discovering that their bankrupt and dishonest employers did not make the requisite fund contributions.[5] Individuals who expected reasonable pension benefits are receiving substantially reduced retirement checks. If the retirement programs of these employees had been jointly administered by union and management trustees, it is more likely that the statutorily prescribed premiums would have been paid.

As the American labor movement begins its second century, it is confronted by challenges that threaten its very existence. In 1954, union members constituted 35 percent of nonagricultural labor force participants.[6] By 1980, this rate had declined to 23 percent, and by 1991, union membership represented a mere 16 percent of nonagricultural workers.[7] Labor organizations that had won 70 to 86 percent of representation elections conducted by the National Labor Relations Board during the 1940s and 61 to 75 percent of the elections held during the 1950s[8] prevailed in fewer than half of the elections held during 1991.[9] If this downward trend continues, unions will represent a mere 5 percent of private sector personnel by the year 2000.[10]

Many people believe that labor institutions possess too much power, support economically inefficient work rules, and provide representational services that are not needed by individuals employed by contemporary business enterprises. Employers disseminate information designed to convince white-collar and professional employees that labor organizations benefit only working class persons. In "classless" American society, the vast majority of individuals consider themselves part of the ubiquitous "middle class"; no one wants to be characterized as "working class."

A significant factor contributing to the erosion of public support for unions is the highly publicized disclosures of illegal behavior by some labor officials.[11] A federal court recently placed the Teamsters Union in a trusteeship to root out corrupt officials; numerous union leaders have been tied to underworld crime families; and various business agents have been imprisoned for the embezzlement of union welfare funds. When labor officials are involved, media stories frequently employ pejorative terms such as "organized crime" and "racketeering" to describe their conduct. When business leaders misuse client or company funds, however, the less opprobrious term "white-collar crime" is generally used.

The unconscionable sweatshop conditions that were pervasive in the early twentieth century have been substantially eliminated, and the labor movement has directly or indirectly[12] established fundamental industrial justice in the workplace. As a result, the moral fervor of the crusading union sympathizers of the past is rarely seen today.[13] The charismatic instigators of social reform and economic equality who previously inspired millions of workers to unite in progressive labor organizations are gone, and few current labor representatives are able to generate similar intensity.[14]

Many contemporary union leaders exude a complacency typified by former AFL-CIO president George Meany, who frequently indicated that he was not overly concerned with the level of union membership:

Why should we worry about organizing groups of people who do not want to be organized? If they prefer to have others speak for them and make the decisions which affect their lives, without effective participation on their part, that is their right. . . . I used to worry about the size of the membership. But quite a few years ago I just stopped worrying about it, because to me it doesn't make any difference.[15]

Numerous lower level union representatives exhibit a similar ideological insouciance.

Changing demographic, industrial, and technological conditions have also undermined labor cohesiveness and effectiveness. During the past several decades, the composition and location of the labor force have dramatically changed. The participation rate for women, traditionally employed in unorganized occupations, has significantly expanded.[16] The labor force participation rate for minority persons has also increased.[17] Labor organizations that have not been historically responsive to the needs of female and minority employees must modify their bargaining objectives to appeal to these new labor force entrants.

One of the most striking demographic trends over the past two decades has been the migration of employees and jobs from the Northeast and North Central areas of the country to the South and Southwest. The population and industrial migration from the Rustbelt to the Sunbelt is likely to continue. More than half of all union members presently reside in Rustbelt states.[18] Unions will have to recruit members in other regions if they are to retain their economic viability.

The increased incorporation of new technologies in the workplace has significantly altered the structure of the American economy. The substitution of capital for labor in the manufacturing area has cost many organized blue-collar personnel their jobs and generated a concomitant increase in nonunion white-collar positions. The employees performing unskilled production functions lack the capacity to exert substantial economic pressure against their automated and diversified employers, and labor organizations have difficulty using traditional bargaining techniques to enhance the employment rights of those individuals.[19]

The technological developments that have significantly modified the structure of the American economy have contributed greatly to the internationalization of the global economic system. By the year 2000, several hundred multinational corporations will dominate world trade. The developed nations provide the capital-intensive technologies, the consumer markets, and the distribution systems, while the developing countries provide low cost labor. The proliferation of low cost "export platforms" has caused the export of many blue-collar production jobs. If labor organizations want to meaningfully influence the employment policies of international businesses, they must coordinate their efforts with unions located in the other countries in which those enterprises operate.

Demographic, industrial, and technological changes do not entirely explain the decline in labor union membership over the past thirty years in the United States. Many of the same industrial and technological phenomena have also occurred in Canada, yet the labor movement there has not suffered a similar fate. Approximately 35 percent of Canadian employees are union members, and 45 percent continue to be covered by collective bargaining agreements.[20] Even the membership rosters of industrial unions such as the Steelworkers and the Automobile Workers have continued to grow during the past twenty years.[21]

A major distinction between American and Canadian business entities is the great antipathy United States employers have exhibited toward the organizational rights of their employees. A recent survey found that 95 percent of private sector companies in the United States actively resist labor organizing efforts.[22] Corporations have developed sophisticated election appeals designed to convince workers that labor organizations merely exact exorbitant dues in exchange for minimal benefits and diminish the professional image of those whom they represent. More aggressive anti-union techniques transcend behavior manipulation and involve overtly unlawful tactics in violation of federal labor law. Key union supporters are regularly discharged, and express or implied threats are made regarding the loss of employment security that would result from unionization.[23] It has been estimated that legal and unlawful management opposition to employee organization accounts for as much as 40 percent of the declining success rate of unions in National Labor Relations Board representation elections.[24]

Is the decline of the American labor movement symptomatic of a terminal condition? Will the country continue its inexorable transition toward the end of the union era? As white-collar employees and technological innovations supplant blue-collar workers and industrial behaviorists humanize employment environments, some observers conclude that union representation will no longer be necessary.[25] Others, however, predict that labor organizations can be rejuvenated if they revolutionize their objectives and modernize their tactics.[26] Before examining the future viability of trade unions, it would be beneficial to acknowledge the impact unions have upon the employment conditions and rights of employees.

When most people think of the benefits provided by labor organizations, they generally consider the economic gains achieved by unionized employees. Such a view is reinforced by empirical data demonstrating that organized workers earn more than their unorganized cohorts.[27] Not only do represented personnel usually receive higher wages, but they also tend to be covered by more generous benefit programs. They are more likely to have health coverage and pension plans. Many have dental and eye coverage, and some even receive limited legal care. The ability of labor organizations to increase labor costs above market levels is normally attributed to the "monopoly" effect that enables unions to restrict the group of individuals who may be employed by a particular firm.

Unorganized employees benefit indirectly from the successful bargaining activities of labor organizations. Their employers frequently provide compensation and fringe benefit packages that are competitive with those enjoyed by unionized employees to dissuade them from organizing.[28] These employers recognize that if the benefits they pay their workers fall too far below those earned by unionized personnel, their employees may contemplate organizational activity.

The economic gains achieved directly and indirectly by labor organizations should not be overemphasized. Through the collective voice exerted by organized groups, workers are also able to advance nonmonetary interests.[29] For example, collective bargaining agreement provisions generally preclude discipline except for "just cause." In the absence of such a contractual restriction, private sector employers are free in the United States to terminate or otherwise discipline employees for good cause, bad cause, or no cause at all, unless such action contravenes a specific statutory proscription.[30] Because private corporations are not "state actors"—i.e., they do not function as governmental entities—they are not subject to the substantive and procedural limitations imposed on federal, state, and municipal employers under the United States Constitution. As a result, private sector employees enjoy no free speech or due process rights vis-à-vis their own employers.

Contractual clauses typically establish orderly layoff and recall procedures. Specific terms often require the application of objective promotional criteria. Seniority provisions normally determine shift, transfer, and vacation preferences. Other employment rights and benefits that would normally be left to employer discretion may similarly be defined in collective bargaining agreements. When unionized employees are not satisfied with the manner in which contractual terms are interpreted and applied, they may seek redress through grievance-arbitration procedures.

Business enterprises depend on the input of three fundamental groups: investors, managers, and workers. As each of these groups competes for a greater share of profits and for more control over corporate decision making, individual employees are at a distinct disadvantage. Investment capital is a highly mobile commodity. For this reason, companies seeking investment capital provide prospective stock or bond holders with detailed information regarding the proposed venture.[31] Federal and state securities statutes also protect investors by mandating the disclosure of relevant financial data to anyone thinking of providing monetary support. When investors become disenchanted with the performance of a particular corporation, they can simply sell their shares and transfer the proceeds to different ventures.

Professional managers may similarly protect their own interests. Those with relatively unique skills can negotiate long-term contracts that provide "golden parachutes" in case the business relationship is terminated prematurely. High-level executives are normally acquainted with their counterparts at other business entities, and they can use those contacts to locate other employment opportunities if they decide to leave their current firms.

Rank-and-file employees do not enjoy such privileges. They are fortunate to have one or two job opportunities at any given time. Prospective employers feel no need to give them detailed information regarding firm affairs. Once workers accept employment with a specific company, they enjoy minimal mobility. They have limited information about other job openings and the transaction costs associated with relocation may be substantial. When workers change jobs, they may lose some or all of their pension rights, and they must forfeit seniority, thus significantly jeopardizing their future employment security.

It is ironic that the individuals who possess the least mobility normally exercise only marginal control over their employment destiny. Unorganized workers are generally powerless to negotiate with employers over their wages, hours, and working conditions. They must accept the terms offered or look for alternative employment. If they are directed to submit to drug testing or to engage in particularly arduous tasks, they have no real choice but to submit or forsake employment with that particular employer. This loss of personal freedom results directly from the considerable inequality of bargaining power that exists between the individual employee and corporate managers.

The substantial decline in union strength over the past several decades has deprived most workers of meaningful collective representation. If labor organizations become wholly ineffective, many employers will undoubtedly exploit their employees by retaining an excessive portion of profits, maintaining substandard working conditions, and subjecting low-level personnel to arbitrary treatment. In the absence of a viable labor movement, federal and state legislators will be less inclined to support statutes protecting worker interests.

Although industrial democracy restricts managerial freedom, it can also enhance economic efficiency. Nonunionized employees who are dissatisfied with their working conditions can only demonstrate their displeasure through resort to the "exit voice."[32] When disenchanted people voluntarily terminate their employment, their employer must assume the costs associated with recruiting and training other workers. In contrast, the collective bargaining process provides employees with the opportunity to modify unsatisfactory conditions.[33] To the extent individuals are permitted to influence employment conditions and business decisions that impact on their economic futures, they are more likely to have a personal commitment to the enterprise. They are more inclined to agree with the final determinations made, and as a result to be more cooperative and productive workers. Unionization not only benefits employees and employers, but also society as a whole.

Although some labor organizations have not always acted as responsible employee representatives, most unions have worked appropriately to advance the rights of workers. If employee organizations can no longer enhance the employment conditions of employees, we will witness a return to traditional master-servant relationships. Individual employees will be unable to influence the terms of their employment, and employers will be able to impose arbitrary conditions. If the balance of power between labor and management is to be maintained at all, labor unions must be preserved. This book explores the actions required if labor organizations are to be rejuvenated.

Chapter 2 traces the historical development of labor organizations in the United States from social and professional orders to business institutions. This background provides a broad perspective on the current plight of unions and an understanding of the measures labor unions must take if they are to function as vital forces in the 21st century. Chapter 3 focuses on the actual extent of union decline and examines the demographic, industrial, technological, sociological, and international trends contributing to that deterioration. Chapter 4 discusses the need for unions to improve their public image and to develop innovative techniques to organize occupations that have traditionally been unreceptive to unionization. Chapter 5 analyzes the means by which labor organizations may increase worker empowerment and advance their employment conditions. It also examines how international union cooperation must be developed to counterbalance the activities of transnational business enterprises. Finally, chapter 6 focuses on the National Labor Relations Act. Specifically, it considers the need for congressional action to revitalize the NLRA by enhancing the organization and collective bargaining rights of employees, deterring unlawful employer conduct, and reaffirming the legislative objectives underlying the original 1935 enactment.

2. THE HISTORICAL FOUNDATION OF AMERICAN LABOR

During the Colonial period, there were relatively few free workers.[1] The great majority of laborers were either slaves or indentured servants. As trade and commerce expanded, there was an increased demand for unconstrained workers. Skilled craftsmen who established small stores preferred to hire nonindentured individuals whom they could lay off when business slackened. As the terms of indentured servants expired and numerous craftsmen immigrated to the New World from Europe, lured by the comparatively high wages paid for skilled labor and the glowing accounts of life in America, the number of unencumbered wage earners steadily increased.

In most early shops, there was no well-defined distinction between the interests of the master and the other workers. Journeymen hoped to become master craftsmen, and apprentices looked forward to the attainment of journeyman status. The product market was localized, and the master bargained directly with customers regarding product pricing. Because of the relative scarcity of competent skilled labor, masters could generally establish noncompetitive prices. As a result, wage rates tended to exceed those available in Europe. This did not, however, guarantee beneficial employment conditions for all journeymen and apprentices. They still had to be concerned with competition from slaves and indentured workers. When business declined, nonindentured workers were frequently laid off.

CRAFT GUILDS

Rudimentary labor organizations existed in the colonies as early as the seventeenth century. They were primarily guilds comprised of artisans who marketed their own products. They endeavored to preserve professional standards by regulating apprenticeship requirements and exerting control over wage rates and product pricing. The few work stoppages that occurred during the colonial period did not involve strikes by workers seeking improved compensation and employment conditions from masters, but protests by master craftsmen against local government regulations that relaxed apprenticeship requirements or established price ceilings.

The first genuine labor strike occurred in 1786, when a group of Philadelphia printers "turned out" in favor of a minimum wage of $6.00 per week. Although the employers initially resisted their demand, the printers ultimately prevailed. Nonetheless, it was not until 1792 that any continuing organization of wage earners was formed. In that year, the Philadelphia shoemakers created a trade union that existed for approximately one year. Other localized craft unions were formed throughout the country. Although many functioned as fraternal social orders, they sought higher wages, shorter hours, the enforcement of strict apprenticeship regulations, and a closed shop precluding the employment of nonmembers.

Initial Judicial Opposition to Organized Labor

Early judicial decisions severely restricted the ability of workers to engage in concerted activity to further their economic interests. Judges found that collective action by journeymen constituted either restraints upon trade in violation of antitrust doctrines or criminal conspiracies against public welfare. Even sympathy strikes and peaceful consumer boycotts were considered illegal.

The first major decision to acknowledge the legitimacy of concerted worker action was *Commonwealth v. Hunt*.[2] Chief Justice Shaw of the Supreme Judicial Court of Massachusetts refused to permit application of the traditional criminal conspiracy doctrine to peaceful group conduct seeking enhanced employment terms. The Court found that allegations that the defendants had agreed among themselves not to work for any master who employed nonunion workers were not alone sufficient to establish criminal liability. The Court further ruled that the mere fact that this association had caused a loss of work to nonunion journeymen was not illegal, so long as inappropriate means were not utilized to injure such nonunion individuals.

Early Labor Involvement in the Political Arena

In 1834, the National Trades Union (NTU), the first national labor organization in the United States, was formed. The delegates approved a platform in favor of manual schools, reduced working hours, and the maintenance of established wage rates, but they opposed the employment of women outside the home. Most of the early craft guilds feared that the employment of female workers would undermine guild wage rates, and they generally discouraged the employment of women. Although the NTU constitution expressly excluded political action, it became apparent that many of the organization's basic objectives could not be achieved without direct political activity. As a result, members formed the Working Men's Party, the first political party of working people in the world. The new labor party was not received warmly by established politicians who endeavored to divert the activist laborers into conventional party channels. The party sought to maintain its own worker identity, but became defunct by 1931.

Despite judicial hostility toward worker collective action, strikes occurred repeatedly throughout the 1840s and 1850s. Some entailed spontaneous employee walkouts protesting unilateral changes in working conditions, while others were orchestrated by labor groups seeking improved employment terms. These work stoppages usually involved skilled personnel. Some achieved limited success, while others ended in failure.

EGALITARIAN ASSOCIATIONS

In 1866, seventy-seven delegates from various craft organizations met in Baltimore to establish the National Labor Union (NLU). The NLU was a loosely connected federation of national trade unions, city trades assemblies, local trade unions, and reform organizations of various kinds. The leaders of the new worker association opposed strikes, which they said were "productive of great injury to laboring classes, . . . have been injudicious and ill-advised, and the result of impulse rather than principle."[3] They alternatively recommended more frequent reliance upon arbitration committees to resolve labor-management controversies. The NLU sought eight-hour statutes, equal pay for equal work regardless of the race or gender of those performing the work, and full employment and organizational rights for both women and blacks. Nonetheless, William Silvis, one of the NLU founders, indicated that while the NLU was obliged to advance the interests of female workers, he did not think that women belonged in the labor force. He also believed that women who were compelled to work outside the home should remain in traditional female occupations. Although many NLU leaders supported a national agenda, most members were primarily interested in local issues. Following the death of William Silvis in 1869, the organization began to decline. By 1872, it had virtually disappeared.

The Knights of Labor

The Panic of 1873 ushered in a six-year period of economic depression that significantly undermined worker organizing. Many existing craft unions experienced both membership declines and financial hardships. The railroad strikes during the summer of 1877, precipitated by wage reductions, were particularly violent. Federal troops and state militia were called out to restore order. These tumultuous work stoppages provided the public with graphic evidence of the dire consequences associated with deteriorating labor-management relationships. Americans began to recognize that they could not escape the conflicts between labor and capital that had begun to challenge the governments of various European nations.

One of the important labor organizations to survive the 1873–79 depression was the Noble Order of the Knights of Labor, established by Philadelphia tailors in 1869. The leaders of this new union realized that the lack of strength that trade unions had exhibited during the depression years was in large part attributable to the lack of real labor unity. They believed that power would come from a consolidation of all labor groups in a single organization that included both skilled and unskilled workers. They welcomed into their ranks all working people, regardless of race or gender, even members of the professions and employers.

The Knights established expansive objectives. They sought to secure for workers "a proper share of the wealth that they create; more leisure that belongs to them; more societary advantages; more of the benefits, privileges and emoluments of the world."[4] The organization called for the establishment of producer and consumer cooperatives, and the creation of cultural orders. It proposed that arbitration procedures be substituted for disruptive work stoppages and advocated eight-hour laws and regulations mandating equal pay for equal work regardless of gender.

The Knights of Labor was a highly structured organization that sought to achieve an amalgam of local unions in a nationwide federation. Since the local union assemblies included both skilled and unskilled workers, they resembled hybrid combinations of craft unions and industrial unions. The sympathy strike became a particularly potent economic weapon, with the collective power of the skilled trades enhancing the clout of the unskilled personnel. The Knights also employed consumer boycotts to further their objectives.

When concerted economic action could not achieve more expansive goals, the Knights resorted to political action. They created various labor parties, which ultimately ran political candidates in thirty-four of the nation's thirty-five states. Some labor party candidates were elected to various state and local offices. The individuals occupying such political positions were able to exercise a degree of authority that transcended the influence possessed by conventional labor union officials.

Terence Powderly succeeded Uriah Stephens as Grand Master Workman in 1879. One of his early accomplishments was an agreement with Cardinal Gibbons that acknowledged that the Knights of Labor was a bona fide labor organization, and not a secret revolutionary society that contravened the teachings of the Catholic church. This accord precluded a church ban that would have severely undermined organizational membership.

Not only did Terence Powderly lead the Knights of Labor until 1893, but he also served three two-year terms as mayor of Scranton, Pennsylvania, from 1879 to 1884. After he stepped down as Grand Master Workman, he was appointed by President William McKinley to a post in the United States Department of Commerce. Powderly did not believe in traditional trade unions and considered the strike an ineffectual and detrimental device, but he worked diligently to enhance the rights of workers. When the Knights established funds to support strikes conducted by local affiliates, despite Powderly's personal opposition to work stoppages, it was agreed that job actions would only be employed when labor and management differences could not be resolved through negotiation or arbitration.

A turning point for the Knights of Labor came when it negotiated employment terms with financier Jay Gould, who operated the southwestern portion of the Wabash Railroad. Gould initially refused to recognize the right of the Knights of Labor to speak for the workers. A strike commenced on August 18, 1885. By the end of the month, Gould had agreed to meet with Powderly and to authorize his executives to negotiate a collective agreement. In early 1886, however, branches of the Gould railroad refused to honor the accord. A strike on the Texas Pacific began on March 1, 1886, but the union was unable to achieve its objective. Gould refused to fulfill a commitment Powderly thought he had made to arbitrate the unresolved issues. When the Knights sought to terminate the work stoppage, the railroad refused to reinstate half the strikers, including those who had been the most active strike supporters. The union thereafter tried to regenerate the work stoppage, but was ultimately forced to acknowledge that the job action had failed.

The Knights of Labor suffered a similar defeat in the anthracite coal fields of Pennsylvania. Union leaders proposed a wage increase, but Lehigh operators refused to bargain over the worker demands. A work stoppage began in September 1887. Workers at nonstruck mines provided sympathy support for the Lehigh strikers, and other coal operators assisted the Lehigh operators by supplying them with coal they needed to satisfy customer demands. Members of the Knights of Labor working for Reading operators who were sending coal to struck Lehigh operators refused to load coal onto Lehigh barges. Railroad employees similarly refused to handle coal being sent from Reading mines to the Lehigh area. The sympathetic Reading miners and railroad workers were discharged, and the affected mine worker and railroad local unions were destroyed.

Private security forces significantly enhanced the ability of companies to withstand strike activity. They ejected union sympathizers from plant premises and employed tough tactics to suppress concerted job actions. When major disturbances occurred, local police and even state militia were called upon to protect the interests of the affected employer. Because employees did not have a legally protected right to strike, companies affected by work stoppages frequently terminated the strike participants. They used private security officers to eject the discharged individuals from plant premises and to ensure that they would not return.

Haymarket Square and the Demise of the Knights

By 1886, membership in the Knights of Labor began to decline. On May 4 of that year, employees of the McCormick Reaper Company went on strike seeking higher wages and reduced hours. Strike leaders called a mass meeting at Haymarket Square to protest police and company tactics. A crowd of 1,000 to 3,000 union sympathizers assembled to listen to various speakers. The Chicago police provided a force of 180 officers to maintain control. After several people spoke and the initial crowd began to depart, a police detachment inexplicably marched toward the wagon on which anarchist Samuel Fielden was speaking. A bomb was tossed among the police by a bystander, causing the death of seven persons, including several police officers. Many well-known anarchists were arrested, with murder indictments being quickly returned against ten, including one person who was never apprehended and another who agreed to testify for the prosecution. Although no defendant was directly connected to the Haymarket Square bombing, all eight were convicted. Seven defendants received the death penalty, while the eighth was given a fifteen-year prison term.

Church leaders and newspaper editors condemned the Haymarket Square incident. Although the person who actually threw the bomb was never identified, many members of the general public attributed the heinous act to labor sympathizers. As a result, public support for organized labor declined dramatically. By the end of the 1880s, the Knights of Labor was no longer a viable organization.

THE TRADE UNION MOVEMENT

By the late 1870s, labor leaders began to recognize the need for a national federation of trade unions. They did not consider the Knights of Labor to be a true labor entity. Unlike most existing trade unions that were organized along narrow craft lines, the Knights of Labor was an egalitarian institution that admitted both skilled and unskilled workers. In 1878, President Joseph Bishop of the Amalgamated Association of Iron and Steel Workers invited other trade unions to send delegates to a special conference that would explore the manner in which such a trade union federation could be established.

On August 2, 1881, a convention of United States and Canadian labor leaders was held in Terre Haute, Indiana, and a follow-up conference was conducted on November 15, 1881, in Pittsburgh. The delegates who attended hoped to establish a trade union federation patterned after the Trades Union Congress in England. Although officials from various Knights of Labor affiliates attended the Pittsburgh conference, the more conventional ideas of the trade unionists prevailed. The Federation of Organized Trades and Labor Unions of the United States and Canada was born.

The preamble for the new Federation contained rhetoric typical of labor institutions of the nineteenth century, declaring that "a struggle is going on in the nations of the civilized world between oppressors and oppressed of all countries, a struggle between capital and labor, which must grow in intensity from year to year and work disastrous results to the toiling millions of all nations if not combined for mutual protection and benefit."[5] The initial Federation objectives were traditional: restrictions on the use of child and immigrant labor; prohibitions against the use of scrip instead of cash to compensate workers; uniform apprentice regulations; eight-hour legislation; and endorsement of protective tariffs.

The Federation initially experienced financial difficulties and minimal growth. The competition between the Federation and the Knights of Labor continued. In 1886, Federation leaders assembled a group of national trade union officials in Philadelphia "to protect our respective organizations from the malicious work of an element who openly boast 'that trade unions must be destroyed.' "[6] A committee drafted a "treaty" that was to be presented to the Knights of Labor. It would have severely restricted the labor activities that could be conducted by the Knights and would have effectively rendered that entity a social and educational order. The Knights did not take definitive action with respect to the Federation proposal.

The American Federation of Labor

On November 10, 1886, the Federation convened a conference of trade unions in Columbus, Ohio. The delegates passed resolutions encouraging the American trade union movement and supporting the establishment of trade assemblies and councils. They also proposed transforming the Federation into an American Federation of Labor (AFL), with Samuel Gompers elected as first president of the new organization. Despite their previous interorganizational rivalry, the AFL convention paid tribute to the past accomplishments of the Knights of Labor.

Gompers had a significant impact upon the evolution of the AFL. With the exception of one year in the mid–1890s, he served as president from 1886 until 1924. Even though he never controlled any national trade union and faced constant opposition to his policies from other AFL officials and members, Gompers dramatically influenced the development of business unionism in the United States. Gompers recognized that the United States economy was expanding and realized that such circumstances would permit the continued elevation of real wages. He acknowledged that American social and political conditions were not supportive of open class hostility, and counseled reliance on political action and traditional trade union collective conduct.

The early years of the AFL were not particularly auspicious. Some of the affiliated trade unions feared that the new federation might expand its power base at the expense of member union autonomy. Other unions complained about the financial cost of AFL affiliation. Gompers attempted to assuage these concerns by emphasizing the degree of organizational freedom retained by AFL affiliates. "The American Federation of Labor avoids the fatal rock upon which all previous attempts to affect the unity of the working class have split, by leaving to each body or affiliated organization the complete management of its own affairs, especially its own particular trade affairs."[7] He also agreed at the 1887 convention to recommend a reduction in the per capita tax contributed to the AFL on behalf of affiliate members.

Unlike the Knights of Labor, the AFL refused to admit to membership organizations that did not function primarily as trade unions. The AFL sought to preserve the craft exclusivity of each affiliate, to avoid injurious jurisdictional disputes. In addition, the AFL refused to endorse the People's Party, which the Knights of Labor supported. Despite the reluctance of AFL leaders to support a separate labor party, they were not indifferent to the political process. They employed traditional lobbying techniques to obtain passage of laws that provided beneficial employment conditions, and they endorsed Democratic and Republican candidates who favored legislation of interest to organized labor.

During the 1890s, organized labor was active in the legislative arena. Through diligent lobbying efforts, the AFL and other unions were able to achieve the enactment of various state and federal laws that were of significant benefit to workers. Some mandated a shorter work day, several sought to eliminate the worst sweatshops by prohibiting manufacturing in tenement dwellings, others abolished the use of company scrip to compensate employees, and a few proscribed anti-union discrimination. Many of these legislative accomplishments, however, were ephemeral. Corporations expeditiously challenged the propriety of such legal restrictions, and they frequently found a sympathetic judiciary. Relying upon such legal doctrines as "freedom of contract" and the sanctity of "property rights," state and federal courts struck down approximately sixty labor and employment enactments by 1900.

By the conclusion of the nineteenth century, Gompers and other labor leaders had to acknowledge that political action could not always provide lasting results. Even when they were able to prevail upon state or federal legislators to enact laws protecting fundamental employee interests, employers could seek the assistance of an accommodating judiciary. By emphasizing the need to preserve complete freedom of contract, business entities were successful in negating the effectiveness of labor lobbying efforts. AFL leaders could no longer rely upon the political process to subdue the "tyranny of capital." "Labor does not depend on legislation. It asks ... no favors from the State. It wants to be let alone and to be allowed to exercise its rights."[8] Trade union officials began to recognize that they would have to secure worker protections through the traditional collective bargaining process.[9]

Despite Gompers' pessimism with respect to the efficacy of political action, the AFL continued to seek legislation favorable to workers. It also continued its effort to convince courts that such enactments should not be considered impermissible infringements on contractual freedom. In 1916, organized labor finally induced Congress to adopt the Adamson Act,[10] which established the eight-hour day principle. In *Wilson v. New*,[11] the Supreme Court sustained the constitutionality of that enactment. Yellow-dog contracts were successfully outlawed in the Norris-LaGuardia Act.[12] In *Phelps Dodge Corp. v. NLRB*,[13] the Supreme Court acknowledged that the freedom of contract reasoning employed previously in cases like *Adair v. United States*[14] could no longer withstand judicial scrutiny.

Anti-Labor Responses to the AFL

As AFL affiliates expanded their organizing activities, they encountered stiff opposition from both employers and government officials. Private guards, state militia, and federal troops were employed to negate the impact of collective worker action. Judges and prosecutors were used to imprison those union leaders with the temerity to defy injunctive orders. Organized labor began to realize how difficult it was to exert sustained economic pressure against major corporations.

By the early twentieth century, most private employers were unalterably opposed to employee unionization. Many companies joined business organizations designed to prevent their workers from becoming trade union members. Businesses were cautioned about the economic power of unions and encouraged to inhibit the spread of organized labor.

Many regional employer associations were developed to assist companies seeking to prevent the spread of unionization.[15] A group of corporations trying to defeat organizing drives conducted by the International Association of Machinists established the Independent Labor League of America. They enrolled machinists who were willing to act as strikebreakers.[16] By 1911, their organization had recruited 6,600 machinists in Chicago alone. With the assistance of private security companies, Independent League members infiltrated unions with spies. Other employer groups also utilized espionage to ascertain secret labor plans in an effort to thwart organizational objectives. Companies regularly required workers to sign yellow-dog contracts barring membership in labor organizations. Individuals discharged as a result of their union membership often had their names placed on "black lists" that were circulated to other companies in the area to prevent their future employment with them.

The American Anti-Boycott Association was formed for the purpose of prosecuting court cases against boycotts and sympathy strikes.[17] Members routinely sought injunctive orders against such collective action, and monetary damages against unions and labor leaders who disobeyed judicial edicts. Businesses also enlisted the aid of state and local police forces. Trespass, disorderly conduct, and traffic obstruction laws were frequently applied to strike conduct.[18]

State and federal judges continued to apply antitrust and criminal conspiracy doctrines to even peaceful collective action. Combinations of workers were regularly found to interfere impermissibly with free trade and commerce. These groups openly endeavored to inhibit the associational freedom that had already been recognized as an inherent right of all free laborers in other industrial nations.

AFL leaders continued to lobby for legislation that would acknowledge the legitimacy of concerted worker conduct and prevent judicial interference with such activities. Organized labor thought it had finally achieved this objective when Congress adopted the Clayton Act[19] in 1914. Section 6 of that enactment provided employees with what Samuel Gompers characterized as the "Industrial Magna Carta."[20]

> The labor of a human being is not a commodity or article of commerce. Nothing contained in the antitrust laws shall be construed to forbid the existence and operation of labor . . . organizations, instituted for the purposes of mutual help . . . or to forbid or restrain individual members of such organizations from lawfully carrying out the legitimate objects thereof; nor shall such organizations, or the members thereof, be held or construed to be illegal combinations or conspiracies in restraint of trade, under the antitrust laws.[21]

Section 20 of the Clayton Act further provided that no federal court could issue a restraining order or injunction in any case involving a peaceful labor dispute between an employer and employees.

Although it appeared that Congress had finally emancipated organized labor from the constraints of the federal antitrust laws, the United States Supreme Court did not entirely agree. In *Duplex Printing Press Co. v. Deering*,[22] the Court severely restricted application of the immunity provided by Section 20 of the Clayton Act. It ruled that the antitrust and injunctive exemptions only applied in situations in which the disputing parties had a direct employer-employee relationship. Because secondary boycott activity necessarily involved participation by persons employed by parties not involved in the immediate labor-management dispute, such conduct was automatically beyond the scope of the Clayton Act exemption.

The Wobblies Challenge Traditional Trade Unions

Despite virulent employer opposition and unfavorable judicial decisions, organized labor prospered. Between 1897 and 1904, union membership increased from 447,000 to over 2,000,000. At this point, the AFL craft union philosophy was challenged by a radically different labor institution. In June 1905, a group of revolutionary activists, including Eugene Debs, William Haywood, Father Thomas Haggerty, and "Mother" Mary Jones, convened a Chicago conference attended by 203 delegates representing 43 associations. The convention voted to create the Industrial Workers of the World (IWW). The opening line of the newly drafted IWW preamble bluntly declared that "[t]he working class and the employing class have nothing in common."[23] The IWW endorsed both industrial and political action.

During the initial years of its existence, the IWW abandoned the most anarchistic Socialists in its ranks, such as the leaders of the Western Federation of Miners. It did not, however, entirely discard its left-wing political ideals. It supported Socialist party candidates, including Debs, who received 900,000 votes in the 1912 presidential election.[24] The Wobblies also employed conventional labor tactics, such as strikes. Nonetheless, they found that their work stoppages were less effective than those conducted by AFL affiliates. This phenomenon was attributed to the greater degree of control exercised by AFL trade unions over their respective crafts, the more experienced AFL union leadership, and the more substantial financial resources available to AFL organizations. By 1915, the IWW had become more conventional in its approach. It sought to organize agricultural laborers and other unskilled workers. It successfully unionized farm personnel in several states.

During World War I, IWW work stoppages in the lumber and copper industries generated severe attacks from citizens' groups and the federal government. Many persons accused the radical IWW leaders of deliberately sabotaging America's war effort. Criminal syndicalist statutes were enacted in various states prohibiting any "doctrine which advocates crime, violence, sabotage or other unlawful methods as a means of industrial or political reform."[25] Several thousand Wobbly supporters were imprisoned, and several immigrant sympathizers were even deported. This relentless prosecution of IWW members and the concomitant loss of public support greatly diminished its organizational strength. By the later 1920s, the IWW had ceased to be a viable labor entity.

Women, Minorities, and the AFL

Although the IWW diligently sought to organize women workers, most AFL affiliates did not vigorously represent the interests of female employees. From 1890 until 1910, the number of female labor force participants grew from 4,005,532 to 8,075,772.[26] Despite this dramatic increase in women workers, females remained an insignificant proportion of union membership. By 1910, only 73,000 women were trade union members.[27] In 1914, the AFL convention almost passed a resolution deploring the gainful employment of women.[28] AFL leaders began to realize that unorganized women workers posed a threat to the negotiated wages and employment conditions enjoyed by male union members. The 1918 AFL convention thus adopted a resolution exhorting affiliated trade unions "to make every effort to bring . . . women into the organizations of their respective crafts."[29] In spite of this more affirmative position, the AFL took no action against gender restrictions imposed by member unions.[30]

The failure of AFL affiliates to unionize women workers was not based upon any apparent female reluctance to participate in labor organizations. In fact, when female leaders recognized that most male trade unions were unwilling to admit women, they got together and formed their own labor organization. In 1903, representatives from the clerks, garment workers, and meat cutters unions drafted a constitution at the AFL convention creating the separate Women's Trade Union League (WTUL). Over the next fifteen years, WTUL affiliates, composed primarily of women workers, grew appreciably.

Unions quickly found that women workers were not afraid of traditional labor-management confrontation. In November of 1909, 150 female employees of the Triangle Shirtwaist factory in New York City were locked out after they joined the International Ladies Garment Workers Union. When the women established a picket line, private security personnel hired by Triangle Shirtwaist attacked them. After the striking employees were arrested, 20,000 unorganized employees responded by walking out of every shirtwaist factory in Manhattan and Brooklyn. When the Triangle Shirtwaist job action commenced, not a single New York garment shop was organized. By the time the strike ended thirteen weeks later, 312 clothing factories had signed union contracts.

The AFL unions' treatment of minority workers was similar to their treatment of female employees. Despite efforts by Gompers to induce trade unions to eliminate constitutional provisions restricting membership to white males, many affiliates continued to exclude minority workers. In his report to the 1900 AFL convention, Gompers warned delegates that if blacks were not permitted to unionize, "they will not only be forced down in the economic scale and used against any effort made by us for our economic and social advancement, but race prejudice will be made more bitter and [result in] the injury of all."[31] The following year, however, when a St. Louis Trades and Labor Council official opposed the granting of an AFL organizer's commission to a black individual, Gompers acquiesced. After World War I, thousands of southern black workers migrated to northern states. Because they were unable to obtain skilled jobs with employers that had closed-shop agreements with trade unions that did not admit black members, many were forced to work as strikebreakers. AFL leaders finally sought to achieve a compromise by issuing separate charters to black unions.

In 1934, a proposal was made at the AFL convention to expel international unions that were guilty of racial discrimination. Many delegates argued that such action would contravene the principle of affiliate autonomy that had been a traditional aspect of AFL existence, and their view prevailed. Even though most AFL unions voluntarily eliminated restrictions against minority membership, it was not until passage of the Civil Rights Act of 1964 that the few remaining affiliates relented.

Time-Study Men and Company Unions

By the 1920s, American companies realized that yellow-dog contracts, black lists, private security forces, and accommodating judges could not always prevent labor organizing. They began to devise more sophisticated union avoidance techniques. "The emerging professional middle class stepped into the fray in the role of peacemakers. Their message to the capitalists was that nonviolent social control would in the long run be more effective than bullets and billy clubs."[32] Acknowledging that "a cadre of professionals was cheaper than an army of Pinkertons" and fearing that skilled workers had assumed control over the production process, many employers implemented the scientific management principles that had been developed by Frederick Taylor.[33] New technology was introduced and the production process was broken down into a series of repetitive tasks that could be assigned to narrowly skilled workers. Corporations were no longer dependent upon highly skilled artisans who could not be easily replaced during a labor dispute. They were now able to employ individuals who could promptly learn to perform limited job functions. Such semi-skilled operatives did not possess the economic influence of the artisans whom they replaced. If they contemplated unionization, they could be terminated and replaced.

During World War I, the Federal Government encouraged employers to adopt shop committees that would provide employees with a greater sense of corporate involvement.[34] Although most companies initially opposed such worker participation schemes, some began to recognize that shop committees could be used to increase productivity and to convince production workers that they did not need labor representation. Employees could always raise issues of concern at shop committee meetings. Trade union officials quickly realized that such worker participation programs were being employed by many companies not to provide rank-and-file production employees with meaningful influence over their daily job functions, but as a means of manipulating worker feelings and discouraging unionization.[35]

The introduction of new technology and the adoption of scientific management programs greatly undermined union strength. Production companies no longer employed the numerous skilled artisans who had historically been members of AFL craft unions. Trade union membership declined, and the narrow craft jurisdictions of such labor unions made it virtually impossible for them to organize the semi-skilled employees operating the new production machinery.[36] As the Great Depression began, many skilled and unskilled workers lost their jobs. By the early 1930s, industrial relations observers predicted the rapid demise of the American labor movement.[37]

The Railway Labor Act

Railroad workers were the first segment of the American economy to be granted statutory labor relations protection. The rail industry had been extensively unionized during the nineteenth century. Work stoppages in the 1880s demonstrated the devastating impact of railroad strikes on the public welfare. Congress decided that legislation was needed to funnel rail disputes into less disruptive channels. The Arbitration Act of 1888[38] established voluntary arbitration procedures, the Erdman Act of 1898[39] provided government mediation, and the Newlands Act of 1913[40] created a permanent Board of Mediation and Conciliation.

During World War I, the Federal Government assumed control of the railroads to guarantee the continued functioning of this vital transportation system. At the conclusion of the war, Congress enacted Title III of the Transportation Act of 1920.[41] These provisions encouraged carriers and railroad brotherhoods to resolve their controversies voluntarily. When mutual accommodations could not be achieved, disputes were sent to a bipartisan board of adjustment or to the Railroad Labor Board. Despite its dispute resolution procedures, the Transportation Act did not expressly protect the right of railroad employees to unionize.

The Railway Labor Act of 1926[42] was the first American enactment to guarantee workers the right to organize and to bargain over their employment conditions. Bipartite adjustment boards were established to resolve grievances that could not be amicably settled. Voluntary arbitration was to be offered to parties that had reached a bargaining impasse, and the President had the authority to appoint emergency boards to resolve contract disputes. The Railway Labor Act, as amended, still regulates railway labor-management relations. In 1936, its coverage was extended to air carriers.[43]

Modern Federal Labor Legislation

In 1933, Congress enacted the National Industrial Recovery Act (NIRA).[44] Section 7a specified that each code of fair competition shall provide that "employees shall have the right to organize and bargain collectively through representatives of their own choosing, and shall be free from the interference, restraint, or coercion of employers." On August 5, 1933, President Franklin Roosevelt created the National Labor Board and appointed Senator Robert Wagner its chairman. Many employers refused to comply with National Labor Board orders, and business groups quickly challenged the constitutionality of the statute. In *Schechter Poultry Corp. v. United States*,[45] a divided Supreme Court invalidated the NIRA. The Court majority found that Congress had impermissibly sought to use its authority to regulate interstate commerce as a vehicle for prescribing rules governing wholly intrastate business activities.

Following the *Schechter Poultry* decision, Senator Wagner introduced legislation to replace the nullified NIRA. On July 5, 1935, Congress enacted the National Labor Relations Act (NLRA).[46] Section 1 emphasized the fact that "[t]he denial by employers of the right of employees to organize and the refusal by employers to accept the procedure of collective bargaining lead to strikes and other forms of industrial strife and unrest." That section declared it the policy of the United States to eliminate such disruptions "by encouraging the practice and procedure of collective bargaining and by protecting the exercise by workers of full freedom of association. . . . " A three-member National Labor Relations Board (NLRB or Labor Board) was established to administer the new law. Employer groups were confident that the NLRA would be invalidated by the Supreme Court. In *NLRB v. Jones & Laughlin Steel Corp.*,[47] however, the Supreme Court rejected the narrow *Schechter Poultry* reasoning and sustained the propriety of the NLRA.

Section 7 of the NLRA guaranteed employees "the right to self-organization, to form, join, or assist labor organizations, to bargain collectively through representatives of their own choosing, and to engage in concerted activities, for . . . mutual aid or protection." Section 8 prohibited employer interference with the exercise of employee rights, proscribed company controlled labor organizations, and mandated good faith negotiations with labor organizations selected by a majority of employees in an appropriate bargaining unit. This enactment finally provided private sector personnel outside the railroad industry with statutorily secured organizational rights.

The Congress of Industrial Organizations

The enactment of the NIRA and the NLRA coincided with an important structural development taking place within the American labor movement that was intended to enhance the ability of unions to organize the emerging mass production industries. Instead of limiting membership to highly skilled artisans, organizations like the United Mine Workers, the Amalgamated Clothing Workers, the Pacific Coast Longshoremen, and the Teamsters began to unionize the skilled, semi-skilled, and unskilled employees working in the coal, clothing, longshore, and trucking industries.[48] Other labor leaders recognized that such a comprehensive program would have to be employed if unions were going to successfully organize the individuals employed in automobile, rubber, steel, chemical, glass, and other industries.

The jurisdictional restrictions indigenous to conventional craft unions made it virtually impossible for such entities to organize mass production industries employing diverse groups of skilled, semi-skilled, and unskilled workers. When AFL affiliates sought to organize such extensive industries, AFL officials usually established a federal labor union that would conduct a coordinated campaign. After the employees had been induced to join the federal labor organization, the skilled workers were assigned to the trade unions having jurisdiction over their respective crafts.

At the 1934 AFL convention, William Green and John L. Lewis proposed the creation of new industrial unions. Following heated debate, however, their industrial union resolution was soundly defeated. The issue was reconsidered at the 1935 AFL convention, generating an unusually acrimonious discussion. When Carpenters President William Hutcheson objected to the presentation by Mine Workers President Lewis in favor of industrial unionization, fisticuffs resulted. The industrial union proposal was again defeated. A month after the 1935 convention, however, officers from the United Mine

Workers, the International Typographical Workers, the Amalgamated Clothing Workers, the International Ladies Garment Workers, the United Textile Workers, the Oil Field, Gas Well and Refining Workers, the United Hatters, Cap and Millinery Workers, and the Mine, Mill and Smelter Workers met in Washington, D.C., to create the Committee for Industrial Organization.

The Committee for Industrial Organization promptly established a series of organizing committees pertaining to the steel, textile, automobile, rubber, chemical, shipping, and electronics industries. AFL President Green contacted the union officials participating in this new committee. He expressed "feelings of apprehension over the grave consequences which might follow from the formation of [such an industrial union] organization within the American Federation of Labor."[49] Although the leaders of the new union indicated that they did not intend to infringe the jurisdictional rights of any AFL affiliates, they proposed to continue their industrial organizing efforts. They subsequently ignored Green's demand that they dissolve their unauthorized group.

By the 1937 AFL convention, trade union leaders were concerned about the fact that the Committee for Industrial Organization was already granting charters to industrial unions. Delegates authorized the Executive Committee to revoke the charters of any AFL affiliates that engaged in "dual unionism" by supporting industrial organizations. In November of 1938, the unions participating in the Committee for Industrial Organization formally split from the AFL and formed the Congress of Industrial Organizations (CIO). During the next two decades, AFL and CIO unions aggressively competed with one another for the right to organize workers employed in the mass production industries.

Many of the industries organized by CIO unions employed numerous minority and female workers. The CIO affiliates welcomed such employees into their ranks and diligently labored to advance their employment interests. The Women's Trade Union League enthusiastically supported the organizing efforts of these industrial unions, graphically demonstrating the desire of female employees to obtain union representation.

Anti-Labor Responses to the Expanding Labor Movement

Competition between AFL and CIO affiliates generated substantial representational gains. Union membership increased from 15 percent of the nonagricultural labor force when the NLRA was enacted in 1935 to over 35 percent by the mid–1950s.[50] Corporations, however, became increasingly concerned about diminishing profits caused by the increased labor costs associated with unionization.[51] As a result, a greater number of unorganized employers redoubled their efforts to prevent unionization.

Businesses also sought Labor Board and court rulings that would narrow the scope of NLRA protection. In *NLRB v. Fansteel Metallurgical Corp.*,[52] the Supreme Court held that sit-down strikes were not protected under the NLRA. Employees who participated in such trespassory job actions could thus be lawfully discharged. Subsequent NLRB and court decisions ruled that employees did not have the protected right to engage in concerted work slowdowns[53] or group refusals to work assigned overtime.[54] Nor could they utilize disruptive "quickie" strikes.[55]

In 1938, the Supreme Court further undermined the ability of employees to engage in work stoppages.[56] Although economic strikes were specifically protected by the NLRA, the Court determined that struck employers possessed the inherent right to hire "permanent" replacements for striking personnel. The Justices found that companies had a legitimate desire to maintain operations, and they inexplicably concluded that the employment of such replacements had a relatively slight impact upon striking workers.

In *NLRB v. IBEW Local 1229*,[57] the Supreme Court held that employees owe a duty of loyalty to their employers when they are involved in labor-management controversies. The Court ruled that individuals who disparage the products or services provided by their employer lose the protection of the NLRA. The Labor Board subsequently held that product disparagement during a work stoppage is impermissible even when the negative representations are entirely truthful.[58]

A further erosion of collective rights occurred when the Supreme Court decided that private property rights take precedence over the organizational rights of workers. In *NLRB v. Babcock & Wilcox Co.*,[59] the Court ruled that businesses could lawfully bar solicitation and literature distribution by nonemployee union organizers on company premises. Fearing that such nonemployee organizers might create discipline or theft problems if they were given access to employee parking lots, the *Babcock & Wilcox* Court ruled that private corporations only have to provide nonemployee organizers with access to company property in those rare circumstances when the labor union is wholly unable to disseminate its organizational message through external channels of communication.

In 1947, the business community enlisted the assistance of the conservative Eightieth Congress. It successfully lobbied for significant changes in the NLRA. The Labor Management Relations Act (LMRA)[60] amendments, which were adopted over President Harry Truman's veto, prohibited most forms of secondary worker conduct. They directed the Labor Board to petition a United States District Court for an immediate restraining order in any case in which a labor organization engaged in unlawful secondary activity. The LMRA also provided parties adversely affected by proscribed secondary activity with the right to sue the responsible labor organization for damages. The NLRA was further modified to provide employees with the protected right to cross a picket line to work during a strike, and made it an unfair labor practice for a labor union to interfere with that privilege.

The LMRA amendments restricted the ability of labor organizations to control the supply of labor. Under the original NLRA, representative labor organizations could obtain closed-shop agreements. Persons denied union membership were simply ineligible for employment with these firms. Under the LMRA, labor organizations could merely require workers to tender their initiation fee and monthly dues within thirty days following their date of employment. This statutory modification shifted the balance of power with respect to hiring decisions from trade unions to employers.

The 1947 Congress responded similarly to an employer desire to limit collective bargaining to rank-and-file employees. In *Packard Motor Car Co. v. NLRB*,[61] the Supreme Court had sustained the extension of NLRA collective bargaining rights to supervisory personnel. Corporations were concerned that such organizational protection might induce higher management officials to unionize, and they asked Congress to avert such a direct threat to supervisor-company relations. Legislators responded by expressly excluding even low-level supervisors from the statutory definition of "employee."

Employers induced Congress to narrow worker rights further in the 1959 Labor Management Reporting and Disclosure Act (LMRDA)[62] amendments to the NLRA. Greater restrictions were imposed upon secondary activity, and organizational and recognitional picketing was severely limited. Congress modified Section 10(1) of the NLRA to require Labor Board attorneys to seek immediate restraining orders in all cases involving unlawful organizational or recognitional picketing. These changes inhibited the ability of labor unions to engage in traditional concerted activity during organizing campaigns.

The LMRDA established substantial restrictions concerning the internal affairs of unions. It required the annual filing of detailed financial reports, and imposed fiduciary obligations upon labor officials. It mandated fair and regular elections of union officers. Union members were provided with free speech protection, and guaranteed procedural due process in cases involving labor organizations seeking to impose discipline. The LMRDA also limited the circumstances in which national or international unions could impose trusteeships on local entities.

The AFL-CIO Merger and Beyond

Soon after the Committee for Industrial Organization left the AFL to form the CIO, AFL leaders realized that a reunification of the labor movement was necessary to preserve organizational strength. The primary impediment to consolidation involved continued AFL insistence upon the concept of exclusive jurisdiction under which the CIO industrial unions would have been required to assign skilled members to appropriate AFL craft entities. Despite their differences, AFL and CIO leaders continued to explore this issue throughout the 1940s. CIO President Murray and AFL President Green repeatedly tried to formulate a plan that would reunite the two labor federations.

In November of 1952, both Murray and Green died. George Meany became head of the AFL, and Walter Reuther ascended to the presidency of the CIO. Both institutions redoubled their efforts to achieve a truce that would eliminate the interorganizational raiding that was benefiting neither group. The monetary costs associated with interorganizational raiding were substantial, and the actual membership gains were marginal. On June 9, 1954, the AFL and CIO finally executed a no-raiding pact,[63] but certain AFL and CIO affiliates refused to honor this agreement. Meany and Reuther, however, worked continually to achieve complete labor unity. They agreed that unions with overlapping craft jurisdictions should be encouraged to merge, and that independent CIO industrial unions should be permitted to maintain their separate identities. In December of 1955, the AFL-CIO merger was achieved, reuniting unions with over 15 million members.[64] All of the constituent unions were thereafter bound by the no-raiding provision set forth in the AFL-CIO constitution.

During the late 1950s, the percentage of labor force participants in labor organizations began to decline. Nonetheless, union political power expanded. Although the American labor movement had decided not to create an independent worker party, it did exert considerable political influence. Political action committees provided substantial financial support to friends of labor. Union officials personally campaigned in favor of pro-worker candidates. AFL-CIO affiliates lobbied for social legislation designed to protect employee interests. Some of the beneficial enactments that received labor support include the Equal Pay Act of 1963,[65] mandating equal compensation for people performing substantially identical work regardless of gender, Title VII of the Civil Rights Act of 1964,[66] proscribing employment discrimination based upon race, color, religion, gender, or national origin, the Age Discrimination in Employment Act of 1967,[67] prohibiting employment discrimination against employees forty and older, the Occupational Safety and Health Act of 1970,[68] protecting the employment environments of American workers, the Employee Retirement Income Security Act of 1974,[69] safeguarding employee pension and welfare benefits, and the recently adopted Americans With Disabilities Act,[70] protecting the employment opportunities of disabled workers. Organized labor has also lobbied in favor of enhanced employee rights under worker and unemployment compensation statutes, and a myriad of other laws designed to enhance worker interests.

Business organizations also expanded their political influence during the past two decades. By the 1970s, corporate lobbyists had regained the leverage they had enjoyed during the 1920s, and they developed the capacity to dominate the legislative process.[71] Labor leaders did not fully appreciate the awesome political strength possessed by corporate America until the mid–1970s. In 1977, the AFL-CIO sought changes in the NLRA that would have provided union organizers limited access to employer premises during unionization drives and enhanced the remedies available to rectify employers' unfair labor practice violations.[72] Labor leaders thought that business officials would not fight these seemingly modest NLRA amendments. They were consequently shocked by the vehement opposition marshalled by business institutions to the proposed legislation.[73] The lobbying efforts of the business community precipitated a Senate filibuster that prevented a vote on the merits of this bill.

During the inflationary years of the 1970s, cost-of-living-adjustment clauses contained in many collective bargaining agreements caused labor costs to increase rapidly. Employers began to consider ways of reducing employee costs. Some transferred production to lower wage areas of the United States or abroad, and some demanded compensation reductions. Others decided to follow the example set by President Ronald Reagan when he discharged thousands of striking air traffic controllers in 1981, by converting their unionized facilities into unorganized plants. Simultaneously, labor organizations were being challenged by significant demographic, technological, industrial, and international changes, all of which hastened a decline in union strength in America.

3. THE EXTENT AND CAUSES OF THE DECLINE OF THE AMERICAN LABOR MOVEMENT

Union membership figures have generally fluctuated over time due to the impact of economic cycles, industrial changes, immigration patterns, and other relevant factors. Between 1897 and 1904, trade union membership increased from 447,000 to over 2,000,000.[1] By 1920, labor organizations had over 5,000,000 members,[2] but over the next three years, membership declined substantially to 3,500,000. During the remainder of that decade, however, union membership decreased at a slower rate to 3,401,000, which constituted 11.6 percent of the 1930 nonagricultural workforce.[3]

The initial years of the Great Depression generated significant unemployment and a corresponding decrease in union membership. By 1934, trade unions had just over 3,088,000 members. The membership decreases of the early 1930s induced some experts to predict the demise of the American labor movement by the end of that decade.[4] Nonetheless, by 1935, when the National Labor Relations Act (NLRA) extended organizational and collective bargaining rights to most private sector employees, trade union membership had rebounded to 3,584,000, which represented 13.2 percent of nonagricultural workforce participants.[5]

Following the enactment of the NLRA, trade union membership grew steadily. By 1940, there were 8,717,000 members, comprising 26.9 percent of nonagricultural workers.[6] At the conclusion of World War II in 1945, labor organizations had 14,322,000 members, representing 35.5 percent of the nonagricultural workforce. By 1954, union membership exceeded 17,000,000. Labor organization members still constituted approximately 35 percent of all nonagricultural workforce participants.

From 1954 through 1980, the absolute number of union members continued to increase slightly. By 1970, union membership exceeded 19,000,000, and by 1980, it was approximately 22,000,000.[7] This growth in union membership did not, however, keep pace with the expansion of the nonagricultural workforce. There were only approximately 49,000,000 nonagricultural workers in 1954. By 1970, there were 70,880,000, and by 1980, that figure exceeded 90,000,000.[8] As a result, the proportion of nonagricultural workforce participants in unions declined steadily from 35 percent in 1954 to 27.3 percent in 1970 and to 23 percent in 1980. Labor organizations that had won 80 to 85 percent of Labor Board representation elections during the 1940s and early 1950s were prevailing in only about 50 percent of such elections by 1980.[9] Yet during the same 1954 to 1980 period, Canadian trade union membership grew from 32 to 36 percent of nonagricultural workers.[10]

During the 1980s, the position of organized labor deteriorated from both an absolute and a relative perspective. By 1984, union membership comprised 18.5 percent of the nonagricultural labor force.[11] By 1990, there were only 16,740,000 trade union members in the United States.[12] They represented a mere 16.1 percent of nonagricultural workers. Although the decline in union membership during the 1980s was substantial, the actual situation today is worse than even these stark figures indicate. Throughout the 1970s and 1980s, there had been a relatively robust expansion of public sector unionization. As of 1990, labor organizations representing federal, state, and local government employees had 6,480,000 members, constituting 36.5 percent of all government workers.[13] Private sector unions only had 10,260,000 members, comprising a meager 12.1 percent of nonagricultural private sector employees.[14] Even though labor organizations represent an additional 2,300,000 private sector workers who are not union members,[15] it is obvious that private sector unions are in a moribund state.

During 1990, labor organizations won only 47.6 percent of the 3,423 representation elections conducted by the NLRB.[16] Although the 1990 percentage was slightly above the 46.7 percent figure for 1986, it is important to acknowledge that the number of Labor Board representation elections declined during that same period from 3,923 to 3,423.[17] The union victory rate was inversely related to the size of the proposed units. While unions prevailed in 52 percent of 1990 representation elections in bargaining units containing from 2 to 49 employees, they won only 37.6 percent of elections in units of 100 to 499 workers and 19.3 percent of elections in units with 500 or more employees.[18]

Recent NLRB election figures, however, provide labor organizations with some positive information. The number of decertification elections, declined from 923 in 1986 to 558 in 1990.[19] The proportion of decertification elections won by labor organizations increased from 24.3 percent in 1986 to 27.2 percent in 1990.

Declining union membership has contributed to two other distressing phenomena. The first is the diminishing political influence possessed by organized labor. During the 1950s and 1960s, union leaders exerted significant political power. Even though they were unable to prevent the enactment of the Labor Management Relations Act of 1947 and the Labor Management Reporting and Disclosure Act of 1959, both of which restricted labor's political and economic activities, unions were able to lobby successfully for statutes prohibiting employment discrimination, enhancing employment health and safety, and protecting employee pension and welfare funds. By 1977, when union officials sought modest changes in the NLRA through the proposed Labor Law Reform Act, they began to encounter the immense political strength possessed by corporate entities.[20] Business organizations were able to prevent the enactment of those AFL-CIO backed amendments to the NLRA.

The second phenomenon associated with the decrease in unionized workers is the diminishing economic clout exercised by organized labor. As fewer firms in basic industries are unionized, labor unions representing workers at the remaining firms are no longer able to negotiate industry-wide pattern agreements. This is already apparent in such traditional labor strongholds as steel and trucking. In 1982, the number of companies covered by the Basic Steel Agreement declined from eight to six. The National Master Freight Agreement, which previously prescribed the employment conditions of most long haul truck drivers, has been supplanted by regional and even firm supplements.[21] The decentralization of collective bargaining makes it increasingly difficult for representative unions to compel unorganized businesses to maintain employment conditions commensurate with those set forth in bargaining agreements in an effort to block unionization by their own employees. In fact, many organized companies have recently demanded compensation reductions and work rule changes designed to enable them to compete more effectively with nonunion companies.[22]

The ability of labor organizations to employ the strike weapon has also declined. With numerous nonunion firms operating in almost every industry, unions are no longer able to constrict production through a general work stoppage. This helps explain the substantial decrease in strike activity over the past fifteen years.[23]

As the economic power of labor unions has waned, the financial influence of corporate America has expanded geometrically. During the 1980s, business mergers and acquisitions caused a concentration of capital in a few major conglomerates. "[T]he centralization of power in the hands of capital owners has resulted in an unhealthy level of economic dependence of all employees on their employers. ... [T]his concentration of employer power poses a serious threat to individual freedom. ... "[24] Such large and diversified business enterprises are frequently able to withstand the pressures indigenous to work stoppages more easily than the employees. Not only do most striking workers lack the monetary resources to survive a prolonged lack of employment, but they face the prospect of "permanent replacement."[25]

By analyzing the factors that have contributed to the decline of the American labor movement, one can determine which trends are likely to continue and which will change in the coming years. In addition, this analysis should suggest ways that organized labor may modify its practices to retain current members and to attract new ones. If labor leaders simply regard these trends as insurmountable barriers to union growth, the American labor movement may indeed become defunct by the year 2000. If, however, they modify their conventional organizing techniques and develop innovative concepts that will appeal to the 90 percent of private sector employees who are not union members, there is no reason why they cannot increase the private sector union participation rate to the 35 to 40 percent range enjoyed by their public sector labor counterparts.

CHANGING DEMOGRAPHIC CHARACTERISTICS OF THE LABOR FORCE

The fluctuating composition and geographical distribution of the labor force will greatly affect union strength and organizational ability during the coming decades. As increased employment opportunities and changing personal expectations encourage greater female labor force involvement, the participation rate for women, who have traditionally remained unorganized, will continue to expand. Today, over 55,000,000 women comprise nearly 45 percent of the nation's work force.[26] Almost 60 percent of all females between 18 and 64 are labor force members. In 1950, only 24 percent of married women were labor force participants, but by the late 1970s, over 46 percent were.[27] The recent increase has been particularly notable among mothers with school-age children. While only 30 percent of women with children were labor force participants in 1960,[28] 63 percent were by the late 1980s.[29] These changes have generated an increased need for day care centers for preschool children and after-school programs for older children. Economic pressure encourages married couples to maintain their dual careers, and financial necessity compels most single women to work, resulting in a labor force containing an even higher proportion of female participants. Between now and the year 2000, experts estimate that two-thirds of new labor force entrants will be women.[30] By the end of the current decade, 61 percent of all adult females are expected to be gainfully employed.

The momentous increase in female labor force participation has not appreciably alleviated gender-based job segregation. Today, 80 percent of women workers are employed in four lower-wage categories: clerical, health and education, domestic service, and "peripheral industries," including light manufacturing and retail trade.[31] Labor unions have not achieved substantial organizational success in these occupational categories. They will have to do so if they want to meaningfully expand female membership. Despite the increasing labor force participation rates of women, earnings obtained by females still lag behind those of their male counterparts. The average full-time female employee earns approximately 60 to 65 percent of the amount earned by her male equivalent.[32] Labor organizations must address this issue if they intend to attract women to their ranks.

Another significant labor force trend is the rapid growth of minority participants. Minority participation rates are expected to increase from 13.6 percent in 1985 to 15.7 percent by the year 2000[33] due to the fact that approximately 30 percent of all labor force entrants over the next decade will be minorities. Minority employees have historically been segregated in low wage occupations, and they have generally earned far less than their nonminority counterparts.[34] Although many minority workers have been organized by industrial unions representing employees in the mass production industries, such as automobile, steel, rubber, and electrical manufacturing, the record of most craft unions has not been very good.

Over the next several decades, declining birth rates and the enhanced longevity of the post-World War II "baby boom" generation will result in a considerable increase in the average age of labor force participants. Although fewer than 10 percent of Americans were fifty-five and older in 1900, 20 percent were by the late 1980s.[35] By 2030, such individuals will constitute almost one-third of the general population.[36] People sixty-five and older will comprise about 14 percent of the population by 2010 and over 20 percent by 2030.[37]

The economic status of older Americans is not commensurate with that of younger persons. People sixty-five and older have a lower average income than do individuals under sixty-five. In 1986, the median income for families headed by people sixty-five and older was $19,932, 61.6 percent of the $32,368 median income enjoyed by families headed by persons twenty-five to sixty-four.[38] The situation for unmarried senior citizens is even worse. The $7,731 median income received in 1986 by persons sixty-five and older in nonfamily settings was only 45.8 percent of the $16,880 median for nonfamily individuals between twenty-five and sixty-four. Married elderly women experience an even greater economic disadvantage. In 1986, the $5,253 median income for married females sixty-five and older constituted a mere 42.8 percent of the $12,265 received by their married male cohorts.[39] This economic disparity partially explains the significant increase in labor force participation by older females.[40]

Through the Age Discrimination in Employment Amendments of 1986,[41] Congress altered the Age Discrimination in Employment Act to prohibit the involuntary retirement of most employees. As more individuals live past sixty-five, an increasing number will continue to work either by personal choice or from economic necessity. Many will seek part-time employment opportunities to supplement their retirement income. Such older, part-time personnel have not been historically inclined to seek union representation. As a greater number of these workers view their positions as permanent, they may become more receptive to appropriate union organizing appeals.

One of the most striking demographic trends over the past two decades has been the explosive growth of the Sunbelt region. The migration of workers and jobs from the Northeast and North Central areas of the country to the South and Southwest is likely to continue.[42] Businesses favor the Sunbelt states when making investment decisions concerning relocating and refurbishing facilities, due to lower labor costs and a less unionized labor force.[43] Over half of all union members currently reside in California, Illinois, Michigan, New York, Ohio, and Pennsylvania.[44] Of these traditional bastions of labor support, only California is expected to experience sustained future employment growth. Labor organizations will have to seek converts in the South and Southwest if they are to expand their membership rolls.

INDUSTRIAL AND TECHNOLOGICAL CHANGES

Workers have historically exhibited resistance to technological advances. As early as 1663, employees in London attempted to destroy new mechanical sawmills that threatened their livelihoods.[45] Ribbon workers implemented similar tactics in 1676, and in 1710, rioters protested the introduction of novel stocking frame equipment. Probably the most notorious example of antitechnological advancement behavior occurred in 1811, when the so-called Luddites destroyed new textile machines in Nottingham.[46]

Despite worker efforts to impede industrial evolution, extraordinary developments have occurred over the past 150 years. The most remarkable aspect of this technological progression has concerned the accelerating rate of change. Although it took fifty-six years (1820–76) to develop the telephone, thirty-five years (1867–1902) to generate the radio, and thirteen years (1923–36) to invent the television, it took only five years (1948–53) to create the transistor.[47] This expedited developmental process will undoubtedly continue. Unimagined technological advancements will significantly transform future employment environments and greatly affect the organizational opportunities of labor unions.

Twenty-first century industrial settings will be highly automated, with computer systems directing the work of technologically advanced robots. The continued substitution of capital-intensive technology for traditional blue-collar workers in most manufacturing facilities will cause significant membership declines among mass production labor organizations. Membership in such basic industrial unions as the United Automobile Workers, the United Steelworkers, and the International Association of Machinists has already declined precipitously.

The pervasive utilization of technology is dramatically altering the composition of the American employment market and directly affecting the continued vitality of the labor movement. The swift introduction of new technology has been creating a "crisis of human obsolescence."[48] As robots and computers supplant skilled and semi-skilled employees, the work force is becoming increasingly bifurcated between sophisticated and highly educated managers and unskilled personnel performing relatively menial tasks.[49] The number of traditional blue-collar production jobs is predicted to decrease even more than it already has, causing a serious erosion among the occupations most supportive of labor organizations.

The reduction in blue-collar positions has seen a corresponding expansion in white-collar and service occupations. Between 1900 and today, the proportion of the labor force consisting of white-collar positions grew from one-fourth to three-fourths.[50] By the beginning of the next century, approximately 90 percent of workforce participants will be employed in white-collar occupations.[51] Such white-collar personnel will probably continue to reflect the kind of management philosophy that has historically caused them to be unresponsive to union organizing appeals. Unless their employment environments become sufficiently onerous that they opt for collectivization, or labor organizations develop innovative programs to persuade such management-oriented employees to view unions as positive factors, the American labor movement will experience a continued decline.

The increased use of computers and other labor-saving technology is also likely to generate a surplus of labor, necessitating a curtailment of the traditional forty-hour workweek.[52] In addition, computer technology permits the creation of individualized employment opportunities, with service personnel earning their income at home in "electronic cottage industries."[53] Such employment arrangements will be particularly advantageous for parents—particularly single parents—who enjoy the flexibility they need to care for young children at home. Other people who wish to avoid protracted commutes may be able to work in "neighborhood centers" that would provide them with the requisite computer equipment.[54]

Because most white-collar employees have historically been unreceptive to unionization[55] and self-employed persons working primarily from their own homes would be difficult to organize, conventional unions may be unable to cope with the restructuring of the American economy. On the contrary, as high-technology service enterprises expand, they may establish more routinized job tasks for many white-collar workers and create highly structured managerial hierarchies.[56] Individuals employed by these types of businesses may experience an increased economic and psychological need for collective behavior.

The technology revolution makes it possible for smaller firms to provide limited products or services designed to satisfy the demands of specialized markets. Smaller companies are able to adapt quickly to changed customer needs, and can thus compete effectively with ponderous corporate enterprises that find it difficult to alter their basic operating structures in response to new customer demands. While these specialty firms are economically efficient from a business perspective and are more amenable to unionization than large companies, labor unions continue to experience diseconomies of scale when they attempt to organize them. The cost per worker for organizational campaigns involving small-scale employers generally exceeds the per capita cost associated with larger enterprises. As a result, many labor leaders do not try to collectivize smaller companies.

GLOBAL ECONOMIC AND INDUSTRIAL TRENDS

The same technological developments that have significantly influenced the structure of the American economy have also greatly contributed to the internationalization of the world economic system. Although the establishment of multinational corporations is not a recent phenomenon,[57] the proliferation of such enterprises has reached extraordinary levels over the past two decades. The major impetus for the creation of transnational ventures has been the desire of business entities in industrialized nations to control and cultivate raw materials indigenous to various underdeveloped countries.[58] New technologies have greatly reduced transportation costs, enabling businesses to move raw materials, manufacturing equipment, and finished products from country to country in an economically efficient manner. As industrial leaders began to appreciate the benefits from generating new markets and exploiting inexpensive foreign labor, the growth rate of multinational institutions accelerated.

By 1973, 140 American multinational corporations had aggregate annual sales of $380 billion, a sum exceeding the gross national product of every nation except the United States and the Soviet Union.[59] Observers consequently predicted that by 1990, 300 immense business entities, two-thirds of which would be American, would dominate non-Communist world trade.[60] At the present time, "USX Corp. imports steel ingot from Korea; General Motors and Ford import cars from Korea; Chrysler imports cars from Mexico; General Electric imports various small appliances from Asia; and IBM imports data processing equipment from Asia."[61] Many United States business entities have become major shareholders in foreign companies. Ford owns 25 percent of Mazda, General Motors owns 34.4 percent of Isuzu Motors, Chrysler owns 15 percent of Mitsubishi, and General Electric owns 40 percent of Toshiba Electronics.[62]

Today, substantial proportions of automobiles, glassware, sewing machines, shoes and textiles, and cassettes, radios, and tape players used in the United States are manufactured in foreign nations on equipment exported from America.[63] The primary stimulus for the transfer of such production functions is labor cost differentials. Clothing is fabricated in Caribbean nations by workers earning 25 percent the wages earned by their counterparts in the United States, and in Mexico by persons earning 10 to 20 percent of American rates of pay.[64] Electrical goods are produced in East Asia by workers who are paid less than 10 percent of United States employees' wages.

So many of the components installed in American products are being manufactured abroad that it has become virtually impossible for consumers to be fully aware of the degree to which they support United States workers when they make a major purchase. For example, the selection of a Honda Accord built in the United States may be more beneficial to American employees than the purchase of a traditionally "American" car.

When an American buys a Pontiac Le Mans from General Motors, . . . he or she engages unwittingly in an international transaction. Of the $20,000 paid to GM, about $6,000 goes to South Korea for routine labor and assembly operations, $3,500 to Japan for advanced components (engines, transaxles, and electronics), $1,500 to West Germany for styling and design engineering, $800 to Taiwan, Singapore, and Japan for small components, $500 to Britain for advertising and marketing services, and about $100 to Ireland and Barbados for data processing. The rest—less than $8,000—goes to strategists in Detroit, lawyers and bankers in New York, lobbyists in Washington, insurance and health-care workers all over the country, and General Motors shareholders—most of whom live in the United States, but an increasing number of whom are foreign nationals.[65]

The governments of developing countries compete for the opportunity to generate American investment. They emphasize their significantly lower labor costs, the docility and dependability of their impoverished workers, the absence of labor organizations, and the minimal or inapplicable employee protection laws.[66] Some nations even establish Free Trade Zones that exempt foreign investment firms employing local workers from export duties and employment taxes.[67]

The United States also encourages the creation of foreign "export platforms." It does not impose an import duty upon the total value of the items finished abroad and returned to America, but only on the value added to the various components on the foreign assembly line.[68] The recent free trade agreement with Canada and the proposed extension of that agreement to Mexico would further promote the development of such transnational production programs. Goods finished in either of those neighboring countries could be returned to the United States for consumption without being subject to import duties.

During the past twenty years, the world has witnessed private enterprise colonization unmatched in this century. Large conglomerates from advanced industrial nations are able to dictate basic economic policy to developing nations desperately trying to enhance the economic interests of their workers through the attraction of foreign investment. While these countries generally attempt to alleviate high unemployment rates among male heads-of-households, the vast majority of multinational corporations operating foreign export platforms employ women of color who are willing to work for depressed wages.[69] These employees frequently work long hours in unhealthy and unsafe employment environments under stressful conditions generated by high production demands.[70]

Throughout the 1980s, American business enterprises accelerated their exploitation of the depressed Mexican economy. In 1965, the Mexican government established the Border Industrialization Program to promote the *maquilladora* system involving factories located opposite one another along the United States–Mexico border.[71] The labor-intensive tasks are performed in Mexican facilities by work forces consisting primarily of females earning less than $0.80 per hour, while the capital-intensive functions are carried out in the high-technology American plants. Multinational firms, such as General Electric, Chrysler, RCA, Xerox, United Technologies, ITT, General Instrument, Eastman Kodak, and IBM use the *maquilladora* program to save billions of dollars each year in aggregate labor costs.[72] Such businesses take advantage of the fact that wage rates in Mexico are lower than they are in most other areas of the world, and benefit from the minimal transportation costs involved. At their Mexican production facilities, they do not have to comply with United States health and safety regulations, worker and unemployment compensation laws, minimum wage and overtime provisions, and the protections set forth in collective bargaining agreements. When a free trade agreement is negotiated with Mexico, the number of *maquiladora* arrangements will increase dramatically.

The availability of foreign production platforms has already caused a substantial loss of American jobs. From 1969 to 1976, 1,200,000 United States manufacturing jobs were lost.[73] Between 1980 and 1985, America lost another 2,300,000 production jobs. A substantial proportion of foreign-based production workers are employed by United States corporations or their affiliates. Whirlpool Corporation currently employs 43,500 people in forty-five nations, with most of these individuals working outside the United States.[74] In 1990, 27,000 of the 40,000 persons employed by California-based Seagate Technology worked in Southeast Asian facilities. Forty percent of IBM's total work force resides in foreign countries, including 18,000 Japanese employees. General Electric is the largest private employer in Singapore, and it has recently completed construction of a $150 million Hungarian light bulb factory.[75] While business leaders are quick to note that these manufacturing job losses were offset by millions of employment opportunities generated in other areas of the economy, it must be acknowledged that "the new jobs are more likely to be less well paid, less skilled, less unionized, only part-time, and located in regions of the country other than those suffering most from job destruction and unemployment."[76]

The continued export of manufacturing jobs from the United States to developing nations further reduces the number of blue-collar production workers who have historically been represented by labor organizations. While capital-intensive technology is a relatively mobile commodity, displaced employees are not easily transplanted to other geographical areas or integrated into new occupations.[77] International business transactions emasculate the job security that unions have diligently sought to obtain for their members. If American labor organizations are unwilling to accept significant compensation reductions and more stressful production schedules, the jobs of their members will continue to be transferred to more hospitable foreign settings. In many cases, United States workers can do nothing to preserve their employment situations because their multinational employers prefer to have their production tasks performed by individuals in developing nations at wage rates equal to less than 20 percent of the $4.25 per hour American minimum wage.

American multinational enterprises are not the only business concerns transferring production jobs to other countries. Over the past decade, foreign corporations have greatly expanded their investment in United States production facilities. For example, Japan's Bridgestone Tire Company purchased Firestone, and Toyota and General Motors established a joint venture to produce automobiles in a Fremont, California, factory.[78] Japan's NEC is producing computer components in California, Sony employs 1,500 workers at its San Diego facility, France's Thompson employs over 3,300 at its Indiana plants, and Dutch-owned Philips has 3,200 employees at its Greenville, Tennessee, factory.[79] These foreign-owned operations are subject to the NLRA because they are located in the United States. Nonetheless, their foreign managers may not view labor-management relations the same way American managers do.

The continued proliferation of transnational business enterprises is also challenging the efficacy and practicality of conventional nation-states.[80] United States statutes prescribing minimum employment standards and guaranteeing employees organizational rights are becoming increasingly irrelevant to international firms. These enactments do not apply to the overseas operations of American business enterprises. Although most American companies have traditionally exhibited ethnocentric behavior, expanding multinational firms tend to function in a geocentric manner. The decision-making process of transnational entities is less likely to include factors of a local or even national nature. When profits can be meaningfully enhanced by closing a United States factory with 2,500 employees and exporting those production jobs to a low-wage facility in a developing country, corporate managers usually choose the profit-maximizing strategy.[81]

The fundamental structure of the American industrial relations system has been undergoing an important transformation in recent years, with capital formations uniting in ever larger entities. As conglomerates of multiproduct and even multi-industry firms have proliferated, the loci of decision-making authority have frequently been transferred from the local to the corporate or conglomerate level.[82] This trend has been especially pronounced with multinational enterprises that have concentrated their managerial authority in centralized locations. These behemoth corporate institutions have thus garnered enormous economic superiority vis-à-vis decentralized labor unions.

Representative labor organizations have found it increasingly difficult to confront such remote managerial centers. Most American bargaining relationships are conducted on a local or regional basis. Few employers and unions negotiate collective contracts that are national in scope, and almost no bargaining agreements have international applicability beyond the United States and Canada. As a result, local and even national labor unions find it impossible to deal effectively with multinational enterprises. They cannot regulate the employment standards followed by American business firms at their production facilities in developing countries.

When a work stoppage occurs at a United States facility of a multinational enterprise, the affected corporation is frequently able to make up the lost production at a foreign plant.[83] If a United States union negotiates a collective contract that provides bargaining unit employees with a fair proportion of firm profits, corporate managers can simply close the affected plants and permanently transfer the manufacturing functions to low-cost production platforms in developing nations.[84] The use of such "runaway" facilities greatly reduces employment costs. It also diminishes the need to deal with labor organizations because organizational and bargaining rights are denied in many developing countries.[85] This approach appeals to American corporations that do not wish to interact with workers on a collective basis.

The radical reorganization of the production process in all Western countries is being orchestrated by enterprises with avowed anti-union sentiments. These corporations have evolved into highly centralized and planned entities, while unions continue to cling to the ideas of decentralization and flexibility. The trade unions have not been able to reformulate their own decentralization and flexibility strategies (economic and industrial democracy) aimed at countering the big corporate interests.[86]

VIRULENT EMPLOYER OPPOSITION TO ORGANIZATIONAL RIGHTS

United States businesses have not been historically inclined to acknowledge the right of workers to organize and to influence their employment terms through collective bargaining. In fact, most corporations have exhibited an overt hostility toward concerted employee behavior. During the nineteenth century, many employers required new personnel to sign yellow-dog contracts that barred them from joining labor organizations. A number of business firms employed private security forces to spy on their employees. Companies frequently enlisted the assistance of police and the judiciary to retain their nonunion status. Courts were quick to enjoin concerted employee conduct, and they swiftly punished those who dared to disobey their proscriptive orders. When state or federal legislatures enacted laws providing minimal employment protections for workers, employer groups successfully challenged the constitutionality of those enactments.[87]

In 1935, the Federal Government established organizational and negotiating rights for workers under the National Labor Relations Act.[88] After businesses failed in their attempt to have this law invalidated,[89] many companies resorted to unlawful tactics. For example, numerous firms created their own "labor organizations" and installed pro-management persons as the officers of those "company unions."[90] Although such employer-dominated institutions contravened the specific prohibition contained in Section 8(2) of the NLRA, those devices enabled many employers to prevent employee unionization by independent labor organizations for several years.

As businesses became accustomed to the rights and obligations set forth in the NLRA, one might reasonably have anticipated a reduction in illegal behavior. On the contrary, the number of unfair labor practice charges filed against companies under Section 8(a)(1),[91] which proscribes employer restraint or coercion of employees with respect to their concerted activity, rose from about 4,500 in 1955 to over 31,000 in 1980.[92] Even though the number of Section 8(a)(1) charges declined to 22,500 in 1985, much of this decrease may be attributed to the reduction in union organizing campaigns during the 1980s. In 1980, the Labor Board conducted 7,296 representation elections, but in 1985, it held only 3,749.[93] While not all unfair labor practice charges are sustained in Labor Board adjudications, a seven-fold increase in alleged violations between 1955 and 1980 is remarkable. Many of those cases undoubtedly involved employer threats to take adverse action against workers who either engaged in informal collective action or contemplated actual unionization.

The NLRB data with regard to retaliatory discharges in violation of Section 8(a)(3)[94] are equally disturbing. Such discriminatory terminations, usually of the most vocal labor organization supporters, represent the most potent anti-union weapon available to employers. If a company is able to eliminate the key organizers during the early stages of a union campaign, the remaining employees generally become extremely hesitant to exhibit enthusiasm for the selection of a bargaining representative. In 1957, the Labor Board directed the reinstatement of 922 individuals found to have been discharged in violation of Section 8(a)(3).[95] By 1970, the number of those discriminated against had risen to 3,779. In 1980, the number of such terminated workers exceeded 10,000, and in 1985, a year with only about half of the representation elections conducted during 1980, the Labor Board directed the reinstatement of 10,905 illegally fired employees.[96] By the late 1980s, unlawful employee terminations occurred in one of every three Labor Board elections, with one of every thirty-six pro-union voters being illegally discharged.[97]

Although it is certainly true that not all of the cited Section 8(a)(3) discharges occurred during union organizing drives, the NLRB figures suggest that most did.[98] Furthermore, even when such unlawful dismissals take place while no labor organization is actively soliciting members, they do diminish the likelihood of future employee organizing efforts. Individuals who have witnessed the illegal termination of fellow workers based upon their exercise of protected rights tend to be afraid to provide open support for unionization. This would explain why "illegal campaign tactics . . . are a major, if not the major, determinant of NLRB election results."[99]

Most American employers that do not employ unlawful tactics to prevent unionization clearly indicate their opposition to labor organizations. They disseminate literature and make "captive audience" speeches to massed assemblages of employees stating their unequivocal desire to remain nonunion. They emphasize the fact that only they possess the power to determine wages, hours, and working conditions, and they frequently note that if representative labor organizations strike to enforce union bargaining demands, the striking individuals may be permanently replaced.

A number of employers retain the services of labor relations consultants who specialize in orchestrating anti-union campaigns. Most consultants develop company programs that involve representations that border on the unlawful. While business firms may lawfully misrepresent the salaries paid to union officials, the manner in which dues money is expended, and the compensation and benefits received by employees of other companies covered by collective bargaining agreements,[100] they may not promise workers special benefits if they oppose the union or threaten reprisals against those who support it. Nonetheless, some consultants recommend the use of overt threats, and a few propose the illegal discharge of primary union supporters.

A number of business firms that have had bargaining relationships for many years have recently decided that they would prefer to regain their former nonunion status. They have taken increasingly tough stands at the bargaining table, and have, in many cases, openly encouraged employees dissatisfied with their present union representatives to conduct decertification campaigns. This would explain the fact that the annual number of decertification elections conducted by the Labor Board grew from about 300 to 400 during the late 1960s and early 1970s to approximately 850 to 900 during the early 1980s.[101] It is also significant to note that incumbent unions lose a greater percentage of decertification elections today than they did twenty years ago. The number of members lost through this maneuver now exceeds 20,000 per year.[102]

Companies that have to decide whether to refurbish existing facilities frequently consider the union status of their plants. Data suggest that business firms are less likely to invest new capital at established locations if the employees at those facilities are organized.[103] Numerous decisions concerning the location of new factories are similarly influenced by unionization factors.[104] The fact that many new production plants have been constructed in the South and Southwest over the past twenty years can be at least partially attributed to the fact that Sunbelt state workers have not traditionally been as supportive of labor organizations as their northern counterparts.[105] This evidence demonstrates that even basic investment determinations are being influenced by the desire of most American firms to avoid unionization.

United States corporations have even formed trade associations designed in large part to discourage worker unionization. Entities such as the National Association of Manufacturers, the American Hospital Association, the Associated Builders and Contractors, the National Retail Merchants Association, and the Master Printers Association have all developed vigorous open-shop programs.[106] They conduct special seminars for members to demonstrate techniques they may employ to keep labor organizations out.

The antipathy exhibited by most American employers toward unionization is especially disturbing when one recognizes that business firms in Western European countries have generally accepted the legitimacy of labor organizations and have not employed similar anti-union tactics.[107] A major reason for the different attitudes toward unionization in America and Western Europe is the impact of unions on organized firms. In most Western European countries, collective bargaining is conducted on a regional or national basis covering most corporations within the relevant industry.[108] Government officials often participate in the negotiations. The terms of the agreements are usually applied to the workers of all industry firms in that region or nation, regardless of the percentage of employees of each company who are active union members. There is thus no significant advantage derived from maintaining a nonunion business.

In the United States, only those corporations that have formal bargaining relationships with labor organizations representing a majority of their respective employees must negotiate collective contracts. More importantly, the terms of such agreements are applied exclusively to work performed by individuals employed within the specified bargaining units. Companies without labor-management relationships remain free to unilaterally establish their own employment terms. Such firms are constrained only by operative market factors. If their wage rates or working conditions are unacceptably low, they will encounter difficulty attracting and retaining qualified employees. Their dissatisfied employees may even contemplate unionization.

The cost of unionization in the United States can be quite high. Management officials must consult their representative labor organizations with respect to matters meaningfully affecting employee wages, hours, and working conditions. There is also a substantial probability that overall labor costs for union shops will exceed those of unorganized competitors. Labor economists estimate that unionized firms have labor costs that are 10 to 30 percent higher than nonunion employers.[109] In the late 1980s, the union-nonunion wage differential exceeded 20 percent in most industries.[110] The fringe benefit costs in organized facilities were over 50 percent above those in unorganized settings.[111] Even though some of this union premium is offset by the greater worker productivity enjoyed by most unionized firms,[112] an increasing proportion of the cost differential is not. This fact places unionized American businesses at a distinct disadvantage compared to their unorganized competitors.

SOCIOLOGICAL CONSIDERATIONS

One of the great deceptions perpetrated on American workers over the past century is the allegedly classless nature of United States society.[113] Children are taught that people born in log cabins can grow up to be president. Horatio Alger stories are used to reinforce the belief that even those individuals raised in the most humble and disadvantaged settings can obtain higher education and rise to the top of American industry. Because most individuals can cite examples of immigrants and first generation children who actually attained professional or entrepreneurial status, it is easy to understand why many persons readily accept the egalitarian legend. This concept accounts for the fact that most working class parents dream of middle-class opportunities for their children.[114] As a result of this myth, few people attribute the success of families with extreme wealth and prominent lineage to the fortuity of birth, considering it instead to be a result of individual achievement.

The American belief in equal opportunity accomplishes several important societal objectives. It induces those born into disadvantaged environments to blame themselves for their failure to escape their surroundings, instead of focusing upon the inequitable educational opportunities afforded them.[115] It helps to delude people into believing that the disparate compensation and employment options available to women and minorities are not the result of invidious gender and racial discrimination, but are the natural consequences of independent choices voluntarily made by those individuals.[116] So long as people in lower socioeconomic circumstances can be made to accept responsibility for their own plights, it is unlikely that the dispossessed masses will revolt against the system that oppresses them.[117]

Those individuals who accept the notion that America has truly achieved the fundamental absence of social stratification should visit a high-technology production facility or a university setting at the conclusion of the normal work day. The rank-and-file personnel will depart in overalls and a work shirt, with many carrying lunch buckets.[118] An inordinate number will be overweight, and most will converse in language suggesting inadequate education. They will be compensated on an hourly basis and be required to punch a time clock each time they enter and leave the premises. Their departing professional colleagues, on the other hand, will generally be dressed in clothing more associated with the middle class, and they will be unlikely to carry lunch boxes. They will receive salaries and not be obliged to account formally for their work time. They will probably speak in a more erudite manner.

The classless deception generates a docility among blue-collar production workers and lower-level white-collar personnel. Such individuals tend to accept their societal positions without questioning the reason for their relative inability to transcend their working class situations. This decreases the likelihood that they will become frustrated by their lack of occupational mobility. It is thus improbable that they will become angry with the limitations imposed upon them by the general American economic system and by the hierarchical structure of their particular employers. As a result, few will conclude that collective action might provide them with a meaningful degree of worker empowerment.

The media and the business community have consistently portrayed union members as "working class," with the implication that such status is synonymous with "lower class" rank. They subtly create the impression that only the "lower class" opts for union representation.[119] Rarely do movies depict labor leaders or organized employees in a favorable light. Only a few films, such as "Norma Rae" and "Matewan," have provided sympathetic portrayals. Far more movies, such as "American Dream," "F.I.S.T.," "Hoffa," and "On the Waterfront," have characterized union officials as corrupt and uncaring, and organized workers as uneducated and violent. Television shows have provided a similar negative image. Most middle- and upper-class Americans consider Archie Bunker the archetypical union member. They view such people as bigoted and semiliterate.

The depiction of union people in newspapers and magazines is no more favorable. Instead of noting the thousands of collective bargaining agreements achieved each year without resort to work stoppages, reporters focus on the relatively few controversies culminating in strikes involving some degree of violence. They usually give extensive coverage to instances of union corruption. Newspapers regularly publish photographs of the old, frequently overweight, cigar-smoking, white, male AFL-CIO leadership each time they gather for AFL-CIO conventions at Bal Harbor, Florida.

Media news reports generally treat wrongdoing by labor and business leaders differently. Union officials who misappropriate money from member pension and welfare funds are described as "embezzlers." They are equated with organized crime figures, even when they act with no connection to any criminal syndicate. When bank officers or brokerage firm agents divert client funds to their own use, they tend to be characterized as "white-collar offenders." The prison terms imposed upon people like Ivan Boesky, Michael Milken, and Charles Keating, each of whom bilked society out of hundreds of millions of dollars, are usually much shorter than the terms given to union officials who have "embezzled" much smaller sums. This type of distinction also fosters the public impression that more union officials are corrupt than business executives. The actual data contradict this stereotypical belief. They demonstrate that union agents are actually less likely to be involved in criminal conduct than their entrepreneurial counterparts.[120] It is especially ironic that the movie and print media continue such stereotypes, because the vast majority of skilled people employed in such information fields are affiliated with labor organizations that function in a professional and lawful manner.

The degree to which the media and businesses have been successful in creating the impression that organized employees are lower class may be seen in the way in which American and Canadian citizens view themselves. Many Canadians respond to public opinion polls by acknowledging their "working class" membership. United States respondents, on the other hand, rarely acknowledge this status. They have been taught to equate such a characterization with "lower class," and few are willing to accept the fact that they are not part of the ubiquitous "middle class."

Most corporations reinforce these class notions among their low-level employees. They try to convince blue-collar production workers that union membership is a clear indication of lower class status. This image increases the likelihood that unorganized personnel will remain so, and it occasionally induces represented employees to decertify their incumbent unions. Over the past two decades, corporate officials have learned that sophisticated appeals to class consciousness work more effectively than crude threats.

Class-based propaganda has been particularly persuasive with respect to white-collar personnel. As the United States has been transformed from a manufacturing economy into a white-collar service society, corporate executives have been careful to provide low-level management workers with the impression that they have more in common with their superiors than they do with their blue-collar compatriots.[121] They have been able to persuade most low level management employees to ignore the fact that they and their production colleagues reside in similar dwellings and have comparable incomes.[122] Whenever labor unions begin to organize banking, insurance, health care, computer processing, and similar industries, the affected employers immediately disseminate anti-union literature disingenuously suggesting that persons employed in such white-collar occupations will lose their professional status if they succumb to unionization.

One of the most striking developments over the past several decades has been the increased concentration of economic and political influence in the hands of a diminishing number of plutocrats.[123] In the early nineteenth century, approximately 80 percent of workers were self-employed entrepreneurs. By the mid–twentieth century, most individuals earned their livings by working for the 2 to 3 percent of the population who owned about half of all private property.[124] During the 1980s, wealth became even more concentrated. The relatively few members of the ruling class have been unwilling to share their power with their subordinates, and sociological circumstances have not favored the development of a united working class. Current labor officials find it difficult to confront the inequities indigenous to the American capitalist system because most of them are unabashedly procapitalist.[125] They are willing to acknowledge the superior rights possessed by corporate owners and their managerial officials.

A somewhat different sociological phenomenon has involved the historical effort of many companies to divide workers along racial and gender lines. Throughout the late nineteenth and early twentieth centuries, companies regularly employed minority and female employees during work stoppages. Because such persons could not obtain membership in many AFL craft unions, they were receptive to strikebreaking overtures.[126] Corporate executives also used the lower compensation acceptable to minority and female workers as a means of moderating union demands for higher rates of pay for white male employees.[127] This attempt to exacerbate such intergroup divisions continues today. Many employers disingenuously blame race-conscious and gender-conscious affirmative action programs when they fail to offer employment opportunities to white males, and they conversely antagonize minority and female applicants when they select white males for vacant positions.

PART TWO

4. THE NEED FOR LABOR UNIONS TO ORGANIZE TRADITIONALLY NONUNION PERSONNEL

The American labor movement has historically derived its organizational strength from northern blue-collar workers. As demographic and structural changes continue to deplete the ranks of these workers and to expand the traditionally unorganized sectors of the workforce, labor unions will be compelled to modify their organizational focus if they wish to retain and broaden their economic vitality in the rapidly approaching post-industrial society. If labor leaders cannot develop programs that appeal to white-collar and service personnel, private sector unions will become increasingly unimportant outside of the shrinking manufacturing sector.

It will not be easy for labor organizations to unionize unorganized occupations. Various factors have combined to discourage collective behavior by workers in these positions. Many nonunion workers are satisfied with their employment circumstances because of the diligent efforts of their employers to avoid the types of employee disapprobation that frequently precipitate collective action. Corporations generally provide unorganized white-collar personnel with compensation and benefit increases as generous as those obtained for their production workers through the bargaining process.[1] Unorganized manufacturing enterprises similarly retain their unfettered managerial discretion by insuring that their employees are as well-off as their unionized counterparts.[2] If labor organizations are to significantly enhance the employment interests of nonunion individuals, they will have to provide more than conventional economic gains. They will have to establish goals that will increase employee participation in managerial decision making and enhance worker dignity.

Although labor organizations may be necessary to preserve previously achieved economic objectives, the critical function of unions in the future will be to prevent the noneconomic exploitation of individuals that results from the inhumane proliferation of industrial technology. White-collar and service personnel will demand a greater degree of influence over their basic terms and conditions of employment, and unions will have to create programs to satisfy such worker expectations. Legislatively prescribed and union-negotiated worker participation plans may provide employees with a greater degree of control over management decisions affecting their employment.

According to some observers, labor unions no longer control their own destiny, because most of the forces that normally increase union membership, such as industrial expansion and northern workforce growth, are now beyond the influence of labor organizations.[3] If unions accept this fatalistic prognosis, they need simply await their predicted demise with uncharacteristic tranquility. If labor leaders recognize, however, that they still exercise considerable control over their fate and exchange their outmoded methods and attitudes for sophisticated organizational techniques and farsighted objectives, they may engender an organizational renaissance in the coming decades.

ESTABLISHING A POSITIVE PUBLIC IMAGE

Many members of the public think that union officials are corrupt, that bargaining agreements establish inefficient work rules that inhibit worker productivity, and that the wages and benefits received by organized employees exceed the value of their services. Although 72 percent of persons questioned by the Gallup organization in the late 1930s expressed their approval of labor organizations, less than 60 percent of the public approved of unions by the mid–1980s.[4] American business leaders and the news media reinforce the negative perception of labor organizations by emphasizing the criminal convictions of union officials and depicting organized workers as unambitious and overpaid. Rarely do media stories indicate the continuing need for collective worker action.

Labor leaders must acknowledge the negative view of unions held by an increasing percentage of the public and work to actively counteract these negative stereotypes. A positive image is the first step to increasing membership and enhancing union power vis-à-vis employers and Congress. Labor organizations must utilize the media to disseminate a pro-union message. The recent "look for the union label" campaign, designed to encourage people to purchase garments manufactured in unionized American shops, and the American Federation of State, County, and Municipal Employees advertisements, showing the various important government functions being performed by organized personnel, were very effective. The AFL-CIO recently conducted a "Union Yes" media campaign to demonstrate how labor organizations respond to contemporary employment issues.[5]

By encouraging news reporters at both the national and local level to disseminate stories about industries that exploit unrepresented employees, organized labor will graphically demonstrate the continuing need for worker representation. For example, the sweatshop conditions indigenous to most apparel manufacturers should be exposed. Unlicensed garment shops in cities like New York, Boston, Chicago, Los Angeles, and San Francisco regularly employ legal and illegal immigrants who are forced to work in unconscionable environments for inadequate wages.[6] Unions need to emphasize that people employed in organized garment factories earn a living wage and toil in relatively healthy and safe surroundings.

Unions should supply media experts with information and statistics about the thousands of conscientious workers who are discharged each year in the United States for no valid reason. People are fired for looking at a supervisor the wrong way, having the audacity to question a seemingly irrational company policy, or even complaining to state or federal officials about unhealthy or unsafe employment conditions. The public should be informed that such incidents occur frequently. They need to know that unsubstantiated discharges are not permitted under collective bargaining agreements that contain provisions prohibiting discipline except for "just cause" and grievance-arbitration procedures that ensure a fair resolution of controverted employee claims.

Many people blame the significant United States trade imbalance on high wage unionized industries. They believe that exorbitant labor costs make it difficult for American businesses to compete effectively in a global economy. Labor leaders must educate the public regarding the higher productivity indigenous to organized firms. They should also point out the fact that recent studies indicate that heavily unionized industries have not contributed more to the American trade imbalance than unorganized industries.[7]

Members of the general public have received the distinct impression from the media that union officials are regularly convicted of criminal activity and that labor unions have connections to organized crime. Most people are unaware that the available data indicate that the conviction rate for union officials is no higher than the conviction rate for their business counterparts.[8] Labor organizations need to improve their public image in this area if they are to earn the trust of the public and potential members. By demanding fair media coverage demonstrating that relatively few union agents engage in unlawful activity and comparing the conviction rates of labor leaders with those of business executives, unions will be able to begin to persuade the public of their beneficial role in society.

While working to show the public the relatively low amount of illegal activity in labor unions, union leaders must also reduce corruption among labor representatives and prevent individuals who have violated their fiduciary obligation toward members from holding union office. Too frequently, AFL-CIO lobbyists seek to prevent the adoption of statutory provisions barring persons guilty of abusing their positions from holding elective union positions. Even though Congress often fails to enact similar prohibitions covering business executives convicted of "white collar offenses," union leaders must recognize that their efforts in this regard undermine public confidence in organized labor. AFL-CIO decision makers must stop viewing Labor-Management Reporting and Disclosure Act provisions that bar persons convicted of certain serious crimes from holding union office[9] as unfair to union agents. They should recognize that preclusive laws actually benefit labor organizations by making it clear that unions will not condone the activities of those individuals who ignore their legal obligations. Union supporters should cooperate fully with federal and state investigative efforts to discover and prosecute the relatively few leaders who have breached their fiduciary obligations toward members as a means of assuring the public that illegal activities within the labor movement will not be tolerated. Only then will they convince the public of their anticorruption stance. Labor lobbyists could even support legislation that would similarly prevent business executives convicted of serious crimes from holding responsible corporate positions.

Organized labor should also sever any connections between local or national unions and organized crime and utilize the media to dispel the public perception that unions are mob-controlled. Honest labor leaders should welcome prosecutions against dishonest persons as a means of strengthening the entire movement. If labor could eliminate this negative public image, it will be able to approach organizing campaigns with more power, unburdened by erroneous public perceptions.

By publicizing the fact that thousands of union officials work conscientiously to further the employment interests of represented workers, at salaries substantially less than their management counterparts, organized labor could focus the attention of the public on who is really getting rich on the backs of American workers. In most instances, union representatives in a particular industry are fortunate to earn 10 to 20 percent of the compensation obtained by corporate managers in the same industry. The most highly paid union officials have traditionally been members of the Teamsters. Under previous Teamsters constitutions, leaders could hold national, regional, and local offices simultaneously, thus enabling many leaders to earn over $100,000 and some to earn over $500,000. At its 1991 convention, the Teamsters Union amended its constitution to place a $225,000 per year limit on total compensation earned by any Teamster officer.[10] In addition, Teamsters activities from 1989 to 1992 were conducted under the supervision of a court-appointed monitor who worked diligently to eliminate corruption within the union. In late 1991, Teamsters elected as their president reform candidate Ron Carey, who has since moved quickly to remove corrupt union officials and restore membership democracy.[11]

Even the limited number of union officers who earn over $100,000 per year pale in comparison to the multimillion dollar compensation packages given to countless business executives. In 1960, the chief executive officers of the 100 largest corporations received gross compensation about forty times the average wage of their respective factory workers, and their after-tax earnings were about twelve times the after-tax earnings of production workers.[12] By the late 1980s, however, the same CEOs received gross compensation that was ninety-three times the average wage earned by their factory personnel, and their after-tax earnings were an astonishing seventy times the after-tax earnings of production employees.[13] The dissemination of this information has already caused some people to shift the blame for the lack of competitiveness of American industry from unions to management. Unions could enhance their own public image by proposing legislation that would prohibit corporations from providing executives with compensation packages that are more than fifteen or twenty times the compensation levels of their respective rank-and-file personnel.

In its effort to increase power, prestige, and membership, organized labor could sponsor television programs and movies that portray unions and union members in a positive light. Documentaries depicting the effective efforts of union leaders or the beneficial work of particular labor organizations would simultaneously enhance labor's image and educate the public. Portraying the lives of people from diverse backgrounds whose jobs have been improved through the collective bargaining process would also help close the gap between the perceptions of organized and unorganized individuals. Surveys have found that more union members view labor organizations as positive factors than do their nonunion cohorts,[14] and members have greater confidence in labor officials.[15] Once labor organizations educate nonmembers about the benefits available through representation, they will be better able to organize traditionally unorganized sectors of the workforce.

Despite the recent decline in union membership, there is evidence to suggest that many unorganized employees would be receptive to appropriate unionization appeals. Even though the persistent efforts of business leaders to depict labor organizations as antiquated and unnecessary have had an impact on organization efforts, over 80 percent of Americans continue to believe that "workers should have the right to join unions," and between 50 and 75 percent of the public still think that "virtually all members of the work force would be better off if they were unionized."[16] Almost 70 percent of respondents in a 1984 Harris poll rejected the notion that labor organizations are only relevant to blue-collar workers.[17] Nonetheless, only about one-third of labor force participants expressed a willingness to vote in favor of unionization if offered the opportunity to do so.[18] Labor organizations must work to encourage the pro-union beliefs held by most Americans and counteract the negative perceptions emphasized by the business community.

Enhancing the Employment Rights of All Workers through the Legislative Process

The labor movement can greatly enhance its public image through legislative activity. AFL-CIO affiliates have generally been considered "business unions" that are primarily interested in enhancing member benefits and protections through collective bargaining. As a result, unorganized personnel often believe that labor unions are not concerned about their employment situations.

AFL-CIO affiliates have lobbied in favor of civil rights laws, legislation establishing minimum wages, maximum hours, workplace health and safety standards, worker and unemployment compensation programs, family leave policies, and statutes protecting worker pension and benefit plans. Most, however, have not worked to provide unorganized employees with rights and protections commensurate with those enjoyed by union members under collective bargaining agreements. This provincial philosophy can be attributed to the belief that the legislative enhancement of employment conditions for all workers would diminish the need for traditional union representation.[19] Labor leaders who cater to this perspective fail to recognize that conventional bargaining procedures are no longer adequate to deal with many of the complex problems created by the inexorable transformation of the American economic system into a post-industrial society and the increasing internationalization of the business world. Corporations in highly competitive markets cannot agree to contractual obligations that would disadvantage them with respect to unconstrained companies. It should thus be apparent to labor leaders that they cannot rely exclusively on collective bargaining to further employee interests. Only legislation covering all workers can provide industry-wide protections.

The economic plight of unorganized workers negatively affects unionized employees. The availability of nonunion individuals, particularly during periods of unemployment, meaningfully threatens the employment standards and job security enjoyed by unionized personnel.[20] This threat is exacerbated by the ability of employers to permanently replace striking workers. Union leaders concerned that legislatively furthering the interests of all employees would undermine the popularity of labor organizations need only consider the fact that European trade unions, which have historically been substantially involved in the political process, have membership rates three, four, and even five times the moribund rate of their politically inactive American counterparts. Even within the United States, the most rapid union expansion in the past three decades has occurred in the public sector, where employees are provided with pervasive statutory protections.

By pursuing legislation that would benefit all workers, whether or not they are unionized, labor organizations would further their objectives in two important ways. To the extent that modern unions demonstrate their dedication to the improvement of the rights of all employees, they will develop a positive public image and increase the likelihood that workers who have traditionally been unreceptive to unionization will reconsider. Furthermore, if unions could obtain statutory provisions defining basic employment terms for all workers, they would substantially decrease the diseconomies associated with unionization. As generally applicable legislative safeguards reduce the artificial labor cost differentials between union and nonunion business enterprises, companies would be less likely to oppose employee organization. The impact of this factor is discernible in Western European countries that apply negotiated employment rights to all workers within a particular industry, regardless of the degree of union support at specific plants. Such a reduction in employer antipathy toward labor organizations would make it easier for unions to recruit new members.

Unorganized employees are frequently more devastated by automation, subcontracting, and production relocation than their unionized cohorts. Even workers covered by conventional bargaining agreements find it difficult to adjust to such changes. Politically astute labor leaders recently lobbied successfully in favor of federal legislation providing employees with sixty days advance notice of mass layoffs and plant closures.[21] In some instances, the personnel threatened with layoff may be able to respond to company concerns by reducing labor costs or increasing productivity and obviate the need for such dislocations. Where such a result cannot be achieved, advance notification enables workers to consider alternative employment opportunities and retraining options while they are still gainfully employed.

Labor organizations could meet this emerging need of contemporary workers by seeking legislation that would establish retraining[22] and relocation funds analogous to unemployment compensation plans that would provide employees with portable rights based upon their previous attachment to the labor market. Individuals facing long-term layoffs would be able to utilize these financial resources to learn new skills and/or relocate to geographic areas with greater employment opportunities. Unions could also serve the needs of unorganized employees by supporting statutes that mandate severance pay and/or special unemployment compensation for employees displaced by an economy moving toward a post-industrial environment. These benefits should definitely be available to individuals dislocated by the transfer of domestic production jobs to foreign export platforms.

Another way to appeal to today's workforce as a means of ensuring the continued vitality of the labor movement is for unions to address issues of employee dignity. Legislation requiring parental leave, employer- or government-sponsored child care, job sharing, and flextime programs would benefit parents. Increasing numbers of single parents and dual-income households have made these "options" essential, and yet employers have failed to provide them unilaterally. Unions could enhance their popularity among traditionally unorganized workers by helping them attain these economic necessities.

Job-sharing plans would obviate the need for layoffs during economic recessions and would permit unions to work for the benefit of employees instead of sacrificing the jobs of some to retain a semblance of power. Labor organizations should therefore promote legislation that would allow workers to reduce their weekly hours to thirty or thirty-five, and enable a greater number of individuals to retain their jobs. Supporting this type of legislation would enhance labor's image with respect to the millions of workers who regularly fear that they are going to lose their jobs.

Union officials must continue to support comprehensive health insurance coverage for all Americans. Approximately 37 million individuals currently lack basic health coverage, and a national program would diminish the financial pressures encountered by private employers in providing such coverage. By lobbying for broad health care coverage, labor organizations can significantly enhance their image among older workers. In addition, unions will be seen by the American public as supporting an issue of vital and increasing national importance.

Labor organizations need to lobby in favor of laws restricting intrusive drug testing. They must seek amendments to the Drug Free Workplace Act of 1988[23] that would limit random drug testing to persons holding safety-sensitive positions. This would enable unions to garner the support of individuals who feel that management has invaded their privacy, while they simultaneously acknowledge the serious nature of the drug problem and the need for employers to protect the safety of their workers and clientele. Demanding that individual drug testing be based on articulable facts that provide a reasonable suspicion of drug or alcohol abuse would prevent employers from abusing drug testing, and help to maintain the dignity of employees.

Many corporations currently rely solely upon the less expensive and less accurate enzyme multiplied immunoassay technique (EMIT). Companies obtaining positive EMIT results should be statutorily obligated to perform the more accurate gas chromatography/ mass spectrometry (GC/MS) test before taking adverse actions against workers who test positive.[24] By working to lower the risk of false positives, unions will show employees that they have the power to protect them against job loss for arbitrary or unfounded reasons. Unions should encourage federal and local governments to establish more rehabilitation programs to assist alcohol and drug abusers, so that even these workers feel that they are important to the labor movement. They should lobby for an amendment to the Drug Free Workplace Act that would mandate rehabilitation for first time abusers to encourage these individuals to become full contributors to American industry.[25]

Labor organizations should cooperate with companies and government agencies to enhance the educational programs available at work and through high schools and community colleges. Employers are finding it increasingly difficult to obtain well-educated workers. Approximately 25 percent of high school students leave before they graduate,[26] and many of the individuals who do obtain high school diplomas lack the basic verbal and math skills required by most companies. Thirteen percent of American adults are considered "functionally illiterate" due to their inability to perform rudimentary mental tasks.[27] Half of all seventeen-year-old students cannot calculate percentages or solve simple equations.[28] Many workers are unable to comprehend verbal or written instructions. Business and labor leaders should jointly lobby federal, state, and local officials to expand the educational and training opportunities available to future labor force participants and to workers who currently need to learn the skills required for new occupations and existing occupations affected by technological changes. In addition, they should jointly encourage the adoption of minimal competency standards that will prevent the continued graduation of functionally illiterate individuals. This investment in human capital would increase productivity and decrease unemployment.

Probably the most significant benefit employees derive from union representation is the "just cause" limitation on discipline expressly or implicitly contained in most bargaining agreements.[29] In the absence of such a restriction and the accompanying grievance-arbitration procedures through which that right is usually enforced, most persons are employed "at will," and can be terminated at any time for any reason that does not contravene a specific statutory prohibition.[30] Although many state courts have evidenced a willingness to impose limited restrictions on unconscionable employee discharges, most judicial edicts have continued to follow the common law "at will" doctrine. They have upheld employers' unfettered ability to terminate employees for even arbitrary and capricious reasons.[31]

"Some 60 million U.S. employees are subject to the employment-at-will doctrine and about 2 million of them are discharged each year.... About 150,000 of these workers would have been found to have been discharged without just cause and reinstated to their former jobs if they had had the right to appeal to an impartial arbitrator as do almost all unionized workers."[32] The American labor movement should lobby in favor of state and federal legislation that would provide all private sector workers with protection against unjust discipline and termination[33] similar to the contractual safeguards available to unionized employees. Unions need not be concerned that the availability of legislative protections would diminish employee enthusiasm for unions, because labor organizations would provide valuable assistance to individuals forced to invoke their statutory rights. They would also insure that wrongfully discharged persons who have been reinstated do not suffer further employment recriminations.

Unions that continue to focus narrowly on the interests of bargaining unit personnel are destined for extinction. The decreasing number of unionized employers will fight more zealously to decertify incumbent bargaining agents they believe are putting them at a critical disadvantage in relation to their unorganized competitors. Labor organizations need to return to their heritage. During the latter part of the nineteenth century, groups like the Knights of Labor and the National Labor Union functioned like social movements dedicated to the advancement of the rights of all workers. AFL-CIO affiliates have generally operated like "business unions" primarily interested in the enhancement of the employment conditions of dues-paying members. As a result, unorganized personnel have often believed that modern labor unions are not concerned with their employment situations.

For the American labor movement to reestablish the social movement approach indigenous to its roots, it must revitalize its alliances with other activist groups. Unions must work more closely with civil rights groups, such as the National Association for the Advancement of Colored People, the Mexican-American Legal and Education Defense Fund, the American Association of Retired Persons, and the National Organization for Women. They should also strengthen their ties with groups concerned with health and safety, the adequacy of worker and unemployment compensation schemes and Social Security benefits, the fairness of tax laws on lower income individuals, the lack of basic health coverage for millions of Americans, and other issues of concern to workers and their families. If these groups coordinate their efforts, they will be able to achieve greater economic and political influence.[34] Unions will be able to utilize their increased power to increase membership and remain a vital force in the American economy.

If labor organizations induce Congress and state legislatures to enact statutes providing all workers with pervasive employment protections, union strength will be enhanced, not diminished.[35] The role of labor organizations would shift to one of providing advice and assistance to individuals challenging discriminatory practices, improper layoffs, or unjust discipline, or to those seeking unpaid wages or overtime pay, the protection of their pension or fringe benefit rights, worker or unemployment compensation, or the enforcement of applicable health and safety regulations.[36] The active participation of union representatives would provide both organized and unorganized personnel with the influence that can only be achieved through collective action. Because most lower level employees lack the financial resources to retain legal representation with respect to such basic employment issues, they would welcome the assistance of labor organization specialists. The costs associated with this representation would be offset by membership dues or service fees imposed upon nonmembers who request such assistance.

Enhancing the Public Perception of Unions through the Collective Bargaining Process

Unions functioning as exclusive bargaining agents must continue to provide bargaining unit personnel with substantive rights that transcend the protections afforded by state and federal enactments or risk losing the support of their members. By providing represented employees with benefits not available to nonunion workers, labor organizations will make themselves more attractive to unorganized personnel and increase their ranks. For example, negotiated wage rates continue to exceed the statutorily prescribed minimum wage. In addition, even if some form of universal health coverage is eventually provided by federal law, unions and employers will negotiate supplementary benefits and claims handling procedures. Prior to the availability of statutory coverage, private parties will discuss cost-containment mechanisms that will enable business entities to provide affordable health insurance.

Labor organizations should seek bargaining agreement provisions covering a myriad of employment-related topics to assist the employees they currently represent and to attract to collectivization those employees not yet organized. Fringe benefit plans could provide legal care, eye care, dental care, child care, care for the aging parents of employees, and parental leave for workers having or adopting children. These programs can be cost-efficient. For example, employers have discovered that the cost of providing child care coverage is outweighed by the savings achieved through reduced absenteeism, improved employee morale, and the enhanced ability to attract and retain qualified workers.[37] Individuals with satisfactory personal lives are generally more productive than those experiencing personal problems.

During the coming years, representative labor organizations should utilize collective bargaining to protect bargaining unit employees from the vicissitudes associated with the introduction of new technology, production transfers, and plant closures. Nonunionized employees will quickly see the benefit of representation if labor organizations are successful in this area. Labor leaders have recognized the need for modern production techniques,[38] and they have the right to demand that business firms reciprocate with the establishment of educational programs that would prepare affected bargaining unit personnel for future occupational demands.[39] Individuals displaced by automation should be entitled to continued compensation during the period of their retraining.[40] The ongoing employment of such workers would be benevolent, would greatly increase employee loyalty to the firm, and would diminish costly employee turnover and guarantee a highly skilled future workforce.[41]

Unions should demand contractual restrictions aimed at diminishing the likelihood of such business transactions. Economically powerful labor organizations will be able to induce employers to accept clauses expressly precluding the relocation or elimination of bargaining unit jobs.[42] Alternatively, agreements should permit such job changes, but ensure displaced workers continued employment security through guaranteed annual wages or some form of job tenure similar to that presently enjoyed by many Japanese workers.[43] Job security programs do not simply benefit the affected employees. When such tenure plans are in effect, workers are less resistant to operational change. This provides managers with greater flexibility, and company loyalty to workers often enhances employee morale.

Unions should demand provisions requiring employers to provide advance notice of contemplated decisions that would directly affect the job security of unit personnel and an opportunity to discuss proposed changes. Even when labor organizations cannot prevent the introduction of labor-saving technology or production transfers, they may be able to protect the interests of adversely affected workers through provisions guaranteeing them intraplant or interplant transfer privileges, retraining opportunities, or severance pay. The availability of these benefits for unionized personnel will encourage collectivization among unorganized workers.

Corporations and unions can jointly establish remedial education programs to improve the basic skills of employees. They could schedule classes before or after work, and employ teachers on a part-time basis to develop the necessary skills of these personnel. Workers who reach higher levels of competence should receive greater advancement opportunities. The extra funds needed to support such programs would be offset by the increased employee productivity associated with a more educated workforce. Unions could negotiate the creation of special funds designed to finance worker retraining.[44] Employees could be reimbursed for the expense of attending relevant classes offered at educational institutions. Bargaining agreements could authorize reimbursement for the cost of attending professional meetings that would enhance personal skills. Investment in "human capital" is as important as investment in new technology.[45] Unions should induce federal and state governments to encourage the development of such educational schemes through the availability of tax credits for participating business firms. Unrepresented workers may seek unionization as a means of obtaining access to these programs.

To provide a sufficient financial base for educational programs and to prevent generous employers from assuming a disproportionate share of retraining costs at the expense of competitiveness, companies within a particular industry should be encouraged to create industry-supported programs similar to those that have been successfully established in Germany.[46] Such expansive training inures to the benefit of all industry participants. Individuals choosing to remain with their present companies learn new skills that enable them to perform broader job tasks and to assume greater decision-making responsibility. Workers who decide to leave their current employers would likely take their enhanced skills to other industry firms that were equally responsible for the costs of the training. More competent employees would enjoy greater professional mobility and higher future earning capacities.[47]

DEVELOPING INNOVATIVE ORGANIZING TECHNIQUES

As the United States continues its transformation into a post-industrial society, the number of white-collar and service positions increases and the number of blue-collar production jobs shrinks. Corporations are opening a disproportionate percentage of new facilities in Sunbelt areas, more women and minorities are entering the labor force, and the average age of workers is increasing. If labor organizations are to survive in the coming decades, they must find new ways to entice white-collar, southern, female, minority, and elderly individuals to recognize the benefits associated with collectivization. If they cannot achieve real gains in these areas, private sector unions will become anemic institutions with limited economic and political influence beyond the contracting manufacturing sector.

Despite the continued decrease in union membership, labor entities have devoted fewer resources to organizing efforts during recent years.[48] Membership declines have left unions with fewer resources to commit to organizing activity. Corporate executives have begun to envision the total demise of American unions. If union membership continues to decline throughout the 1990s, these executives may be able to generate a business environment in which labor unions will no longer be relevant. Management officials would be able to determine all employment conditions unilaterally, because individual employees would have no significant influence over the terms of their employment.

Business leaders are not likely to decrease their opposition toward unions. When the Supreme Court recently sustained the authority of the Labor Board to promulgate rules defining the bargaining units for health care institutions,[49] the American Hospital Association immediately pledged to fight union organizing efforts on all fronts.[50] A prominent management attorney suggested that "employers should use every waking moment to assess their vulnerability to organizing and begin the process of 'hardening the target.' "[51] Labor entities will have to devise novel methods of countering such management tactics and appealing to workers who might be contemplating collective action to retain their current strength and build a foundation from which to grow.

The American labor movement will also have to cope with recent Labor Board and court decisions that have made it more difficult for unions to organize workers. In *NLRB v. Yeshiva University*,[52] the Supreme Court held that persons who meaningfully influence corporate policies constitute "managerial employees" excluded from NLRA coverage. Although the university professors in that case possessed the authority to formulate and implement institutional policies, they lacked any real control over their wages, hours, and working conditions. The Court thus ignored the fact that unionization would have provided these "managerial" personnel with input regarding their fundamental employment conditions. Following *Yeshiva*, the Labor Board ruled that when a representative labor organization negotiates a bargaining agreement providing nonmanagerial workers with significant influence over management policies, the workers become "managerial" personnel and forfeit their statutory right to continued representation.[53] This type of decision will make it increasingly difficult for unions to organize nonsupervisory persons.[54]

In recent years, management labor relations specialists have significantly modified their methods of discouraging employee unionization. The overt threats and palpable economic intimidation of the past have been replaced with highly sophisticated techniques developed by professional behaviorists.[55] Corporations have combined more aesthetic employment environments with subtle appeals to workers' class consciousness to convince employees of the obsolescence and lower class nature of union representation. Employers urge that wages and working conditions will not be improved through collective bargaining, because employees can only obtain what employers are willing to provide.[56] They emphasize that the NLRA does not oblige them to agree to any union proposals, and they note that employees who decide to engage in a work stoppage in support of bargaining demands may be permanently replaced. The success of these measures can be attributed, in large part, to the fact that many union organizers continue to utilize the provincial proselytizing techniques that were developed during the late 1930s and early 1940s to appeal to blue-collar production personnel.[57] While the traditional approaches may still appeal to unskilled and semi-skilled service sector workers, they are unlikely to appeal to more educated, white-collar personnel. Unions must modify their organizing techniques to successfully respond to the onslaught of management.

American labor unions must revitalize their organizing practices if they are to expand their membership and remain a vital force in the American economy. They must reconsider their sources of leadership and act upon statistical trends in organizing data. Tailoring their organizing efforts to particular groups of workers will slowly but surely enable labor to capture the power it needs to successfully propound its new agenda.

Union Leadership

Unions have historically recruited their leaders from the rank-and-file membership to ensure that such officials would identify with and understand the concerns of the workers they represent. This politically sagacious practice unfortunately fails to guarantee the selection of the well-educated and charismatic personnel necessary to counter management's innovative anti-union techniques.[58] The minimal financial remuneration and relatively low prestige accorded most trade union officials by society, however, make it difficult for labor organizations to attract new talent. This syndrome frequently causes the protégés of aging former leaders to continue established practices without regard to their current efficacy.

The established union leadership has not been adept at organizing recent labor force entrants.[59] Many labor officials have failed to comprehend the problems and aspirations of burgeoning white-collar occupations.[60] As labor officials encounter more affluent and better educated workers, they must be able to understand and reflect the concerns of those individuals. Vast technological, educational, and societal changes have pervasively influenced most occupations over the past several decades. Organizers must also recognize the impact of the dramatic increase in labor force participation by women and minorities.

Unions must employ energetic and charismatic individuals who are committed to the advancement of worker rights. They should hire some people who have obtained degrees in industrial relations and have studied organizational behavior. These people will bring new strategies to the labor movement and will be able to enhance the organizing skills of representatives promoted from the rank and file. New organizers should be provided with special training to familiarize them with the unique needs of the union's members and the behaviors of the business entity at issue. Some labor organizations may have sufficient resources to develop their own educational programs. Other unions may take advantage of courses taught at the George Meany Center for Labor Studies, which was established for this purpose by the AFL-CIO in 1968.[61] Special classes are also offered at university institutes of industrial relations. The types of training available are diverse:

> Organizer training has shifted from information giving (about the law and merits of unionization) to in-depth practice skills required for effective enlistment of members—speaking, planning, interpersonal and group relationships. How to cope with "union-busters" is another feature. Case studies and simulations immerse trainees in problem solving and interpersonal skills development.[62]

Trained organizers must be able to empathize with the occupations being targeted. It is generally beneficial for the organizers or their families to have worked in the industries involved. This increases the likelihood that the organizers will be respected by the group being organized. It also makes it easier for the organizers to reflect the concerns of those people.

During the formative stage of a campaign, union organizers must determine which workers are most respected by their colleagues. By enlisting the support and assistance of these individuals, their task will be greatly facilitated. These leaders can distribute union literature and proselytize effectively in favor of collectivization due to their influence among their peers. Their co-workers would be more likely to listen to their appeals than to the claims of outside organizers.

Focusing on the Needs of Targeted Employees

Labor unions must acknowledge that collectivization is a grass-roots movement involving rank-and-file personnel. Successful organizers are generally able to elicit the views and assistance of workers in the proposed bargaining unit because "[e]mployees have strong views about their jobs that they are eager to tell to someone they think really cares."[63] Individuals generally contemplate unionization because of their lack of influence with respect to their basic employment terms. Organizers must understand these frustrations and indicate to all workers the degree to which they can gain empowerment through a collective voice. Organizers must also realize that many employees are more concerned today with issues pertaining to employment dignity than with traditional economic matters. They need to emphasize the way in which workers can enhance their feelings of self-worth through collectivization.

Organizers must spend substantial time in the communities being organized to show prospective members that they are personally concerned about the employees involved and are readily accessible to them. A study conducted by the AFL-CIO Department of Organization and Field Services recently found that unions prevail in 78 percent of elections in which regular house calls are made to target employees.[64] The victory rate is only 40 percent when communication is carried out primarily through telephone calls and 39 percent when mass mailings are employed.[65] The use of house visits is likely to stimulate grass-roots enthusiasm. By taking the time to listen to each employee's concerns, organizers can demonstrate a respect for each person's viewpoint and formulate collective objectives that reflect the actual desires of bargaining unit personnel.

AFL-CIO data similarly indicate that other "rank-and-file intensive" organizing techniques significantly increase the likelihood of union victory. For example, the conducting of small group meetings involving bargaining unit personnel, the establishment of representation committees comprised primarily of unit workers, and other regular involvement of rank-and-file employees in the organizing campaign greatly increase the union success rate.[66] "Solidarity demonstrations" are also beneficial. If organizers induce bargaining unit workers to wear union buttons or T-shirts or to participate in campaign rallies, they increase the probability of an election victory.

The recent organizing success of the Harvard Union of Clerical and Technical Workers (HUCTW) provides a model that could be emulated by other labor entities. HUCTW sought worker support through one-on-one personal contacts, and it carefully recruited organizing leaders from within the targeted work force.[67] Although HUCTW focused upon economic concerns, it also stressed issues of power and self-respect.[68] It recognized the need to imbue clerical personnel with a sense of dignity. The individuals who supported HUCTW concluded that they could only enhance their employment interests in a unified manner. One HUCTW member eloquently summarized the feelings of many: "The underlying issue is our right to a voice in decisions which affect our lives. Individually we can only whisper, together as a union we can roar."[69]

Developing Organizing Strategies

Before a labor union begins an organizing drive, it must confirm that the targeted group is amenable to unionization. The union must look for employers with unsatisfactory personnel practices and employees who are not pleased with their existing employment circumstances.[70] Formal or informal preliminary surveys can be conducted to identify units likely to vote in favor of union representation. If labor organizations carefully choose worker aggregations that are inclined to collectivize, they will significantly increase election victory rates.

Too many labor unions limit their organizing efforts to large units because of economies of scale. The problem with this approach is that unions prevail in only 28 percent of the representation elections carried out in units with over 500 employees, while they win over 50 percent of the elections held in units with under 50 people.[71] This disparity may be attributed to several factors. Corporations with large units are more likely to have the financial resources necessary to conduct aggressive anti-union campaigns. In addition, it is difficult for organizers to personally contact a significant number of the individuals in a large unit. They instead resort to less successful tactics such as pamphlets or telephone calls.

Future employment settings will not be likely to include large numbers of workers in single locations.[72] An increasing number of firms will be service-oriented. These businesses tend to be smaller than their manufacturing counterparts. Although it will cost more per employee to organize small units, the additional cost is outweighed by the higher success rate. As more units are organized, unions will benefit from the increased dues received from new members that will provide them with greater economic and political power, and enable them to develop more extensive organizing programs.

When several labor organizations compete for the right to represent the same group of employees, it is likely that these workers will be unionized at the end of the campaign. The union victory rate in contested elections is almost 75 percent.[73] While this phenomenon may reflect the fact that the target group is especially receptive to unionization, AFL-CIO affiliates should consider the benefits to be achieved from coordinated campaigns conducted by different unions. Joint efforts may increase the probability of a pro-union result, and the prevailing organization could share some of its additional dues revenues with the losing union.

Although AFL-CIO members are not permitted to organize individuals already represented by another AFL-CIO affiliate,[74] there are times when such conduct should not be proscribed. If an incumbent union is inadequately representing bargaining unit personnel, it is likely to be decertified. By allowing another union to organize such disaffected workers before decertification of the existing union, the AFL-CIO may prevent a decertification campaign that would probably preclude unionization of that unit in the near future.

ADAPTING TO DEMOGRAPHIC CHANGES

The Shift from the Rustbelt to the Sunbelt

The continued migration of workers to the Sunbelt states[75] and to rural areas[76] will force unions to devise new organizing strategies that will appeal to the needs of people residing in these environments. Although it may be more expensive for labor organizations to seek rural converts, collectivization could enhance the economic circumstances of rural workers, and socially active labor unions could provide the kinds of personal services associated with traditional fraternal organizations.

Unions have historically found the southern and southwestern regions of the country difficult to organize.[77] Recent trends, however, indicate that this situation is changing.[78] As more northern workers who have traditionally supported the labor movement migrate to the Sunbelt and discuss the benefits of union representation with their new co-workers, union organizing should be facilitated. During the late 1980s, unions that had the assistance of the AFL-CIO Industrial Union Department achieved highly respectable certification results in southern states. Those labor organizations prevailed in a remarkable 63 percent of representation elections conducted in Alabama, North Carolina, South Carolina, Georgia, Mississippi, and Tennessee.[79]

The unions assisted by the AFL-CIO committed substantial resources to the southern organizing campaign.[80] They established employee committees within each targeted plant, and secured a substantial degree of worker participation. The greatest impediment to organization involved worker ignorance of their legal rights and fear of employer reprisals. Through carefully structured education programs, union organizers apprised individuals of their statutory prerogatives and dispelled their unfounded apprehensions. Labor organizations can develop similar programs that would enable them to unionize a greater proportion of Sunbelt employees.

Changes in Workforce Composition

Approximately two-thirds of the labor force entrants during the next decade will be women, and almost 30 percent will be minorities.[81] By 2030, one-third of Americans will be fifty-five and older.[82] Labor unions will have to expand their appeals to these individuals if they are to achieve sustained growth. Even though labor unions have not historically achieved significant organizational success with female and minority workers, there is reason for union officials to be more optimistic today. Recent AFL-CIO statistics indicate that unions prevail in 60 to 66 percent of Labor Board elections involving bargaining units comprised primarily of female and/or minority employees.[83]

Women Workers. The record of organized labor with respect to female employees has certainly been undistinguished. Although 30 percent of organized workers are women, only 12 percent of national union leadership positions are held by females.[84] In 1980, Joyce Miller, President of the Coalition of Labor Union Women, became the first woman to serve as a member of the AFL-CIO Executive Council.[85] Despite the dearth of female union officials, the proportion of women union members has actually increased since the mid–1950s.[86] In addition, 41 percent of women workers have indicated that they would support a union if they had the chance to do so.[87] AFL-CIO affiliates must encourage the election and appointment of more female officials, employ more women organizers,[88] and work more closely with the Coalition of Labor Union Women,[89] 9 to 5, and other groups of working women to broaden their appeal to the increasing number of organizable women entering the labor force.[90]

The labor movement needs to confront issues important to female workers to attract them to unions. Labor organizations must continue to seek legislation and bargaining agreement provisions designed to eliminate gender-based compensation differentials[91] and challenge artificial barriers to the advancement of qualified women. In addition, union officials should support parental leave programs and flexible hour plans, and strive to obtain government and/or employer sponsored day-care centers to facilitate the movement of women into the labor force. If unions are responsive to the needs of women, they will benefit from the membership dues of millions of new labor market participants.[92]

Many women continue to be segregated in traditionally female occupations,[93] and earn substantially less than their male cohorts in equivalent positions.[94] They regularly experience a lack of meaningful control over their employment situations. Unions should make female employees aware that women workers who have collectivized earn 39 percent more than their nonunion cohorts[95] and tend to have a greater sense of occupational empowerment.[96] This factor may induce the millions of women employed in traditionally female occupations to contemplate the benefits to be derived from unionization.

Minority Workers.   Blacks and other minorities were responsive to organizing efforts during the late 1930s, particularly in heavy industries being collectivized by industrial unions, but their enthusiasm subsequently waned due to the vestiges of discrimination in many craft unions.[97] The enactment of Title VII of the Civil Rights Act of 1964[98] required the offending labor organizations to abandon their discriminatory practices and impelled recalcitrant union leaders to recognize their legal and moral obligations toward minority employees. If labor organizations can affirmatively act to ensure equal employment opportunities for all persons regardless of their race or nationality, minority workers could become a cornerstone in the rebirth of the labor movement. A recent survey disclosed that 69 percent of minority employees would support a union if they had the opportunity.[99] This propensity should facilitate organizing minority workers in all sectors of the economy.

AFL-CIO affiliates should emphasize to potential minority union members that most labor organizations have historically supported equal rights for minority workers. Representative labor organizations must continue to seek and enforce bargaining agreement provisions proscribing discrimination. They should continue their efforts to eliminate race-based wage and job disparities. Unions should hire more minority organizers to demonstrate their unequivocal commitment to equal employment opportunity. During new organizing campaigns, they should emphasize the fact that the average earnings of unionized minority workers exceed those of their unorganized counterparts by approximately 30 percent.[100] Unions that are committed to the eradication of all forms of employment discrimination will be able to appeal to the increasing number of minority labor force participants.

Older Workers.   As the American labor force continues to age, labor unions will have to formulate new bargaining objectives that reflect the interests of older workers or else forego a growing source of members. Labor organizations can attract these workers by strengthening pension plans and negotiating supplemental health insurance to protect retirees from expenses not covered by Medicare. Many individuals fear that their employment opportunities will be reduced as they age, but bargaining agents can win the support of these workers by seeking provisions guaranteeing qualified senior employees the advancement rights they deserve.[101]

Some older workers want the chance to move toward retirement on a phased basis. Labor unions should negotiate contractual provisions with employers that permit senior personnel to opt for part-time employment on a two-thirds or half-time basis as they approach retirement. Unions can counsel management to develop work-sharing programs that would enable two older employees to share the same position. This arrangement would allow employers to benefit from experienced workers, and the individual employees would work the flexible schedules suited to their employment needs. Senior workers have generally been enthusiastic union supporters. If labor organizations continue to protect the employment interests of older persons, they will retain their support and even increase their power as this segment of the labor force increases.

THE ABILITY TO ORGANIZE WHITE-COLLAR AND SERVICE PERSONNEL

To enhance their economic and political vitality in the coming decades, labor organizations will have to develop programs designed to appeal to the burgeoning ranks of white-collar and service personnel. Only about 10 percent of service industry and office workers have been organized.[102] Union officials must concentrate their efforts on the major white-collar and service industries: insurance, health care, banking and finance, and retail. To reach these workers, the labor movement will need to undergo an organizing revolution similar to the industrial union movement of the late 1930s and early 1940s[103] and the public sector movement during the 1960s and 1970s.[104] Because many government unions have successfully organized white-collar and service employees,[105] they can provide a model for private sector unions. The AFL-CIO should establish a Professional and Service Employee Department that would include new organizations in each of the targeted industries. Existing unions—such as the Retail Clerks International Association (RCIA), the Office and Professional Employees International Union (OPEIU), and the Service Employees International Union (SEIU), all of which have already demonstrated the ability to collectivize retail, office, and health care workers—should be charter members of the new department.

Service employees are generally locked into low-paying and routinized jobs with minimal opportunities for personal advancement. Although worker turnover is usually high, thus negating a perceived need among employees for unionization, service personnel are optimal targets for collectivization because of the poor economic and environmental conditions associated with their positions. Union representation could enhance their economic circumstances and improve their employment surroundings. Labor organizations could be less concerned with significant foreign competition, because most service jobs are necessarily performed in the United States. AFL-CIO affiliates should learn from unions like the RCIA and the SEIU, and develop programs that will appeal to service personnel who wish to improve their employment circumstances regardless of whether they view their jobs as short-term or long-term.

White-collar workers have not been inclined toward union membership primarily because of their perceptions of the labor movement and their own employment situations. These workers historically enjoyed an upward mobility that induced them to identify more with the interests of their employers than with those of their rank-and-file colleagues.[106] Their middle-class socioeconomic status caused many white-collar workers to question the benefits to be derived from membership in blue-collar trade unions.[107] Manipulative managers determined to convince their white-collar employees that labor union participation would be both unprofessional and personally demeaning.

As the United States has moved toward a post-industrial society, white-collar positions have significantly changed. Businesses have become more bureaucratized. Global firms control local operations through the concentration of managerial authority in centralized administrations that function on a strictly hierarchical basis. As a result of these changes, many lower-level management employees have had their discretionary authority circumscribed. They receive directives from regional, national, or even international officers who tell them the exact manner in which they are to carry out their managerial tasks.[108]

The employment situation for nonmanagerial professionals has similarly deteriorated. Restrictive corporate policies have reduced their autonomy and limited their exercise of professional discretion.[109] The computer revolution has also curtailed white-collar employee freedom. As the United States has evolved into an advanced information-processing economy, the individuals performing the requisite computer functions have experienced less occupational autonomy. Supervisors can electronically monitor employee keystrokes, break periods, and error rates.[110] Even the work of problem-solving analysts has become routinized, and scientists and engineers find themselves subjected to greater business constraints.[111]

The economic circumstances of white-collar personnel have eroded during the past decade. Between 1977 and 1990, the remuneration received by upper executives rose by an astonishing 220 percent, while the compensation levels for mid-level managerial employees and hourly workers increased at a much more moderate rate.[112] Top corporate officials no longer pretend that they share a common bond with lower-level white-collar personnel. Business leaders believe that they deserve to receive financial rewards reflecting the profits generated by their efforts. Because they no longer provide managerial employees at the plant and regional levels with full autonomy, upper management is no longer willing to attribute enterprise gains to the decision-making functions of those people.

Corporate executives now regard lower-level white-collar employees as analogous to blue-collar production workers. When economic conditions deteriorate, such white-collar professionals become as disposable as their production colleagues.[113] This reduced job security makes it more difficult for companies to convince white-collar personnel to identify with long-term enterprise interests and weakens the belief of lower and middle management in their potential for upward corporate mobility.

As white-collar employees increasingly find their situations similar to their blue-collar compatriots,[114] they may contemplate the benefits of collectivization. Labor unions must recognize that these individuals are not concerned solely with economic issues. They want to participate in the decision-making process of the firm and to enhance their employment dignity.[115] Many no longer believe that corporate employers respond to their interests, exhibit concern about their job security, or provide employment environments as pleasant as those they previously experienced.[116]

The baby-boom generation has experienced an additional barrier to upward mobility. Although the number of well-educated professionals has increased dramatically, the number of desirable corporate positions has not. Individuals in their late thirties and early forties thus have fewer opportunities for advancement. A study of technicians and engineers in the French electrical industry revealed that union militancy was directly related to diminished employee mobility.[117] As American professional workers react to similar barriers, they may begin to identify more closely with their blue-collar colleagues than with the corporate managers who have contributed to their declining employment status. This development may persuade growing numbers of white-collar employees to yield to unionization entreaties.[118] United States labor organizations should be encouraged by the fact that white-collar personnel in other industrial countries have been unionized for many years.[119]

If labor unions want to successfully organize white-collar personnel, they must devise strategies that will specifically appeal to them. Their campaign materials must be drafted to interest highly educated people who are as concerned with self-actualization as with economic gain. Labor unions must employ erudite organizers who can relate effectively with professional employees. Organizers must emphasize issues pertaining to worker dignity. They should formulate bargaining objectives that involve employee autonomy, worker participation in managerial decision making, and the opportunity for professional advancement.[120] Campaign literature might include demands for paid educational leave and greater opportunities to attend professional conferences.[121]

The unionization rate for white-collar professionals now exceeds the rate for nonprofessional workers.[122] This indicates that many white-collar personnel want to enhance their employment influence and view unionization as an appropriate vehicle to accomplish this objective. Even though a substantial share of organized white-collar people are government employees, labor organizations should be able to similarly advance the employment interests of private sector professionals. As the American industrial system becomes more automated and professional jobs become more routinized, highly educated but underutilized employees will increasingly experience dampened aspirations and professional dissatisfaction. To counteract their loss of individual autonomy and regain the respect and dignity eroded by organizational changes and technological advances, many private sector white-collar workers may resort to collective action. As more professionals, such as physicians, lawyers, and accountants, experience a similar loss of control over their employment destinies, they too will contemplate unionization.[123]

During the past several decades, the socioeconomic situations of blue-collar and white-collar employees have become intertwined. Changing employment circumstances have caused the simultaneous "embourgeoisement" of blue-collar workers and the "proletarianization" of professionals.[124] White-collar workers who previously viewed themselves as "upper-middle class" are more likely to consider themselves "middle class" today, while blue-collar employees who formerly saw themselves as "working class" now think of themselves as "middle class."[125] Both groups share a feeling of powerlessness that may be alleviated through collective action.[126] If American labor organizations can demonstrate their capacity to preserve professional values while advancing joint employment interests, they will experience significant growth among white-collar personnel.

THE ASSOCIATIONAL APPROACH

One of the unique aspects of the American industrial relations system is the exclusivity doctrine. Under Section 9(a) of the NLRA,[127] a labor organization may only become the statutory bargaining agent for the employees in a proposed unit if a majority of the individuals in that unit indicate their wish to be represented by that union.[128] The NLRA does not require employers to recognize labor entities that do not enjoy such majority support. As a result, millions of workers who support unions remain unrepresented because they are employed in settings in which a majority of their colleagues do not presently want a bargaining representative. If labor organizations can provide tangible benefits for union adherents who are employed in these environments, many of these sympathizers will formalize their relationship with unions and expand their economic and political strength. As the fellow workers of such individuals notice and appreciate the services provided by labor organizations, they may ultimately decide to support unionization. If unions reestablish the associational approach initiated by the early worker guilds, they will enhance their institutional influence over the employment relationship, regardless of the representational status of any given employee.

American workers have consistently recognized the benefits derived from associational endeavors by joining occupational guilds and forming social and fraternal entities such as the Workmen's Circle and the German Workmen's Benefit Fund.[129] Contemporary professional employees join organizations such as the American Bar Association (ABA), the American Dental Association (ADA), the American Medical Association (AMA), the American Nurses Association (ANA), the National Education Association (NEA), the American Association of University Professors (AAUP), and various scientific and technical groups. These institutions have promulgated rules governing professional standards, and created career development programs and continuing education curricula. They have lobbied successfully for licensing requirements designed to restrict occupational entry.[130] Their control over the supply of labor in their respective fields has enabled most of their members to realize considerable financial reward for their efforts.

Some of the traditional professional entities have become formal labor organizations over the past several decades. The NEA, the ANA, the AAUP, and similar groups are now the legal bargaining agents for millions of professional employees. Other professional associations are likely to move in a similar direction. Thousands of American lawyers and physicians are already represented by labor organizations that serve federal, state, and local government personnel.

In 1985, a special committee established by the AFL-CIO to explore innovative techniques to enhance worker involvement in the labor movement recommended the creation of associational memberships for individuals not included in traditional bargaining units.[131] The AFL-CIO accepted this suggestion and instituted an "associate membership" program.[132] Associate members pay an annual fee and receive institutional benefits. The AFL-CIO established the Union Privilege Benefits Corporation to provide associate members with discount-rate credit cards, reduced-cost investment assistance, and group-rate health and life insurance.[133] It also created a home financing plan in partnership with the Federal Home Loan Mortgage Corporation that makes it easier for members to qualify for advantageous federally backed mortgage terms.[134] The AFL-CIO could offer additional benefits to associational members. For example, it could provide legal services to associate members who wish to challenge discriminatory personnel policies or unjust discipline.[135] It could assist associate members with property transactions, marital dissolutions, or the development of estate plans.

The AFL-CIO hopes to appeal to the 28 million former union members who are currently employed in unorganized work environments[136] and to other individuals who have never experienced union representation. If the associate membership program is successful, millions of employees may take advantage of the opportunity to become affiliated with the AFL-CIO. Once they discover the economic benefits and collective strength attainable through labor organizations, they may view labor unions more positively. Associate members who acknowledge the personal and occupational gains that can be achieved through the collective bargaining process[137] may decide to support union organizing efforts.

Unfortunately, the judicial branch has already begun to undermine the viability of the AFL-CIO associate membership approach. In *American Postal Workers Union v. United States,*[138] the court ruled that the annual $35 "dues" payment made by associate members to the tax-exempt American Postal Workers Union constituted taxable income to that entity because Section 511(a)(1) of the Internal Revenue Code[139] imposes a tax on the "unrelated business taxable income" of otherwise tax-exempt organizations. The court found that the associate member payments were "not substantially related (other than through the production of funds) to the organization's performance of its exempt functions."[140] Although the annual fees paid by associate members directly qualified them for group insurance coverage, those contributions also indirectly enhanced the economic vitality of the union and increased its capacity to lobby for legislation promoting the employment interests of the associate members. It is thus questionable whether the court should have viewed those payments as "unrelated business taxable income." If this decision is not reversed by the Supreme Court, the AFL-CIO should seek an amendment to the Internal Revenue Code that would specifically exempt from the taxable income of a union the reasonable fees charged to associate members. This amendment would enable unorganized employees to obtain some of the advantages of unionization, and increase the capacity of AFL-CIO affiliates to advance the interests of all workers.

5. ENHANCING ORGANIZED LABOR'S ECONOMIC AND POLITICAL POWER

Employees who select a bargaining agent under the NLRA are guaranteed negotiating rights with respect to issues pertaining to wages, hours, and conditions of employment. While their representative labor organization may insist upon negotiations concerning these "mandatory" topics, the NLRA expressly provides that the duty to bargain "does not compel either party to agree to a proposal or require the making of a concession."[1] It is generally impermissible for an employer to modify working conditions unilaterally. Nonetheless, once a good faith impasse is reached, a company may unilaterally implement terms that it has offered the representative union at the bargaining table.[2]

The NLRA merely protects the right of employees to select a bargaining agent and engage in collective bargaining. It does not regulate the substantive terms that will govern the negotiations. The Labor Board is only empowered to regulate the bargaining process. It lacks the authority to review the merits of substantive proposals advanced by the participants.[3] The Labor Board may not require either side to agree to a specific term or to make a particular concession, even when it determines that a party has failed to satisfy its obligation to engage in good faith bargaining.[4]

Private sector employees enjoy a statutory right to engage in work stoppages. Nonetheless, while individuals may not be discharged by their employer as a result of their protected concerted conduct,[5] economic strikers may be "permanently replaced" by other workers.[6] Replaced strikers are not entitled to automatic reinstatement once the work stoppage concludes, but only receive preferential recall as vacancies occur.[7] An increasing number of employers are willing to hire permanent replacements for striking workers. A recent AFL-CIO study found that 11 percent of the 243,300 American employees who participated in major work stoppages during 1990 were permanently replaced.[8] Such corporate action significantly undermines the willingness of workers to support strikes.

Even if employers did not have the right to hire permanent replacements for economic strikers, increasingly diverse and technologically advanced business enterprises are now finding it easier to withstand the impact of work stoppages. Managerial personnel can frequently maintain minimal levels of output by keeping automated equipment functioning. For example, when the Communications Workers Union strikes American Telephone & Telegraph, most telephone users hardly notice any attenuation in service. Computerized equipment handles most local and long distance calls. Only those few individuals who require operator assistance or technical staff services suffer an inconvenience, and managerial personnel are able to satisfy most of their needs.

When one facility of a complex business is shut down, operations can often be transferred to another location. Even if all of a firm's employees located in the United States decide to participate in a work stoppage, a growing number of multinational enterprises are able to recover lost production at foreign plants.[9] When service workers decide to strike, their functions can be performed either by temporary replacements or by temporary employment agency personnel who are retained during the work stoppage. Revenues lost through a partial or total shutdown at one location or division can frequently be offset by profits earned by other corporations.

The hierarchical structures of variegated business organizations also affect the bargaining process. Although representative labor unions can generally obtain relevant information regarding local operations, they are frequently unable to procure pertinent information concerning overall enterprise profitability.[10] Decisions affecting local employment conditions are frequently made at corporate headquarters by managers with no personal knowledge of the operative circumstances. Furthermore, labor organizations find it difficult to engage in meaningful negotiations regarding bargaining unit terms of employment when the participating company representatives lack the authority to make agreements that conflict with overall corporate employment policies.

As the efficacy of the conventional strike weapon continues to decline, organized labor will have to develop new techniques that will enhance its economic and political power. Labor unions must resort to corporate and community campaigns to exert pressure against target firms. Employee influence may be greatly enhanced through negotiated and legislated worker participation programs that provide rank-and-file personnel with the right to be meaningfully involved in the management decision-making process. Labor organizations can also use the billions of dollars in pension funds to reward employers with beneficent employment conditions and penalize companies that do not treat their workers decently. American labor organizations must increase their political activity, in recognition of the fact that statutory protections are generally more lasting than negotiated benefits. Because national unions can no longer regulate the global operations of transnational business enterprises, they must form international federations that can counterbalance the increased power of multinational firms.

CORPORATE AND COMMUNITY CAMPAIGNS

Most companies are concerned about the dissemination of adverse information regarding their business activities. They fear that prospective customers may decide to do business with their competitors, and are afraid that creditors will hesitate to provide them with additional financial support. Consequently, tactics that generate negative publicity about a target business can often be quite effective in accomplishing bargaining goals.[11]

Unions should enlist the assistance of local media representatives at the onset of a labor dispute. The labor organization needs to prepare press releases and make spokespersons available to forcefully and succinctly explain the underlying issues. Union representatives who are fortunate to receive sixty seconds on an evening news program must be able to summarize their position and demonstrate that their demands are reasonable and easily satisfied by the recalcitrant employer. A union on strike should convey its message through newspaper, radio, and television advertisements. By placing the company on the defensive, labor representatives will enhance their bargaining situation.

During a strike, unions can use publicity picketing and consumer handbilling to inform the public about their cause. Striking employees should picket their employer with placards concisely explaining the circumstances of the controversy. Leaflets describing the employment dispute should be distributed to all persons entering or leaving the employer's premises. Picketers may lawfully ask truck drivers, delivery persons, and service personnel to honor the picket line,[12] and they may generally request prospective customers to refrain from dealings with the offending employer during the labor dispute.[13] The disruption of deliveries or loss of customers to competitors will put economic pressure on the struck employer. Publicity picketing can be employed to generate public sympathy even if the union does not go so far as to strike the employer. Placards and leaflets should clearly indicate the basis of the dispute and encourage people to compel the affected business entity to accept the labor organization's demands.

Labor organizations should not hesitate to utilize tactics that harass uncooperative employers. For example, recalcitrant corporations should be charged with failing to bargain in good faith. Union officials should file complaints with state and federal authorities regarding possible health and safety act violations. Employment discrimination claims should be referred to state fair employment practice agencies or the federal Equal Employment Opportunity Commission. Businesses that might be violating state or federal pollution regulations should be cited. The cost to the employer of defending such claims is high, and the monetary sanctions and adverse publicity that result from established violations can be significant. These legal means can be effectively utilized by employees to penalize employers that treat their employees unfairly.

Labor organizations dissatisfied with particular companies should isolate those firms from the business community by asking corporate leaders to resign from the boards of directors of the offending enterprises, and inducing financial institutions to sever their ties with those companies. Regional AFL-CIO affiliates can threaten to withdraw health and pension fund money from banks that continue to support the targeted businesses. Union officials could purchase stock in the offending corporations and put the relevant issues before the shareholders at stockholder meetings. A public relations campaign of this type was successfully conducted by the AFL-CIO against Litton Industries during the early 1980s when Litton refused to honor its obligations under the NLRA.[14]

Labor unions need to reestablish their ties with other community organizations to enhance their power in the community. By working closely with civil rights entities, environmental groups, religious bodies, and other similar institutions, unions will be able to engender crucial public support during employment controversies and produce effective consumer boycotts.[15] The threat of a community boycott during the 1980s motivated General Motors to retain a Van Nuys, California, plant it had planned to close.[16] If these community coalitions can enlist the assistance of media representatives, they can increase the pressure exerted against target companies.

INCREASED EMPLOYEE PARTICIPATION IN CORPORATE MANAGEMENT

In a technologically advanced society in which employees exercise little discretion in their jobs, employers can easily regulate the employment environment to discourage worker initiative and autonomy.[17] Highly trained and educated employees, however, desire to participate in managerial decision making. Sophisticated personnel are reluctant to accept supervisory directives without question, and are not satisfied with mere financial remuneration.[18] As real wages rise and workers feel relatively secure, the marginal utility of additional income declines and employees become more concerned with personal job satisfaction.[19] Workers want meaningful occupational challenges and the opportunity to exercise control over their employment destinies.

Workers have historically participated in American industry indirectly through the collective bargaining process, but employees attempting to affect their employment circumstances in this way have never been considered managerial partners.[20] Some observers have noted that bargaining can be a mere facade that only provides workers with "pseudo-participation," because final determinations regarding fundamental matters continue to be made unilaterally by corporate officials.[21] Others have noted that collective bargaining has become overburdened by a myriad of issues constantly addressed on a confrontational basis.[22]

Labor organizations and employers in the United States have traditionally regarded collective bargaining as a confrontational, rather than cooperative, process.[23] Each considers a victory for the other a loss for their own cause.[24] Through resort to such antediluvian economic weapons as strikes and lockouts, unions and corporations have fought to achieve bargaining supremacy over each other. Only during dire economic circumstances threatening the continued viability of business enterprises have workers and management utilized cooperative systems that have permitted more direct labor involvement.[25]

American labor leaders have generally been unsupportive of and even hostile to arrangements designed to provide workers with more direct participation in corporate management,[26] believing that it is the function of managerial officials to manage the enterprise and the duty of trade union representatives to act as responsible adversaries.[27] Union leaders also fear that labor-management ventures are designed by business enterprises to surreptitiously increase productivity.[28] Employers disingenuously convey the impression to workers that their views are important in exchange for greater productivity.[29]

In addition, labor-management committees created to regulate employment environments and employee job tasks could render shop stewards and other local union officials obsolete.[30] If workers are induced to substitute joint committees for conventional trade unions, the need for employees to join and support what appear to be superfluous labor organizations will be diminished.[31] Corporations could utilize such "humanistic" devices to convince workers that management is concerned about their employment circumstances to the extent that labor representation is no longer necessary.[32]

Many managers are equally unenthusiastic about employer-employee cooperative programs, believing that such ventures permit workers to encroach inappropriately upon management prerogatives. They fear that workers may ultimately use such joint plans to take over the entire managerial function.[33] Business enterprises see union and employee involvement in the decision-making process as a concession of power. They believe that these schemes will undermine the ability of business firms to compete successfully.

Despite the recalcitrance of labor and management officials, it is likely that increased labor-management cooperation will occur. American business firms must maximize productivity and efficiency to compete successfully in a global economic system. Corporate executives have begun to recognize that innovative ideas can be provided by shop-level employees who are intimately familiar with basic operations.[34] Businesses can enhance productivity in two critical ways by developing formal programs encouraging worker participation in the decision-making process. First, they can increase the likelihood that operations are being conducted in the most efficient fashion. Second, they can improve employee morale by demonstrating their respect for the mental capabilities of rank-and-file personnel, thereby increasing worker effort and reducing turnover and absenteeism.[35] To be truly effective, employee involvement programs must establish a genuine intent to redistribute managerial authority.[36] Companies that create illusory employee participation committees will at best see no change in the efficacy of their operations and at worst will undermine what positive morale had previously existed among their employees.

There is no evidence that agreements by labor organizations and corporations to establish cooperative worker participation programs will lead to the eventual demise of employee associations as feared by union leaders. Although the relationship between representative unions and management is certainly altered when the parties progress from the antiquated era of direct confrontation to the enlightened era of cooperation, the need for traditional employee representation will not disappear.

The trade union is not superfluous in a factory with a system of workers' management, because the two bodies, though both representing the worker, represent different functions and different interests of the workers. The function of the trade union is to protect the worker as employee; the function of the (worker self-management) council is to protect the worker as producer. Insofar as these functions are distinct, two organizations are justified and neither is redundant; insofar as these functions conflict with one another—as they must at times—there is room for negotiations, for "labor-management negotiations."[37]

Labor and management officials at companies including AT&T, Honeywell, Xerox, and Helene Curtis have found that cooperative programs have enhanced, rather than detracted from, collective bargaining relationships.[38] Similar experiences have occurred at automobile plants.[39] Direct labor-management confrontation has been replaced by mutual problem-solving systems that provide a more efficient and harmonious method for resolving industrial disputes.[40] Worker-manager communication has greatly improved, and employees have the opportunity to participate directly in the structuring of their daily job functions.[41]

Conventional collective bargaining has primarily been a reactive process, with representative labor organizations reacting to employer initiatives.[42] If workers are to influence management decisions before they are formulated, direct input is necessary. Increased worker participation in corporate management may begin with shop level committees, extend to semi-autonomous work groups, and culminate with labor representation on boards of directors.[43] These systems should provide employees with complete information concerning corporate affairs, the ability to influence the manner in which jobs are structured, and even the right to vote on fundamental business decisions.[44]

Shop Level Cooperation

Contemporary American workers are better educated, more affluent, and more mobile than their predecessors.[45] These factors have induced modern employees to become increasingly independent and individualistic. They are less tolerant of job boredom and uncomfortable employment environments.[46] The majority of today's white-collar personnel believe that they should have the right to participate directly in management deliberations that will affect their daily working conditions.[47]

Employees in most Japanese companies have long enjoyed the opportunity to participate in corporate decision making. Workers and supervisory personnel have eschewed the adversarial labor-management relationship indigenous to United States employment settings in favor of a cooperative system of consensus management that permits employees to directly influence shop-level decisions.[48] Japanese managers work diligently to maintain harmonious employer-employee relations based upon joint respect.[49] Both labor and management representatives strive for mutually beneficial results in recognition of their symbiotic circumstances.

Business enterprises in many Western European nations provide their employees with similar forms of participatory management, either voluntarily or pursuant to statutory obligations.[50] In 1891, Germany enacted the *Arbeiterschutzgesetz*, which provided company owners with the right to unilaterally establish work rules. If a permanent workers' committee existed, however, the owners had to conduct a hearing on proposed rules before that committee.[51] In 1900, Article 91 of the *Bayrisches Berggesetz* created statutorily mandated worker committees, but required them only for mines with more than twenty employees.[52] The *Betriebstategesetz*, or Works Councils Act of 1920, directed the election of employee representatives on supervisory boards, and provided for the use of worker committees throughout German industry.[53] In 1972, The Federal Republic of Germany enacted the Works Constitution Act, which directed the election of works councils in all enterprises with five or more permanent employees.[54] The works councils are entitled to information regarding contemplated management changes affecting employee interests. Company officials are encouraged to achieve mutual accords with respect to worker terminations and the consequences of reorganizations, partial or total plant closures, and the introduction of new technology. Impasses are resolved through mediation by a tripartite conciliation board or the labor court.[55]

Corporate laws in the Netherlands mandate employee participation in work-related deliberations through both lower level works councils and higher level management boards.[56] Before making decisions that could meaningfully affect the work environment, job security, or other areas of employee concern, Dutch managers must consult with the relevant works councils.[57] Labor-management relationships in Austria, Denmark, Norway, and Sweden provide employees with similar forms of plant level participatory management.[58]

Some European companies have gone beyond the formal cooperative systems mandated by statutory provisions and have voluntarily established shop floor production groups that determine how day-to-day operations are to be managed. In various Saab and Volvo manufacturing facilities, for example, conventional assembly lines have been replaced by work stations where individual employees decide how the requisite job tasks are to be accomplished.[59] Saab and Volvo workers exercise significant control over their fundamental employment circumstances, minimizing their boredom and enhancing their feelings of self-worth.

An increasing number of American corporations have begun to acknowledge the benefits of cooperative management schemes. Although shop floor labor-management committees were established in some United States industries in the 1930s,[60] most of the American developments in this regard have occurred more recently.[61] General Foods,[62] Harmon Industries,[63] Rushton Mining,[64] and AT&T,[65] as examples, have "humanized" their production facilities by providing workers with a considerable degree of job autonomy. They have also created systems that enable individual employees to influence directly the manner in which their work is structured through committees in which workers participate in managerial deliberations. Such cooperative ventures should eventually replace many of the traditional confrontational methods of labor-management relations still used in other business enterprises.

The reorganization of work environments through the establishment of joint employee-management committees can evoke substantial anxiety among supervisory personnel who are accustomed to conventional superior-subordinate relationships between themselves and rank-and-file workers.[66] Managers must develop a new style that will motivate employees to accept their leadership out of respect for their professional expertise rather than out of fear of their disciplinary authority.[67]

Cooperative job enrichment or "quality of work life" programs are beneficial for both workers and employers because they open new channels of communication between employees and managerial personnel, and enable labor representatives to expand the scope of issues over which they can exercise meaningful influence.[68] These plans insure that the "human aspects" of the work process will be considered during management deliberations, and they provide employees with the enhanced sense of dignity associated with industrial democracy and the satisfaction of having influenced decisions directly bearing upon their existence.[69]

United States corporations that have instituted labor-management codetermination programs have generally experienced positive results.[70] Job satisfaction usually improves, and employee absenteeism and turnover decline.[71] Cooperative systems also make it easier for businesses to respond optimally to economic crises, because worker input frequently provides managers with ideas they might not otherwise consider.[72] Employee participation in decision making increases worker support for final decisions.

If a business enterprise wants a harmonious and productive employment atmosphere, it should adopt policies that provide for employee involvement in decision making. Labor organizations should support employer-employee programs, understanding that they continue to perform important functions for members who work in settings with such cooperative arrangements. Unions can provide workers with the information and expertise they need to participate meaningfully in cooperative labor-management schemes. In addition, unions must continue to utilize collective bargaining to enhance employee interests with respect to matters not subject to resolution through employer-employee committees.[73] Labor officials must realize that cooperative industrial-relation plans can beneficially supplant many of the inefficient practices associated with conventional adversarial labor-management relationships.

Representation on Corporate Boards

Fundamental corporate policies have traditionally been determined in American business enterprises by professional managers who are directly responsible to the shareholder/owners, but not to the rank-and-file employees. Some contemporary observers have appropriately suggested that corporate managers should have a responsibility toward workers similar to that owed to stockholders.[74] "[N]o company can function without workers any more than it can operate without capital. Capitalists contribute money to the company; workers contribute half their waking lives."[75] Rank-and-file employees are less able to protect themselves against business vicissitudes than are shareholders, who can diversify their investment portfolios.[76]

If employees are to participate meaningfully in decisions that affect their employment destinies, they must alter the conventional labor-management relationship. Representative unions can no longer simply respond to the employment ramifications of business determinations that have already been formulated, as they do through the collective bargaining process.[77] Workers who are inextricably involved with the generation of business profits deserve the opportunity to have their interests understood and considered prior to the development of crucial corporate policies.[78]

Joint sovereignty, if it is to mean anything at all, must mean a redefinition of the incidents of ownership, which entails both an attack on private property and a rejection of technological determinism. It must involve a relinquishment by management of what it has heretofore regarded as its exclusive decisionmaking prerogatives, even in such "vital" areas as investment decisions. Giving unions a voice in matters like wages and hours is of limited value if they have no say in matters that affect the competitive position of the firm, for that is what ensures the firm's ability to pay any wage at all. For the union to participate meaningfully in any matter that concerns workers, it must address issues that lie at the core of entrepreneurial control.[79]

Many Western European nations have already acknowledged the right of workers to participate on corporate boards. In Germany, business enterprises are controlled by a management board (the *Vorstand*) and a supervisory board (the *Aufsichtsrat*).[80] Daily managerial functions are performed by the management board. The supervisory board is responsible for overseeing the management board, and it directly appoints and may remove members of that body. Under the *Mitbestimmung* (Codetermination) Act of 1976,[81] one-half of the supervisory board members in a large corporation (*Aktiengesellschaft*) must be elected by the employees of the enterprise. Each class of personnel is entitled to at least one representative on the supervisory board, with seats reserved for separate blue-collar, white-collar, and middle-management delegates. The codetermination systems found

in most Western European corporations guarantee worker representatives the opportunity to participate in managerial deliberations
affecting not only wages and working conditions, but also fundamental business matters that could affect their job functions and
future employment security.[82]

Employees could achieve participation on corporate boards in the
United States in three ways.[83] First, a worker representative can be
elected to a board of directors on an ad hoc basis. Second, a representative labor organization might accomplish a similar result
through the collective bargaining process, as recently occurred with
respect to the appointment of UAW President Douglas Fraser to the
board of the Chrysler Corporation.[84] Finally, state or federal legislation could provide for employee delegates on corporate boards.

Employee representation on managerial boards provides workers
with vital information not traditionally available to them, and permits them to discuss their interests directly with shareholders.[85]
Management officials receive greater input than they would otherwise with respect to employee concerns and ideas. Communication
channels are enhanced throughout the corporate hierarchy due to
employee participation in decision making.[86]

Direct worker participation may alter the conventional role performed by labor organizations. "If unions have members on company
operational boards of directors and the management and worker directors jointly decide on a policy, how can the unions then object
to the policy and with whom do they negotiate?"[87] Representative
labor organizations can minimize such problems by either electing
union-sponsored persons to corporate boards or coordinating their
efforts with worker delegates serving on corporate boards. Union
officials and employee delegates can share information and ideas
before critical issues are debated and decided by management boards.
Both approaches enable union leaders to include managerial board
deliberations in the bargaining process.

Worker representation on corporate boards blurs the sharp distinction between labor and management.[88] International Association
of Machinists President William Winpisinger has suggested that "as
worker representatives on directing boards become more and more
involved in management's problems, they are likely to become less
and less responsive to the needs of those they represent."[89] This
pessimistic view assumes that worker delegates will fail to remember
their rank-and-file roots. If employee directors continue in their jobs,
they will continue to provide worker perspectives to management

that might induce shareholder directors to reassess their own predilections.[90]

Employee representation on corporate boards does not supplant conventional collective bargaining but complements negotiations by providing workers with input and influence not found in traditional adversarial labor-management relationships. Collective negotiations are still necessary to define and protect basic employment terms, and grievance-arbitration procedures must continue to be employed to ensure management compliance with contractual obligations. Worker participation on corporate boards should actually facilitate the collective bargaining process, because it stimulates harmonious employer-employee relationships.

Legal and Practical Ramifications

Labor proposals for worker representatives on corporate boards or shop-level committees raise legal questions under several labor relations statutes, the antitrust laws, and corporate enactments. Federal legislation mandating the establishment of codetermination programs would eliminate any legal impediments to employee delegates on managerial boards or works councils. Even in the absence of such enabling provisions, however, voluntarily adopted worker participation plans should be sustained.

Corporate boards are empowered to select and remove managerial officials who are responsible for employer collective bargaining and grievance adjustment. If worker-elected directors were able to impermissibly influence this process, problems might arise under Section 8(b)(1)(B) of the NLRA,[91] which makes it an unfair labor practice for a labor organization or its agents "to restrain or coerce" an employer with respect to its selection of representatives for collective bargaining or grievance adjustment purposes. Because this provision only precludes labor organization interference accomplished by restraint or coercion, it should not be held to apply to board of director deliberations. If worker delegates are selected directly by the employees themselves, they would not be acting as union agents when they perform their managerial duties. Their conduct would thus not be attributable to a labor entity. Even if the delegates are chosen through labor organization procedures, the proselytizing that worker directors would engage in during board meetings would be unlikely to be sufficiently outrageous to constitute restraint or coercion within the meaning of Section 8(b)(1).[92] So long as such individuals did not resort to threats or similarly opprobrious behavior, their actions would be beyond the scope of Section 8(b)(1)(B). A labor organization would only subject itself to Section 8(b)(1)(B) liability if its officers threatened a corporate director with respect to the board's selection of bargaining or grievance adjustment representatives, or if it sought to discipline union members because of the manner in which they voted on such matters. A union may not impose sanctions on members as a result of the way in which they carry out their managerial functions.[93]

Codetermination programs might be challenged under Section 8(a)(2) of the NLRA,[94] which makes it unlawful for an employer "to dominate or interfere with the formation or administration of any labor organization...." The potential problem is caused by the fact that Section 2(5) of the NLRA[95] broadly defines "labor organization" to include "any organization of any kind, or any agency or employee representation committee or plan, in which employees participate and which exists for the purpose, in whole or in part, of dealing with employers concerning grievances, labor disputes, wages, rates of pay, hours of employment, or conditions of work." If the Labor Board or courts were to decide that joint employer-employee committees constitute "labor organizations" under Section 2(5), the presence of management representatives on such committees might be considered unlawful domination under Section 8(a)(2). Even though Section 14(a)[96] permits supervisory personnel to be members of representative labor organizations, such management agents are not allowed to hold union office.[97] So long as worker participation programs are conducted on an egalitarian basis without being subject to supervisory control, Section 8(a)(2) should not preclude such cooperative ventures.

Section 8(a)(2) was primarily designed to outlaw "company unions" that had been established by business firms to prevent the selection of independent bargaining agents.[98] Early Labor Board decisions concluded that Congress not only intended in Section 8(a)(2) to outlaw company unions, but also to proscribe employee committees that were created to enable workers to participate in the adjustment of individual grievances. In *NLRB v. Newport News Shipbuilding & Dry Dock Co.*,[99] the Supreme Court sustained this statutory interpretation. Although the employer-assisted worker representation plan operated to the apparent satisfaction of the employees, the Court concluded that Congress required a strict separation between workers and management.[100] The Court further found that the employer's motivation when it created the shop-level committee was not controlling.

In *NLRB v. Cabot Carbon Co.*,[101] the Supreme Court reaffirmed the principles that had been adopted in *Newport News Shipbuilding*. Cabot Carbon had established employee committees at various plants for the express purpose of meeting regularly with management officials to discuss problems and handle grievances. The committees also considered "seniority, job classifications, job bidding, makeup time, overtime records, time cards, a merit system, wage corrections, working schedules, holidays, vacations, sick leave, and improvement of working facilities and conditions."[102] Even though the employee committees did not "bargain with" Cabot Carbon with respect to these basic employment issues, the Supreme Court found that they existed for the purpose of "dealing with" the company regarding such matters and that this factor was sufficient to render the plans "labor organizations" within the meaning of Section 2(5).[103] Because the committees had been created by management personnel, they were employer-dominated entities that contravened Section 8(a)(2).

If the *Newport News Shipbuilding* and *Cabot Carbon* rationales are applied to contemporary worker participation programs, even egalitarian shop-level committees would be rendered unlawful. Fortunately, more recent Labor Board and court decisions have appropriately recognized that Congress could not have intended to preclude enlightened forms of employer-employee cooperation that are not designed to discourage worker unionization. For example, in *Hertzka & Knowles v. NLRB*,[104] the Ninth Circuit decided that a Section 8(a)(2) violation must "rest on a showing that the employees' free choice . . . is stifled by the degree of employer involvement at issue."[105] The court went on to observe that the condemnation of innovative forms of codetermination involving worker participation "would mark approval of a purely adversarial model of labor relations. Where a cooperative arrangement reflects a choice freely arrived at and where the organization is capable of being a meaningful avenue for the expression of employee wishes, . . . it [is] unobjectionable under the Act."[106] A similar rationale was employed by the Sixth Circuit in *NLRB v. Streamway Division of the Scott & Fetzer Co.*[107] to uphold the legality of "in-plant representation committees" that were designed "to provide an informal yet orderly process for communicating Company plans and programs; defining and identifying problem areas and eliciting suggestions and ideas for improving operations."[108] Rather than constituting "labor organizations" that were "dealing with" the employer, the court decided that the committees were merely a "communicative device" through which employees and managers could discuss issues of mutual interest.[109]

In *Mercy-Memorial Hospital Corp.*,[110] the Labor Board found that a joint employer-employee committee was not a "labor organization" within the meaning of Section 2(5), even though it made grievance determinations and actually made recommendations regarding working conditions. The Board concluded that the committee existed not to "deal with" management but to provide workers with a voice in the resolution of grievances raised by fellow employees.[111] The NLRB expanded the legitimacy of worker participation plans in its subsequent *General Foods Corp.*[112] decision. General Foods had created a "job enrichment program" that divided employees into four teams. Each team operated on a consensus basis to determine job assignments, job rotations, and the scheduling of overtime work. Although the teams did not possess disciplinary authority, they did occasionally conduct job interviews. First line supervisors usually attended team meetings, and they often accepted team recommendations. The Board found that the teams were "nothing more nor less than work crews established . . . as administrative subdivisions of the entire employee complement" and that they "were not established to head off incipient organizing drives by outside unions nor did they come into existence in response to any unrest in the bargaining unit. . . ."[113] Finding that the teams were merely intended to facilitate communication between workers and management, the Board held that the company's delegation of managerial functions and responsibilities to employees did "not involve any dealing with the employer on a group basis within the meaning of Section 2(5)."[114] In the more recent *Anamag* case,[115] the NLRB followed the *Mercy-Memorial Hospital* and *General Foods* approach, and sustained the legality of employer-established work teams that were intended to reflect the Japanese "team concept" of management. The Board emphasized the fact that because committee decisions were jointly made, there was no evidence of managerial domination.[116]

The Labor Board and the courts should generally accept shop-level worker participation programs that have been created in organized business environments and assume that the representative unions will be able to prevent inappropriate employer domination of employee committees. A violation should only be found where the evidence demonstrates that a dominant employer has imposed a shop floor program on an anemic union and completely controlled the work of that group. Cooperative arrangements unilaterally developed in unorganized settings should be subject to greater scrutiny. If employee participation schemes have been created in good faith to provide workers with the opportunity to influence their employment conditions and there is no indication that management officials are effectively regulating the deliberative process, the committees should be sustained.

The appointment of employee or labor delegates to corporate boards should not raise problems under Section 8(a)(2). The participation of one or two employee representatives on a managerial board having many members would not convert that management entity into a "labor organization" under Section 2(5). Even though worker directors could raise issues of interest to rank-and-file personnel, the board would not exist for the purpose of "dealing with" the employer with respect to such matters. It would instead exist as a managerial entity responsible for the development of corporate policy. When unionized companies agree to place labor delegates on managerial boards, this should similarly be found lawful under the NLRA. The participation of union representatives on such boards would not create circumstances involving any meaningful risk of employer domination of the representative labor organizations. Although the other board directors could certainly outvote the labor members, they would not normally be able to control internal union affairs or the conduct of union agents at the collective bargaining table.

Section 202(a)(5) of the Labor-Management Reporting and Disclosure Act (LMRDA)[117] requires every officer and employee of a labor organization to file reports with the Secretary of Labor regarding "any direct or indirect business transaction or arrangement" between them and any employers whose workers their union represents. The Department of Labor has indicated that the filing of annual reports describing union participation on managerial boards would satisfy the Section 202(a)(5) requirement.[118] The Labor Department has also stated[119] that so long as such employee delegates do not accept remuneration from the relevant corporations for their board of director services, no problems would arise under either Section 302(b)(1) of the Labor-Management Relations Act (LMRA),[120] which prohibits officers and employees of labor organizations from accepting payments from employers whose workers are represented by their respective unions, or Section 501(a) of the LMRDA,[121] which precludes union officers or agents from acquiring any pecuniary or personal interest in employers that would conflict with the interests of their respective unions.[122]

LMRA Section 302(c)(1) excludes from the coverage of Section 302(b)(1) compensation received for work performed in one's capacity as an employee of the company involved, but it is not certain that remuneration offered for service on a corporate board would be covered by this provision. Because corporate directors are not normally considered "employees" of those business firms, it is possible that the Section 302(c)(1) exemption would not be applicable. Section 302(c)(3)[123] similarly exempts payments "with respect to the sale or purchase of an article or commodity at the prevailing market price in the regular course of business." Even though the services of a director are not "an article or commodity" in the ordinary sense, a Department of Labor official has suggested that this provision might permit union officials serving on corporate boards to accept the same compensation given to other directors.[124] To avoid unexpected liability under Section 302(b)(1), union agents serving on managerial boards may wish to reject compensation for those activities.

Some experts have suggested that labor representation on corporate boards might create difficulties under federal antitrust statutes.[125] While labor organizations that enter into combinations or agreements with employers enjoy a rather substantial exemption from antitrust liability arising under Section 1 of the Sherman Act,[126] which proscribes contracts, combinations, and conspiracies in restraint of trade, this immunity is not absolute. If unions enter into contractual arrangements with business enterprises not to further the legitimate employment interests of their respective members but to further anticompetitive objectives in the product market, their exemption is forfeited.[127] Because trade unions initiating and/or participating in jointly established labor-management codetermination programs usually act solely to enhance the job security and employment rights of their employee-members, and such cooperative ventures constitute a direct means of achieving appropriate labor objectives, immunity under the so-called nonstatutory exemption should preclude Sherman Act liability.[128]

Another potential legal impediment to board level worker participation is Section 8 of the Clayton Act,[129] which provides that "[n]o person at the same time shall be a director in any two or more corporations ... if such corporations are or shall have been theretofore ... competitors."[130] Although the Federal Trade Commission has indicated in an advisory opinion that Section 8 was not intended to apply to labor unions that negotiate seats on the managerial boards of competing companies,[131] the Justice Department has declined to endorse this interpretation unequivocally.[132] Because this provision was almost certainly not designed to preclude labor participation on the boards of competing corporations, the more carefully considered view of the Federal Trade Commission should be accorded judicial acceptance. Until this controversy is finally resolved, however, labor organizations can circumvent the potential difficulty by ensuring that the same individuals are not selected to sit on the managerial boards of competitor firms.[133]

The directors of a publicly held corporation have traditionally been under a fiduciary obligation to represent the interests of the corporation and its shareholders.[134] Even though one might argue that worker delegates on managerial boards would not violate their fiduciary duty to stockholders merely because they advance employee interests to the apparent detriment of shareholders,[135] the possibility that such behavior might be found to contravene the fiduciary obligation of such representatives cannot be ignored.

Employee delegates can avoid fiduciary duty problems by merely posing worker views about issues with the potential to engender conflicts between the desires of workers and the interests of stockholders. They do not have to vote on those matters. This approach, however, would not wholly satisfy either the employees or the corporate owners. To accommodate the changes associated with transition from confrontational labor-management relationships to cooperative arrangements, the historical fiduciary obligations should be judicially or legislatively modified with respect to labor delegates on corporate boards. They need to acknowledge that these representatives are appointed to managerial bodies with the expectation that they will advance the interests of the employees being served.[136] This approach would provide workers with the opportunity to achieve meaningful codetermination, and shareholder concerns would continue to be adequately protected through the remaining directors who would still have a fiduciary obligation to the stockholders.

As state corporate law doctrines are altered to permit labor representatives on managerial boards to be responsive to worker interests, new principles should be developed recognizing that such delegates owe a fiduciary duty to the employees for whom they speak.[137] If labor directors breach this obligation, injured employees should be able to obtain redress against them similar to that available to shareholders aggrieved by fiduciary violations by ordinary board members under existing corporate legal rules. Unionized workers could also argue that managerial board members selected by their representative labor organization owe them a duty of fair representation under the NLRA with respect to the actions they take as corporate directors.[138] Courts should recognize, however, that "[a] wide range of reasonableness must be allowed a statutory bargaining representative in serving the unit it represents, subject always to complete good faith and honesty of purpose in the exercise of its discretion."[139]

The inclusion of worker representatives on corporate boards will create some practical problems because of the inherent conflicts of interest that exist between labor and management. When collective bargaining procedures supplement codetermination systems, employee directors should certainly not participate in managerial board deliberations pertaining to the formulation of company bargaining strategy.[140] This dilemma can be easily resolved, as it has been by Chrysler Corporation and the UAW, by excluding the labor delegate(s) from meetings at which such matters are to be discussed.[141] Furthermore, because the collective bargaining process will probably remain confrontational, and participatory management arrangements are adopted to achieve cooperative results, expediency militates in favor of a rule barring the appointment to managerial boards of any individual who is directly involved in the negotiation of collective contracts.[142] This practice would minimize the risk that someone would attempt to act as both a cooperative director and an adversarial negotiator.

Worker appointees on corporate boards must be denied access to information that would compromise management bargaining positions. Even though union negotiators are entitled to review company financial records in those rare situations when management bargainers rely upon an inability-to-pay theory to support their low offers,[143] labor representatives generally do not have the right to inspect such business records. If employee-selected directors were denied access to confidential information, the integrity of the conventional bargaining process would be preserved, and labor representatives would not be deprived of financial data to which they would otherwise have a legitimate claim.

Worker delegates on managerial boards should be entitled to review material of substantial interest to business competitors. Because the same labor organization might be the bargaining agent for the employees of competing firms, management officials might initially fear the improper disclosure of trade secrets to other enterprises.[144] Experiences in Western European countries that have codetermination systems indicate that this employer concern is unfounded. Employee board members, recognizing the fiduciary obligation owed to their immediate corporation and their concomitant duty to avoid behavior that might disadvantage the workers they represent on the board, have maintained the confidentiality of secret business data.[145]

People who are skeptical regarding the benefits of worker participation on managerial boards note that such representatives might not support the acquisition and retention of efficient managers or the introduction of labor-saving technology. Evidence obtained from business enterprises that have adopted participatory management programs indicates that these trepidations are unsubstantiated. German observers have discovered that labor representatives are as eager as shareholder directors to retain highly qualified supervisory personnel, and researchers have found that codetermination systems do not necessarily impede technological progress.[146] Worker-selected directors must recognize the need to maintain corporate competitiveness if job security and beneficial compensation levels are to be preserved.

EXPANDING THE INFLUENCE OF WORKER CAPITAL

Employment relationships have traditionally involved employees working for corporate enterprises owned by outside shareholders who select the managerial personnel. Although working class people historically have not possessed economic power vis-a-vis their employers, employees are beginning to recognize that they are able to wield financial influence. Through pension fund leverage and employee stock ownership plans, workers may eventually be able to seize control over the business enterprises that employ them.

Pension Fund Leverage

During the past thirty years, worker pension programs have grown geometrically. Employee pension funds currently constitute the largest single source of investment capital in the American economy and represent the greatest source of private wealth in the world.[147] There are presently over 500,000 private pension plans in the United States, with aggregate assets of approximately $2 trillion. This sum is expected to exceed $3 trillion by the mid–1990s.[148] Pension funds currently own twenty to twenty-five percent of the stock of the corporations listed on the New York and American Stock Exchanges.[149] The money available in American pension funds already exceeds the combined gross national product of the United Kingdom and France.[150]

Most employees covered by retirement programs have no idea where their pension funds are invested, and have evidenced little interest in the management of such assets.[151] In actuality, substantial portions of retirement investments are used to finance anti-union companies and transnational business enterprises that use such capital to expand their foreign operations to the detriment of their American employees. Of the twenty-five corporations in which pension funds have been most extensively invested, sixteen are primarily nonunion entities.[152] It is therefore apparent that if employees and representative labor organizations became directly involved with the management of their pension funds and the manner in which such economic leverage is being used, they could significantly influence the policies of many corporate employers. The 1977 AFL-CIO convention adopted a resolution urging that "the substantial financial power of [union negotiated pension funds] be entrusted to financial institutions whose investment policies are not inimical to the welfare of working men and women."[153]

Pension fund managers have begun to acknowledge the propriety of considering the social benefits to be derived from prospective investments. In Hawaii, public employee pension money is partially used to finance low interest mortgages for state workers.[154] The Building and Construction Trades Department of the AFL-CIO has approved a new pension fund investment strategy aimed at the creation of construction jobs for unemployed union workers.[155] In 1987, Carpenters Union Local 33 became the first labor organization in the United States to use its pension fund dollars to open a full-service, federally chartered bank providing financial services to members as well as the general public.[156]

Through the exercise of pension fund power, unions and their members can influence the election of corporate management boards to ensure the selection of benevolent business leaders. Workers can use their leverage to influence corporate board decisions that concern matters of interest to employees.[157] Even though unorganized businesses would probably object strenuously to such union "interference" in internal management affairs, many unionized companies might welcome investment strategies that favored employers that maintain humane employment environments.[158]

Only 40 percent of negotiated retirement programs have jointly administered trust funds under Section 302(c)(5) of the LMRA.[159] The remaining 60 percent involve funds that are managed solely by the employers of the covered workers.[160] If labor organizations are to meaningfully expand their influence in this area, they must use the collective bargaining process to obtain control over the assets currently managed by the companies. Unions should also encourage unorganized employees covered by pension plans to demand that their employers appoint fund trustees who will make socially responsible investments that will reward corporations maintaining beneficial employment situations.

Labor organizations attempting to influence the investments being made by pension fund managers must be careful not to violate the fiduciary obligations imposed upon fund trustees by the Employee Retirement Income Security Act of 1974 (ERISA).[161] Section 404(a)(1) of ERISA mandates that (1) pension fund assets be utilized for the exclusive benefit of plan beneficiaries, and (2) investments be made in a prudent manner.[162] If pension fund trustees make investment decisions in a manner intended to enhance the rights of workers generally, they arguably are no longer acting solely to further the interests of the plan beneficiaries.[163] Such conduct might similarly be viewed as contravening the fiduciary duty imposed upon fund managers. Nonetheless, "[a]s long as the principles of maximum return and prudent investment are faithfully followed, there is nothing to preclude the trustees from exercising other considerations in their investment strategies."[164] When fund managers consider several investment options involving relatively equal risks and financial returns, they can select the alternative that would optimally advance the interests of working people without concern that they are contravening the mandates of ERISA.

The NLRA restricts the ability of labor organizations to negotiate agreements that preclude the use of pension funds to finance non-union business firms. Such an accord would constitute a "hot cargo" agreement in violation of Section 8(e),[165] which makes it an unfair labor practice for a union and an employer "to enter into any contract or agreement, express or implied, whereby such employer ... agrees ... to cease doing business with any other person. ... " So long as unions merely seek to prevent the use of pension fund money to support business entities that have ignored the statutory rights of their employees or maintained substandard employment conditions, and do not merely try to preclude all investment in nonunion companies, they will not violate Section 8(e) of the NLRA.

Union leaders must recognize the substantial power associated with the control of pension fund resources and anticipate the increased importance of this strategy in the coming decades. Union officials can significantly advance the rights of organized workers by inducing fund trustees to make investment decisions that do not unnecessarily assist anti-union corporations to obtain competitive advantages at the expense of their members.

Obtaining Corporate Control

In 1847, following an unsuccessful work stoppage, twenty members of a Cincinnati iron molders union established one of the first industrial cooperatives in the United States.[166] Since that early experiment with worker ownership, other groups of employees have decided that it is preferable to work for establishments that are owned and operated by the people who perform the requisite production or service tasks than for traditional employers. During the 1920s and 1930s, cooperatives were created in Oregon and Washington by plywood workers, and many of those enterprises still flourish today.[167] Similar ventures have been launched by the Vermont Asbestos Group,[168] the Saratoga Knitting Mill,[169] South Bend Lathe,[170] Rath Packing,[171] and the Chicago and North Western Railway.[172]

Although the primary motivation for early industrial cooperatives was the desire of individuals to work for themselves, other factors have provided the impetus for more recent employee ownership developments. Corporations facing financial difficulties have begun to recognize that their own labor forces can provide crucial sources of operating capital. Workers threatened with layoffs and plant closures have realized that partial or total employee buyouts of the affected facilities are the optimal means of guaranteeing continued job security. Through the use of employee stock ownership plans (ESOPs), Chrysler,[173] Pan American World Airlines,[174] Acme Markets,[175] Wierton Steel,[176] Western Airlines,[177] and various over-the-road trucking concerns,[178] for example, have generated the funds necessary to remain in operation while simultaneously extending limited entrepreneurial control to their respective employees.

In 1974, Congress concluded that specific legislation was needed to regulate the establishment and operations of ESOPs. Section 407(d)(6) of ERISA[179] articulates the basic rules regarding such plans. Congress realized that the Section 404(a)(1)(B) prudent investment requirement[180] and the Section 404(a)(1)(C) diversified portfolio mandate of ERISA would substantially impede ESOP development.[181] As a result, Congress designed Section 404(a)(2)[182] to expressly exempt investments in ESOPs from the prudent fiduciary and diversification requirements of ERISA.[183] The enactment of this provision and the tax benefits associated with the creation and financing of ESOPs have provided the impetus for the establishment of greater numbers of worker stock ownership programs.

ESOPs may encounter legal impediments under labor statutes. The Labor Board has recognized that the decision to create an ESOP constitutes a mandatory subject for collective bargaining under the NLRA.[184] Employers and representative labor organizations are thus obliged to negotiate the creation of such programs. Once parties agree to establish some form of worker ownership, however, other NLRA issues are raised. Should individuals who own part of their employer be entitled to the rights of "employees," and be included in bargaining units with employees who are not stockholders? The NLRB has appropriately resolved the first inquiry by determining that shareholder-workers are to be regarded as protected "employees" under the NLRA, except in those unusual situations in which their ownership interests are so substantial that it gives them an "effective voice" in the formulation of corporate policy.[185] The Labor Board has also acknowledged the propriety of including stockholder-employees and nonstockholder-employees in the same bargaining unit, so long as no preferential treatment is accorded the stockholder-employees because of their shareholder status.[186]

When workers effectively own the enterprise that employs them, questions may arise under Section 8(a)(2) of the NLRA[187] concerning possible owner domination of the employee members of the managerial body that determines compensation levels and working conditions. ESOPs could be considered "labor organizations" within the meaning of Section 2(5).[188] Section 8(a)(2), however, was enacted for the purpose of precluding external management interference with worker representational organizations and not to inhibit the right of employees to participate in industrial cooperatives that permit them to influence their employment circumstances. Based on this purpose, bona fide worker ownership programs should not constitute a violation of Section 8(a)(2).[189] If the Labor Board or a court decision were to reject this analysis, Congress should amend Section 8(a)(2) to clarify that it does not apply to ESOPs.

Section 501(a) of the LMRDA[190] imposes certain fiduciary obligations upon union officers and agents and provides that such individuals must neither hold nor acquire any pecuniary or personal interest which conflicts with the interests of their labor organization. It further requires such people to account for any profits they receive from transactions conducted by them or under their direction on behalf of their union. So long as such individuals carefully transact business with the managers of employee cooperatives in a professional manner and appropriately report any profits they might personally derive from stock owned by them as worker participants in the cooperative that employs them, these officials should not be hindered by Section 501(a).[191]

Worker control over industrial cooperatives has often diminished or eliminated the hierarchies and inequalities that separate rank-and-file employees and managerial personnel in conventional employment environments.[192] These ventures have frequently enhanced job security through the institution of cost-saving measures implemented without layoffs.[193] Most individuals working in cooperative businesses have evidenced increased job satisfaction, better communication between managers and workers, and enhanced enthusiasm for their tasks.[194] As a result of these factors, employee turnover has declined and productivity has increased.[195]

Some observers have questioned the actual degree of control exercised by rank-and-file personnel in corporations that are partially or even wholly owned by the employees themselves, suggesting that professional managers continue to operate such businesses.[196] Empirical research, however, refutes this notion. One study found that 36 percent of ESOP enterprises have employee representatives on their managerial boards, while 77 percent of worker cooperatives have such direct employee participation.[197]

Although workers support employee ownership schemes, most labor leaders lack enthusiasm toward such ventures fearing that these programs will ultimately be detrimental to employee interests: "[s]ooner or later the workers will become managers themselves, and they'll start acting like managers. It [will pit] worker against worker."[198] This pessimistic perspective has not been borne out in actuality. For example, the plywood cooperative personnel have not found such worker transformations to be a problem. In those rare instances when selected directors do not fulfill constituent expectations, they simply are not reelected.[199]

Some union officials have equated ESOPs and worker cooperatives with antilabor environments, and maintain that these systems are instituted by employers in an effort to reduce employee support for union representation.[200] Commentators have also pointed out that most of the plywood cooperative workers are not union members,[201] but this condition is probably attributable to the fact that those enterprises were established prior to the enactment of the NLRA in 1935. The Vermont Asbestos Group employees, who did not form their cooperative until 1975, have maintained their union solidarity and become more involved with their representative labor organization since their company's metamorphosis.[202]

Even where workers possess the right to participate directly in the selection of management officials, they continue to require supplemental union representation. Many crucial business decisions must be made from among competing alternatives. Employees are not monolithic. They have diverse needs and aspirations that cannot always be simultaneously satisfied. Through their representative bargaining agents, competing worker groups can express their concerns to management and endeavor to obtain beneficial results.[203] Labor organizations can also improve employee attitudes by teaching them to understand the difference between worker and manager functions, and by educating supervisory personnel about humanistic management techniques.[204] Thus, instead of being rendered obsolete by employee ownership programs, labor unions will continue to perform an important role. This fact explains why it is highly unlikely that workers at employee-owned firms will vote to decertify their representative labor organizations.[205]

INCREASED POLITICAL ACTIVITY

The American labor movement must recognize the need to expand its political influence if it is to retain its vitality in the coming decades. During the 1980s, the business community seized control of two of the three branches of the federal government. Business expends substantial sums of money through direct contributions, political action committees, and indirect support to ensure the election of pro-business presidents. By controlling the White House, the business community is also able to influence the development of a judicial branch favorably disposed toward business interests. By the end of the Bush administration, approximately three-fourths of all federal judges will have been appointed by conservative Republican presidents. The Supreme Court may no longer have a single justice who could reasonably be characterized as "liberal."

By controlling the executive branch, entrepreneurs prevent the enactment of legislation that would benefit rank-and-file employees at cost to employers. The president can be depended upon to veto any laws that are unacceptable to business executives, and it has been rare for Democrats to obtain the votes needed in the House and Senate to override such presidential action. Even if a pro-worker statute were enacted, the business community can be confident that an ultra-conservative judiciary will narrowly interpret the legislation, negating the impact of such a law. For example, during the 1988 Term, the Supreme Court eviscerated Title VII of the Civil Rights Act of 1964[206] and Section 1981 of the Reconstruction Era Civil Rights Act.[207] The Court made it significantly more difficult for plaintiffs challenging discriminatory personnel practices to prevail under Title VII than it had been before its decisions,[208] and effectively rendered Section 1981 irrelevant except for cases involving intentional hiring discrimination.[209]

Organized labor must show workers that they have been harmed by the pro-business environment that has prevailed in the United States since 1981, when Ronald Reagan became president. Unions must demonstrate that neither workers' collective employment situations nor their individual economic interests have been advanced by conservative politicians who are primarily beholden to wealthy corporate contributors. During the past decade, the effective tax rate for the affluent has declined appreciably, while the overall rate for most lower- and middle-income people has either remained constant or grown due to increases in regressive sales, gasoline, and social security taxes. Union officials must persuade working class individuals, including lower-level managers and professional employees who lack meaningful control over their job functions, to support politicians who are likely to strengthen laws protecting worker rights, guarantee an equitable tax structure, vote in favor of comprehensive medical coverage for all Americans, and support other policies that will enhance the economic circumstances of lower- and middle-income Americans. "If unions take the lead in articulating these new interests, and do so in a fashion that presents a clear vision and a role for workers in the governance of the American corporation and in the future economic strategies of the nation, employees may see new and compelling reasons to join Unions."[210]

Although the AFL-CIO and its various affiliates have supported pro-worker legislation and politicians sympathetic to labor goals, they have not been sufficiently active politically. Labor officials must acknowledge that conservative, pro-business representatives are not going to vote for laws that would truly enhance the interests of working class people and campaign for the election of more liberal, pro-employee candidates. Unions should contemplate forming or supporting a third party, perhaps a Workers party, that would nominate individuals to run in elections in which neither the Republican nor the Democratic candidate has shown any respect for the rights of the working class.

The more than 16 million union members in America today[211] and the millions of unorganized employees are likely to support political candidates inclined to advance their employment and economic interests. The AFL-CIO and its affiliates must mobilize these people to proselytize in favor of pro-employee nominees. While workers most likely do not possess the economic wealth of corporate executives, they clearly outnumber them. By providing personal services, these campaigners can offset the financial advantage enjoyed by pro-business candidates.[212] Union members can become campaign workers, operate telephone banks, run copy machines, and conduct get-out-the-vote drives.[213] Labor organizations can maintain computer lists on a district-by-district basis of members willing to work for appropriate candidates, so that people in relevant geographical areas can be mobilized efficiently.[214] They should also encourage employees to vote in all elections, because high worker turnouts can counterbalance the economic advantage possessed by business-backed candidates.

Union leaders must raise funds to support and reward the politicians whom they support. Only those groups providing meaningful financial support to political candidates can obtain effective access to elected officials, because in elections in the United States, "votes are not as important in campaigns as money."[215] The fact that labor political action committees (PACs) have existed for almost fifty years[216] attests to the fact that organized labor has already been aware of this reality.

Despite the declining membership figures over the past thirty years, labor political action committees have succeeded in raising significant amounts of money in recent years. Actual contributions from union members rose from $1.43 million in 1960 to $11.82 million in 1987.[217] Even after inflation is taken into account, real political contributions rose approximately 2.5 times over that same period.[218] To accomplish this objective, labor organizations were forced to raise membership dues, assessments, and fees. Even though this measure enabled labor unions to increase their political expenditures during a period of declining enrollment, it caused them to become less attractive to prospective members and provided employers with another negative factor to be utilized during anti-union campaigns. If labor organizations double their membership ranks over the next ten to twenty years through more diligent and innovative organizing techniques, they will be able to double the amount of political contributions received from members without increasing dues, assessments, and fees. If unions simultaneously convince unorganized employees to provide monetary support for pro-worker political candidates, the economic power of working individuals will be greatly enhanced.

Labor leaders should not be afraid of offending incumbent officeholders by supporting their opponents. Ultra-conservative, pro-business incumbents are unlikely to support pro-labor or pro-worker legislation that is opposed by corporate executives. By organizing grass-root support for the opponents of such politicians, unions can intimidate incumbents into moderating their views or succeed in getting their choice of candidates into office.

COUNTERACTING THE POWER OF MULTINATIONAL BUSINESS ENTERPRISES

During the past several decades, hundreds of transnational business entities have been created. This economic phenomenon has challenged the ability of domestic labor organizations to protect the rights of individuals employed by such corporate institutions and the capacity of traditional nation-states to regulate the global operations of such firms. American union leaders consider many multinational manufacturers to be "runaway" businesses that are ceaselessly seeking inexpensive labor in developing countries.[219] These global enterprises maintain that their activities have not caused a diminution in employment in the United States, because their technological developments and market planning have generated new white-collar jobs to replace the manufacturing positions being exported to foreign nations.[220] Multinational businesses also contend that if they did not establish foreign production facilities, business firms from other countries would fill the void and prevent American institutions and workers from benefiting from expanding foreign markets.[221] To the extent that American firms develop production facilities abroad to supply markets that would probably not be served through the exportation of goods produced in the United States, due to import barriers or other cost factors, such endeavors do not decrease employment opportunities for American workers. However, where products that would otherwise be manufactured in the United States for domestic consumption are produced in low-wage foreign countries by American subsidiaries for importation back to the United States, such business activities generally reduce the number of American production jobs.

To counteract these economic developments, some myopic unionists may attempt to limit transnational expansion through legislation designed to prevent such global institutions from reaping the benefits of their foreign operations. Although protectionist legislation might generate short-term benefits for American workers, the long-term ramifications would likely be negative. International trade conflicts among historically interdependent nations could easily precipitate a nationalistic world environment that would culminate in a Pyrrhic victory for organized labor. The United States would have difficulty obtaining needed raw materials, including petroleum, from abroad, and conventional American export markets could be eliminated. Union officials should consider remedial measures that would have less devastating international, and ultimately domestic, consequences.

A possible solution is "content" legislation that would require foreign manufacturers that wish to sell their products in the United States to have a certain percentage of those goods produced in America.[222] Even though such content requirements would not be as restrictive as import quotas or substantial import tariffs, they could similarly limit the importation of goods manufactured by other than American workers. Foreign companies serving American markets would be forced either to establish new production facilities in the United States or associate themselves with American manufacturers. This practice has already occurred in both the automotive and electronics industries.

Labor leaders should accept the inevitability of an interrelated and symbiotic international economic system. Instead of trying to prevent the development of foreign production facilities that might erode American job security, labor organizations should seek legislation that would directly assist displaced workers. For example, taxes imposed on transnational enterprises that export jobs and monies obtained from conventional import duties could be used to finance special adjustment assistance programs. In addition, Congress could provide training that would enable displaced blue-collar personnel to learn the high technology skills associated with the jobs created by multinational expansion. Unions should support legislation that establishes relocation funds to assist individuals who have had to move to other geographic areas to find work. Labor organizations should work for unemployment benefits to be given to displaced individuals until they are able to procure positions commensurate with their capabilities.

International Labor Cooperation

Despite the Malthusian proliferation of multinational enterprises and the increasingly significant impact of such institutions upon the employment conditions of many American workers, most labor leaders have evidenced little enthusiasm for internationally coordinated collective bargaining tactics.[223] Unions have ignored the stark labor-management power imbalance created by transnational firms. By operating on a global basis, corporate structures can minimize the efficacy of wholly domestic labor organizations.[224] To counteract this trend, prophetic unionists have emphasized the necessity for transnational labor cooperation.[225]

The movement toward international union cooperation will encounter many obstacles. During the developmental stages of a global labor federation, corporations may exploit organizational weaknesses. Union strength will vary substantially from country to country, making it difficult to sustain unified job actions which transcend national borders.[226] If labor representatives press too vigorously for bargaining concessions in one geographic area, management officials may decide to relocate the enterprise to a national environment that is less supportive of worker solidarity.[227]

Union leaders may find it arduous to maintain transnational employee unity. Professors Northrup and Rowan have suggested that "[t]he idea that workers in one country will enthusiastically, or even reluctantly, support the cause of their brothers and sisters in another country is a figment of the intelligentsia imagination that persists over the years without either occurring to or permeating the thoughts of those who are expected to lose pay to make it come true."[228] Some evidence, however, indicates that this cynicism is not entirely justified. Labor organizations from different nations have already engaged in limited international cooperation. For example, in February 1971, French Michelin workers demonstrated and ceased work in support of a strike by Michelin's German employees.[229] That same year, workers in Belgium, Holland, Germany, and Italy collaborated to prevent Air Liquide from diverting production from a struck French plant to the facilities at which these individuals were employed. Similar union solidarity was demonstrated by British and German employees to enhance the position of striking French Kodak personnel.[230]

Probably the most dramatic incident of transnational union cooperation occurred in 1969 against the French-based international glass manufacturer, St. Gobain. The International Chemical and General Workers Federation (I.C.F.) established a committee comprised of labor leaders from each of the twelve countries in which St. Gobain operated. These representatives decided that no national union would execute a bargaining agreement with any subsidiary without committee approval. Information concerning the various negotiations was shared, a mutual strike fund was created, and each of the labor organizations agreed that none would perform any overtime to compensate for production lost because of work stoppages in other plants.[231] The I.C.F. unions also asserted that local workers should not have their compensation levels determined solely by reference to the recent profitability of their respective facilities, but should instead share in the overall prosperity of St. Gobain's global operations. Even though a few observers have questioned the degree of success actually achieved through international union efforts,[232] these endeavors demonstrate that transnational labor cooperation can be successfully carried out. If trade unions hope to influence meaningfully the operations of multinational enterprises, they must establish transnational organizations that can confront multinational companies on an international basis.

Despite the obvious need for expanded labor coordination, the growth of transnational collective bargaining has not occurred as rapidly as many observers initially anticipated.[233] The various differences in ideology and practice among labor movements that must be overcome before unions can establish successful joint ventures primarily explains this undistinguished record of trade union collaboration. While American labor organizations have generally accepted the capitalist system, many of their European counterparts have embraced a socialist philosophy.[234] Furthermore, unions that principally represent workers employed by parent corporations expected to export jobs to foreign countries do not share the same protectionist interests as the organizations whose members will be the beneficiaries of such job relocations. Some transnational facilities will be located in highly organized areas of the world, while others will function in basically nonunion environments. American labor organizations operate in a highly decentralized industrial environment in which most plant rules are determined at the local level, whereas most European trade unions function in more centralized economies in which fundamental employment conditions are established through industry-wide collective bargaining.[235] Transnational union cooperation will also have to accommodate the difference between exclusive representation rights available in the United States and the nonexclusive representation in most European countries, where employees are generally free to select their own negotiating agents regardless of the representational preferences evidenced by their fellow workers.[236] Despite these differences, however, the need for unified labor action to counterbalance the increasing power of multinational enterprises should impel union leaders all over the world to emphasize their common interests while minimizing their dissimilarities.

Labor organizations that represent workers of multinational enterprises must realize that domestic bargaining will not effectively regulate the transnational operations of such firms. These employee associations must join together with their foreign counterparts to create formal and informal labor confederations to achieve basic objectives. Unions in industrialized countries need to cooperate to avoid whipsaw tactics by global business institutions designed to induce workers in different nations to compete against one another. Information exchanges will enable labor leaders to know what unions and employers in various areas of the world are doing.[237] Electronic databases can provide immediate knowledge concerning the production figures, wage rates, fringe benefits, and working conditions of international employers. Such networks also enable labor organizations to prevent transnational production transfers intended to thwart job actions conducted by workers at particular facilities.[238]

Unions desiring to reduce the exportation of jobs from developed to developing nations must organize the workers in the developing countries. In this way, unions can ensure that such individuals are not denied employment dignity or forced to accept unconscionable working conditions. As such labor movements develop, international worker federations should seek the harmonization of compensation, fringe benefits, and working conditions throughout multinational enterprises. Such a long-term objective may currently appear naively optimistic given the extremely heterogeneous nature of the world economy.[239] Nonetheless, as developing nations become more industrialized this goal will become attainable.

International worker organizations can create information clearing houses. The International Chemical and General Workers Federation and the International Metalworkers Federation already provide extensive research and database services for their transnational member unions to facilitate employment condition comparisons among subsidiary companies, between subsidiaries and parent corporations, and among global business ventures.[240] Worker associations such as the International Conference of Free Trade Unions, the World Federation of Trade Unions, and the International Federation of Christian Trade Unions should be encouraged to provide business information on a worldwide basis.[241] Intelligence networks like these would enable national unions to engage in traditional collective bargaining on a highly informed basis, in addition to providing the foundation for a system of coordinated transnational bargaining.

Unions from different countries representing workers in related industries should consult with one another to maximize their negotiating effectiveness and strive toward greater uniformity of wages and employment conditions. Cooperation should include common contract termination dates within each industry and guarantees that work that would otherwise be performed at struck facilities cannot be transferred to other locations,[242] to enable labor organizations to coordinate their bargaining techniques on a transnational scale. Labor officials should simultaneously demand consultation rights with multinational enterprise managers concerning all of their international operations, with the ultimate objective of truly global collective bargaining.[243] Employees could then confront multinational business institutions on a relatively equal basis and counteract the ability of transnational employers to induce workers in different countries to engage in internecine competition with one another in a frequently futile effort to achieve job security and reasonable employment terms.

The maturation of the European Community (EC) will provide the impetus and structure for coordinated collective bargaining by labor unions within the EC. Although various European labor organizations have conducted a "social dialogue" with employers for many years and negotiated informal agreements pertaining to diverse topics of mutual interest,[244] the unified EC should presage formal transnational bargaining.[245] The new EC procedures will affect the foreign operations of many United States corporations.

As the emergence of the EC fosters cooperation among European labor organizations, changing circumstances within North America militate in favor of regional labor cooperation. Once the United States and Mexico conclude a free-trade agreement, a relatively unified Canadian–United States–Mexican free-trade zone will be established. As more corporations establish *maquilladora* arrangements in Mexico to take advantage of reduced labor costs, labor organizations representing United States and Canadian workers will need to develop closer ties with their Mexican counterparts. AFL-CIO officials have already initiated discussions with Mexican union leaders to formulate a joint strategy designed to protect the employment rights of American and Mexican employees.[246] By the early 21st century, North American labor institutions should become closely aligned with the European entities functioning within the EC countries. Such international labor cooperation would enable unions to effectively challenge the awesome economic power possessed by global corporate enterprises.

International Government Regulation

Although parent nations have occasionally sought to prevent or limit the exportation of jobs and technology and some host nations have adopted policies to enhance their own interests,[247] political units with limited jurisdictional scope lack the authority to govern meaningfully the transnational operations of nationless institutions. Corporations can easily circumvent legal restraints imposed by one country through the transfer of existing or future investments to regions without such restrictions.[248] Multinational corporations are geocentric entities that do not owe allegiance to any particular country.[249] If global entities are to be effectively regulated, government organizations with international jurisdiction will have to be utilized.

Nations in developed regions are in the best position to formulate uniform labor codes applicable to transnational business establishments. Labor organizations may initiate multinational regulation

through devices presently available, such as the EC or through treaties similar to the General Agreement on Tariffs and Trade (GATT).[250] EC nations previously attempted to impose information and consultation obligations upon transnational companies with respect to various employment matters through the Vredling Directive.[251] Although that directive generated substantial opposition from business firms and was never formally adopted,[252] it is likely that similar duties will ultimately be prescribed through the EC Social Charter.[253] By the time a unified EC is established, there will undoubtedly be uniform regulations governing the operations of transnational firms and mandating collective bargaining rights for the employees of such enterprises. As Canada, the United States, and Mexico create a North American free-trade region, they will be forced to develop a joint governing body that can prescribe the organizational rights of employees. By the early 21st century, labor organizations should be able to negotiate on behalf of the individuals employed by corporations doing business in all three countries.

6. THE NEED TO REFORM THE NATIONAL LABOR RELATIONS ACT

Throughout the first 150 years of its existence, the United States officially discouraged collective worker action. When individual employees joined forces with other workers, they were subject to antitrust or criminal conspiracy liability.[1] Courts did not hesitate to enjoin such collective efforts.[2] On those infrequent occasions when judicial edicts failed to prevent concerted employee conduct, affected employers might employ the national guard, the state militia, or private security forces to put an end to the employees' efforts.[3] When state legislatures attempted to pass laws proscribing yellow-dog contracts, which required employees to promise that they would not join unions, or provisions guaranteeing individuals more healthful work environments, pro-business courts invalidated those statutes as impermissible infringements upon the freedom of contract of both employers and employees.[4]

When Congress attempted in the Clayton Act of 1914[5] to divest federal courts of jurisdiction to issue injunctive orders pertaining to peaceful labor disputes, the Supreme Court narrowly construed that enactment to prevent striking employees from enlisting the sympathetic support of other workers by limiting the statutory exemption to disputants in direct employer-employee relationships.[6] It was not until 1932, when the Norris-LaGuardia Act[7] finally deprived federal judges of the authority to enjoin even sympathy action indigenous to labor disputes, that the federal government provided lasting affirmative support for collective worker behavior. In 1933, Congress tried to grant employees organizational rights through the enactment of Section 7a of the National Industrial Recovery Act,[8] but the Su-

preme Court found that act unconstitutional based on the impermissible legislative attempt to regulate intrastate commerce.[9] Congress responded in 1935 by passing the National Labor Relations Act (NLRA),[10] which successfully provided private sector personnel with organizational and collective bargaining rights.

Congress specifically indicated in Section 1 of the NLRA that "[t]he denial by employers of the right of employees to organize and the refusal by employers to accept the procedure of collective bargaining lead to strikes and other forms of industrial strife and unrest...."[11] Congress further emphasized "[t]he inequality of bargaining power between employees who do not possess full freedom of association...and employers who are organized in the corporate [form]...."[12] Congress sought to alleviate these problems "by encouraging the practice and procedure of collective bargaining."[13] The propriety of this theme was acknowledged by the Supreme Court when it sustained the constitutionality of the NLRA.[14]

The NLRA has provided significant rights for millions of American workers. Over thirty-three million employees have voted in the 345,000 representation elections conducted by the Labor Board since 1935.[15] The NLRB has processed almost 800,000 unfair labor practice charges and has issued more than 46,000 decisions.[16] During the past fifty-seven years, millions of workers have taken advantage of the NLRA right to influence their wages, hours, and employment conditions through the collective bargaining process. Millions of collective agreements have been negotiated—most without resort to work interruptions. Even though the duty to bargain does not compel either party to agree to any proposal or make any concession,[17] unionized employers and representative labor organizations have achieved innumerable accommodations of their competing interests pertaining to a multitude of topics.

During the first several decades of the NLRA, Labor Board and court decisions judiciously protected the Section 7 right of employees to form, join, and assist labor organizations and to select exclusive bargaining agents. The NLRA covered individuals with tenuous employment relationships who needed collective strength to counterbalance corporate power. Worker participation in management decision making through the bargaining process was expanded to include most relevant subjects pertaining to the employment relationship. Remedial orders were devised to rectify the effects of unfair labor practice violations. As the NLRA became more established, however, employer groups lobbied in favor of amendments designed to curtail employee rights, and court decisions began to erode important statutory protections.

THE EARLY EXPANSION OF STATUTORY RIGHTS AND PROTECTIONS

NLRA coverage was initially extended to diverse groups of workers. In *NLRB v. Hearst Publications, Inc.,*[18] for example, the Supreme Court upheld the extension of collective bargaining rights to newspaper sellers who would have been considered "independent contractors" under traditional legal principles. In *Packard Motor Car Co. v. NLRB,*[19] the Court sustained the authority of the Labor Board to provide statutory rights for supervisory personnel. In *Hearst Publications*, the Court adopted the "economic realities" test to determine which individuals really needed organizational strength to counterbalance the economic power possessed by those for whom they worked.

Unless the common-law tests are to be imported and made exclusively controlling, without regard to the statute's purposes, it cannot be irrelevant that the particular workers in these cases are subject, as a matter of economic fact, to the evils the statute was designed to eradicate and that the remedies it affords are appropriate for preventing them. . . . Interruption of commerce through strikes and unrest may stem as well from labor disputes between some who, for other purposes, are technically "independent contractors" and their employers as from disputes between persons who, for those purposes, are "employees" and their employers. . . . Inequality of bargaining power in controversies over wages, hours and working conditions may as well characterize the status of the one group as of the other. The former, when acting alone, may be as "helpless in dealing with an employer," as "dependent . . . on his daily wage" and as "unable to leave the employ and to resist arbitrary and unfair treatment" as the latter. . . . In short, when the particular situation of employment combines these characteristics, so that the economic facts of the relation make it more nearly one of employment than of independent business enterprise with respect to the ends sought to be accomplished by the legislation, those characteristics may outweigh technical legal classification for purposes unrelated to the statute's objectives and bring the relation within its protections.[20]

The Supreme Court thus concluded that seemingly independent newspaper sellers and lower level supervisors were entitled to "employee" status under the NLRA.

During the formative years of the NLRA, the Labor Board and the courts promptly defined and enforced basic substantive rights. Employers began to refrain from overt forms of intimidation as the NLRA proscribed coercive threats and discriminatory treatment. Labor organizations quickly used Section 8(a)(2) to challenge management-dominated employee committees, and the Labor Board directed these "company unions" to be disestablished.[21] The NLRB and the courts developed legal doctrines to protect the unfettered choice of employees who were the targets of union organizing campaigns. The Labor Board determined that even conduct not constituting an unfair labor practice could provide the basis for setting aside election results where the challenged action may have prevented a fair representation election.[22] Under the *Hollywood Ceramics*[23] doctrine, elections that may have been influenced by pre-election distortions were nullified when material misrepresentations of fact emanated from parties in positions to know the correct facts and the opposing party did not have sufficient time to correct the misstatements before the balloting.

As the NLRA matured, the NLRB and the courts prohibited more subtle forms of employer restraint on employee collective action. For example, pre-election benefit increases that might induce workers to vote against representation were proscribed, even when there was no evidence that the employer intended to impermissibly influence the election process.[24] Companies were also prohibited from discharging union supporters for alleged misconduct that occurred during organizing campaigns where no unprotected behavior actually occurred. Because the alleged misconduct was inextricably intertwined with the privileged organizing activities, the Court believed that those erroneous terminations would have a chilling effect upon other employees who desired to exercise their protected organizing rights.[25]

When employers rejected union requests for voluntary recognition based on claims of majority support and then engaged in unfair labor practices designed to dilute the majority support that had been obtained by the organizing unions, remedial bargaining orders were generally issued.[26] The Supreme Court subsequently intimated that where "outrageous" and "pervasive" employer unfair labor practices had significantly deterred employee organizing efforts, the NLRB could, in extraordinary circumstances, issue remedial bargaining orders even in the absence of evidence that the organizing labor entities had ever achieved majority support.[27] The Court theorized that these labor organizations would have attained majority strength but for the chilling effect of the employer's conduct. The Labor Board issued bargaining orders in favor of minority unions only in cases involving extraordinary circumstances,[28] because of the need to balance an efficacious deterrent to flagrant employer unfair labor practices against the right of employees to be free from representation by non-majority unions.[29]

The Labor Board expanded the definition of protected "concerted activity" to include individual conduct that was found to advance the employment interests of other employees. Thus, an individual employee asserting a right contained in a collective contract would automatically be considered to be acting on behalf of the other workers covered by that agreement.[30] In *Alleluia Cushion Co.,*[31] the Labor Board extended this doctrine, ruling that an individual's complaint under a safety and health statute constituted "concerted" activity even without a bargaining agreement or evidence of co-worker support.

In *NLRB v. Weingarten, Inc.,*[32] the Supreme Court sustained the extension of Section 7 protection to employees requesting union representation during employer-initiated investigatory interviews that workers reasonably fear might result in disciplinary action. Whenever individual employees are called in for investigatory interviews that they believe may culminate in discipline, they may lawfully insist that a shop steward be present before any questioning may occur. The Labor Board subsequently extended the right to co-worker assistance at such investigatory interviews to persons employed in nonunion settings in *Materials Research Corp.*[33]

Even though Section 10(c) of the NLRA, as amended by the Labor-Management Relations Act (LMRA), provides that the Labor Board shall not order the reinstatement of any employee who has been terminated for cause, the NLRB appropriately recognized that this rule should not preclude reinstatement orders in all cases of worker misconduct. When significant employer unfair labor practices provoked acts of unprotected misbehavior by employees protesting the unlawful employer actions, the Board balanced the seriousness of the protester misconduct against the seriousness of the employer violations. If the antecedent employer unfair labor practices were far more serious than the unprotected employee responses, the Board directed reinstatement.[34]

Section 8(d) expressly provided employees who selected an exclusive bargaining agent with the right to negotiate over "wages, hours, and other terms and conditions of employment."[35] Although the NLRA does not include a specific definition of mandatory bargaining topics, administrative and judicial decisions recognized the prerogative of representative labor organizations to insist upon discussions pertaining to such fringe benefits as vacations,[36] pension plans,[37] group insurance programs,[38] and paid sick leave provisions.[39] Other areas determined to be obligatory subjects of bargaining covered employee discounts,[40] safety rules,[41] employee workloads,[42] grievance procedures,[43] layoff and recall rights,[44] and certain subcontracting decisions.[45] By the late 1960s, labor organizations expected to negotiate about most topics that had any meaningful impact upon worker interests.[46]

The Supreme Court acknowledged the need for representative unions to maintain bargaining unit solidarity during labor disputes in *NLRB v. Allis-Chalmers Manufacturing Co.*,[47] by sustaining the right of labor organizations to impose judicially enforceable fines upon members who cross picket lines to work during lawful work stoppages. The *Allis-Chalmers* Court reviewed the legislative history underlying the LMRA amendments to the NLRA and concluded that Congress did not intend the Section 8(b)(1)(A)[48] proscription against union restraint and coercion to preclude the enforcement of internal union disciplinary rules against strike-breaking members:

Integral to [the] federal labor policy has been the power in the chosen union to protect against erosion [of] its status . . . through reasonable discipline of members who violate rules and regulations governing membership. That power is particularly vital when the members engage in strikes. The economic strike against the employer is the ultimate weapon in labor's arsenal for achieving agreement upon its terms, and "[t]he power to fine or expel strike-breakers is essential if the union is to be an effective bargaining agent. . . ."[49]

In *NLRB v. Boeing Co.*,[50] the Supreme Court held that the magnitude of the penalties imposed by labor organizations upon members who violate legitimate union rules does not affect the propriety of such actions under the NLRA. Even though an excessive fine is more coercive than a reasonable assessment, the Court believed that Congress did not authorize the Labor Board to regulate such internal union matters. The NLRB employed similar logic to find that it did not possess the power under the NLRA to evaluate the fairness of the internal union procedures through which a fine is imposed.[51] By the early 1970s, it was clear that the Labor Board and the courts would not interfere with the right of labor organizations to impose discipline upon members who violated legitimate union rules.

Representative labor organizations were also provided with significant discretion with respect to the expenditure of dues money collected from employees pursuant to lawful union security arrangements. Although the Supreme Court held in *Railway Employees Dep't. v. Hanson*[52] and *Machinists v. Street*[53] that unions provided with exclusive bargaining rights under federal enactments could not constitutionally expend the compelled dues money of objecting bargaining unit members for political or ideological causes, the scope of these holdings was limited.

THE EROSION OF NLRA PROTECTIONS

Judicial Limitations on Union Activities

The NLRA was enacted during the depths of the Great Depression. The Supreme Court had recently invalidated the extension of bargaining rights to workers under the National Industrial Recovery Act, but it finally acknowledged the need for special legislation to help bring the country out of the depression. Although the Court began to sustain the constitutionality of various enactments that advanced the rights of working people, including the NLRA, it remained a conservative institution that did not believe that rank-and-file employees should be permitted to exert undue influence against their respective employers.

In *NLRB v. Mackay Radio & Telegraph Co.*,[54] the Court decided to limit the primary economic weapon available to employees. Even though the *Mackay Radio* case directly concerned the propriety of an employer's refusal to reinstate along with other returning strikers several individuals who had been particularly active union supporters, the Court took the opportunity to address an issue that had not been raised by the parties.

Nor was it an unfair labor practice to replace the striking employees with others in an effort to carry on the business. Although §13 provides, "Nothing in this Act shall be construed so as to interfere with or impede or diminish in any way the right to strike," it does not follow that an employer, guilty of no act denounced by the statute, has lost the right to protect and continue his business by supplying places left vacant by strikers. And he is not bound to discharge those hired to fill the places of the strikers, upon the election of the latter to resume their employment, in order to create places for them.[55]

The Court decided that an employer's need to continue operations during an economic strike outweighed the rather slight impact upon the permanently replaced strikers. This opinion was a devastating infringement on the statutorily protected right to engage in concerted activity and clearly illustrated the Court's determination to provide businesses with the leverage they needed to neutralize the strike weapon that Congress had granted to workers.

The Supreme Court was not willing, however, to allow employers to use any device to negate the efficacy of a lawful work stoppage. Economic strikers could not be terminated, because they were engaged in protected concerted activity.[56] Even when they were lawfully replaced, economic strikers retained their "employee" status under the NLRA and enjoyed preferential recall rights as soon as positions for which they were qualified became vacant.[57] Nonetheless, in 1959, Congress amended Section 9(c)(3) of the NLRA[58] to provide that permanently replaced economic strikers may only vote in representation elections conducted within twelve months from the date the strike commenced. This statutory change made it easier for a business firm that had broken a work stoppage to decertify the incumbent union one year after the strike began, because only the replacement personnel and reinstated strikers, parties not necessarily amenable to unionization, could vote in that election.

In the 1963 *Erie Resistor* case,[59] the Supreme Court held that an employer could not offer striker replacements twenty years of "super seniority" to use in future years during layoffs to displace reinstated strikers with greater actual seniority. In *Giddings & Lewis, Inc. v. NLRB*,[60] however, the Seventh Circuit completely ignored the *Erie Resistor* rationale. It decided that an employer that had hired permanent replacements during an economic strike did not violate the NLRA when it promulgated a rule providing that members of the existing workforce would be recalled in the order of their seniority, ahead of more senior, unreinstated strikers, in the event of a layoff.[61] This practice effectively provided replacement personnel with the "super seniority" that the *Erie Resistor* Court had found impermissible.

In *Trans World Airlines, Inc. v. Independent Fed'n. of Flight Attendants*,[62] the Supreme Court established a new rule that further undermines worker solidarity during strikes. A closely divided Court held that less senior "crossover" employees who either refuse to honor the initial strike call or decide to return to work during the work stoppage may retain the higher positions they obtain while their more senior colleagues remain on strike, even after the labor dispute has been resolved. This decision encourages less senior personnel to work during a strike to obtain an employment advantage over more senior employees who choose to strike, and causes more senior workers to fear that their participation in a lawful work stoppage may jeopardize the job status they previously earned through years of seniority.

Congressional Restrictions on Labor Organization Strength

Businesses also petitioned Congress for relief from the economic weapons made available to employees under the NLRA. For example, the NLRA had allowed labor organizations to utilize secondary tactics to further worker interests. A union involved in a labor dispute could lawfully picket a supplier or customer of the affected employer even if the supplier or customer was not directly involved in the labor discord, to pressure the affected employer. The LMRA[63] amended the NLRA in 1947 to prohibit most forms of secondary activity. New Section 10(1)[64] directed the Labor Board to seek immediate injunctive relief against unions employing secondary tactics to prevent the continuation of the secondary conduct during the pendency of NLRB unfair labor practice proceedings. The LMRA also provided primary and secondary employers that were affected by unlawful secondary boycotts with the right to seek monetary damages in federal court.[65]

Congress further expanded the area of proscribed secondary activity in the 1959 Labor Management Reporting and Disclosure Act amendments to the NLRA.[66] One provision outlawed peacefully obtained "hot cargo" agreements in which a secondary employer and a union agree that the employer will not do business with a business firm directly involved in a labor dispute.[67] The 1959 amendments also imposed severe restrictions on peaceful picketing designed to organize employees or to obtain voluntary recognition of a representative labor organization from the employer,[68] making it more difficult for labor entities to unionize new workers.

Narrowing the Scope of NLRA Coverage

In 1947, businesses induced Congress to amend the NLRA definition of "employee" to exclude both "independent contractors" and "supervisors."[69] Congress thus rejected the "economic realities" test formulated in *Hearst Publications* to determine those individuals most in need of NLRA protection. The Supreme Court further narrowed the statutory definition of "employee" in *Allied Chemical & Alkali Workers Local 1 v. Pittsburgh Plate Glass Co.*[70] At issue was whether retired individuals continued to enjoy "employee" status following their retirement to the extent they wished to bargain over their pension rights. The Court ruled that these people were not "employees" within the meaning of the NLRA, because they were no longer actively seeking reemployment with their former employer.

In *Yeshiva University,*[71] the Supreme Court substantially reduced the NLRA protection available to white-collar personnel. The Court noted that "managerial" employees, who "formulate and effectuate management policies by expressing and making operative the decisions of their employer,"[72] have historically been excluded from NLRA coverage by Labor Board decisions due to their close alignment with corporate management. Since the university professors who sought to organize for collective bargaining purposes fit this definition of "managerial" employees, despite their lack of control over their "wages, hours, and other terms and conditions of employment," they were found ineligible for NLRA coverage. In *College of Osteopathic Medicine & Surgery,*[73] the Labor Board extended *Yeshiva University* by finding that organized college faculty members who obtain meaningful control over academic matters through collective bargaining become "managerial" personnel and thus, ironically, forfeit their negotiation rights under the NLRA.

Thwarting Organizational Tactics

Over the past two decades, the Labor Board and the courts have made it easier for corporations to prevent the unionization of their employees. Under the traditional *Hollywood Ceramics*[74] approach, the NLRB refused to permit employers to use material misrepresentations to adversely affect the manner in which employees voted in representation elections. Following the publication of a limited empirical study that suggested that employee voting was not meaningfully influenced by employer misrepresentations or threats,[75] the Labor Board abandoned the *Hollywood Ceramics* doctrine. In *Shopping Kart Food Market,*[76] the NLRB announced that election rules "must be based on a view of employees as mature individuals who are capable of recognizing campaign propaganda for what it is and discounting it."[77] As a result, the Board no longer evaluates the impact of misleading campaign statements upon worker free choice.

It simply assumes that individuals whose employment destiny is substantially controlled by their employer are not influenced by employer campaign recitations suggesting that unionization may cause a loss of business and jobs.[78]

The Labor Board recently decided that it will no longer issue bargaining directives in favor of nonmajority unions under *Gissel Packing*.[79] A labor entity seeking such an order must now demonstrate that it actually achieved majority support. An employer that quickly thwarts an incipient organizing campaign through unlawful threats and discharges may thus be able to chill the organizational propensities of the remaining workers sufficiently to prevent the campaigning union from attaining majority support. Even though this employer would incur backpay liability for the unlawful discharges, it would succeed in avoiding the duty to recognize and bargain with a labor union.

In its 1984 *Meyers Industries* decision,[80] the Labor Board narrowed the Section 7 protection afforded to individuals who protest adverse employment conditions. The NLRB determined that individuals who question safety conditions or file complaints with state or federal regulatory agencies are no longer insulated from retaliatory employer discipline under the NLRA, unless they either act in direct concert with other workers or assert rights codified in existing bargaining agreements. Personnel who are not covered by a collective contract or do not associate themselves with other workers are thus unable to challenge resulting discharges under the NLRA. In 1985, the NLRB decided that the right of employees to request representation at investigatory interviews would no longer be available to unorganized employees despite the absence of language in Section 7 restricting the definition of concerted activities to those in which formally organized employees participate.[81]

The NLRA protection afforded to individual employees was eroded further in *Clear Pine Mouldings*.[82] The Labor Board discarded the "provocation" doctrine that had preserved the reinstatement rights of employees who engaged in nonflagrant misconduct in response to serious employer unfair labor practices. Strikers who protest extreme employer unfair labor practices now forfeit their right to reinstatement if they engage in "excessive" behavior.

When the doctrine enunciated in *Clear Pine Mouldings* is combined with the remedial rule established in *Gourmet Foods*, it becomes clear that immoral employers willing to ignore their legal obligations under the NLRA can significantly disenfranchise employees exercising their protected right to organize. A company can instruct its supervisory personnel to alert it to incipient organizing efforts. It can readily ascertain the names of the primary union organizers and terminate them in a public and humiliating manner. If the employer is fortunate, its openly provocative method of termination may precipitate unprotected responses from those discriminated against, causing them to forfeit their right to reinstatement under *Clear Pine Mouldings*. Such overtly intimidating conduct would discourage further organizing activity by the remaining workers. This would probably prevent the campaigning union from attaining majority support. The *Gourmet Foods* doctrine would thus preclude issuance of any remedial bargaining order.

Restricting the Issues Subject to Bargaining

Currently organized employees may no longer influence their employment circumstances to the extent unionized workers could in the past, due to recent Labor Board and court decisions that have narrowed the scope of mandatory collective bargaining. In *First National Maintenance Corp. v. NLRB*,[83] the Supreme Court held that a company decision to close part of a business does not constitute a mandatory subject for bargaining. The Court used language that could potentially preclude employee participation in many other important management decisions affecting terms and conditions of employment:

Management must be free from the constraints of the bargaining process to the extent essential for the running of a profitable business. It also must have some degree of certainty beforehand as to when it may proceed to reach decisions without fear of later evaluations labeling its conduct an unfair labor practice.... [I]n view of an employer's need for unencumbered decisionmaking, bargaining over management decisions that have a substantial impact on the continued availability of employment should be required only if the benefit, for labor-management relations and the collective bargaining process, outweighs the burden placed on the conduct of the business.[84]

The Court now requires collective bargaining of management decisions having a significant impact upon employment security only when it is likely that the representative labor organization will be able to satisfy employer concerns at the bargaining table.

In *Dubuque Packing Co.*,[85] the Labor Board held that a business entity is only obligated to bargain about a prospective decision to relocate production from one facility to another when (1) the management decision does not involve a change in the basic operation of the business; (2) the work to be performed at the new location will not differ substantially from that performed at the existing plant; (3) labor costs are a significant factor with respect to the company's proposed relocation; (4) the representative union may be able to offer concessions that will satisfy the employer's financial concerns; and (5) there are no unusual circumstances that require a prompt corporate decision that would be unduly delayed by collective negotiations.

Intrusions into Internal Union Affairs

Recent Labor Board and Court decisions have eroded union disciplinary authority. In *NLRB v. Textile Workers Granite State Joint Board*,[86] the Supreme Court held that a union could not discipline individuals who had crossed a lawful picket line to return to work during a strike when they had resigned from the labor union prior to their strike-breaking activities. Following this decision, several labor organizations amended their constitutions to restrict the right of members to resign during ongoing labor disputes. In *Pattern Makers' League of North America v. NLRB*,[87] however, the Supreme Court held that the proviso to Section 8(b)(1)(A), which gives unions the right "to prescribe [their] own rules with respect to the acquisition and retention of membership,"[88] did not indicate a congressional intent to permit labor organizations to restrict member resignations. The Court further determined that the Section 7 right of an employee to cross a picket line to work during a strike could not be limited by union provisions limiting membership withdrawals.

In *Ellis v. Brotherhood of Railway, Airline & Steamship Clerks*,[89] the Supreme Court held that while unions could expend the dues money received from objecting bargaining unit members to support conventions and social activities, they could not use such resources to organize other groups of workers or to prosecute civil suits that did not directly involve members of the bargaining unit. The Court simply ignored the fact that a union's capacity to organize the employees of competitor firms directly affects the job security and employment benefits enjoyed by organized personnel. It also disregarded the fact that test litigation prosecuted on behalf of one bargaining unit may inure to the direct benefit of employees in other units. For example, a victory under the wage and hour laws, the health and safety statutes, or the civil rights acts could establish a precedent that would greatly advance the employment rights of all employees.

Lehnert v. Ferris Faculty Ass'n.[90] further restricted the right of labor organizations to use the funds received from objecting bargaining unit members. The Court determined that for challenged activities to constitute properly chargeable endeavors, they must (1) be "germane" to collective bargaining; (2) be justified by the government's vital interest in labor peace while avoiding "free riders" who benefit from representational efforts without paying for union services; and (3) not significantly add to the burdening of free speech inherent in the allowance of a union security agreement. The Court disallowed expenditure of compelled dues money for lobbying, electoral, or other political activities. In 1992, President Bush increased the pressure on labor organizations through Executive Order 12,800 that requires federal contractors to post notices apprising employees of their right to object to the impermissible expenditure of their union dues.[91] Proposed Department of Labor regulations will require unions to break down the expenditures contained in annual LMRDA reporting forms into distinct categories: contract negotiation and administration, organizing, safety and health, strike activities, political maneuvers, lobbying, promotional efforts, and other.[92] These rules are designed to make it easier for workers to challenge union dues expenditures, and they will create expensive accounting problems for many labor organizations.

NECESSARY LABOR LAW REFORMS

Over the past several decades, business and government antipathy toward unions have combined with demographic, industrial, and global factors to threaten the continued viability of the American labor movement. If this negative trend is not reversed in the near future, labor organizations will become relatively insignificant institutions by the beginning of the 21st century. Union officials need to modify their organizing techniques to appeal to white-collar employees, women, minorities, and managerial personnel. Labor leaders must also develop techniques that will increase the economic and political strength of their organizations.

Union leaders cannot revitalize organized labor without the crucial assistance of Congress, the White House, and the judiciary. Organized labor should use its new-found economic and political power to persuade Congress to amend the NLRA to provide affirmative support for trade unions. The United States must reconfirm the congressional objectives underlying the original Wagner Act if it seriously believes that vital labor organizations constitute an important component of a strong democracy. The amended NLRA should expand the rights of employees, protect employee choice in representation elections, enhance the economic options available to representative unions, broaden the scope of bargaining, and modify the remedial provisions of the NLRA to discourage illegal employer opposition to employee organization.

Substantive Changes

Statutory Coverage. Congress must amend Section 2(3) of the NLRA,[93] which defines the term "employee" to reflect the economic realities characteristic of the post-industrial society America has become. Individuals who perform services for businesses and might constitute "independent contractors" under archaic legal doctrines should be provided with statutory coverage to reflect the true economic relationship between them and the entities for whom they work. Modifying Section 2(3) to incorporate the *Hearst Publications* "economic realities" test would enable individuals who do not fall within the traditional definition of "employee" but nevertheless retain little or no control over the terms and conditions of their employment to benefit from the protections of the NLRA.

Congress must also amend Section 2 to limit the scope of the supervisory exclusion. The Labor Board presently finds supervisory status in individuals who possess the authority to influence the terms and conditions of other employees, even when that authority is rarely exercised.[94] The statutory definition should be altered to exclude only those persons who actually make determinations with respect to the employment of other employees and who do so regularly. Lower level "supervisors" who exercise such powers infrequently or merely make recommendations to higher management officials should not be excluded from NLRA coverage. Their employment interests are more closely aligned with their rank-and-file colleagues than with corporate managers,[95] and they require collectivization to advance their employment rights.[96]

Section 2(3) should explicitly exclude "managerial officials," defined to include only those persons "who regularly and meaningfully participate in the formulation or effectuation of fundamental labor or personnel policies directly pertaining to wages, hours, or other terms and conditions of employment." Employees who may be able to influence company rules not immediately related to basic employment conditions should not be excluded from NLRA coverage.[97] Because such individuals lack the capacity to decide those issues that would be the subject of collective bargaining, they should have the statutory right to advance their employment interests through organized efforts.

Representation Elections.   The statutory right of employees to organize is meaningless without the opportunity to participate in fair representation elections. The Labor Board should prohibit tactics by employer or union agents that are likely to infringe employee free choice. Employers should be prohibited from disseminating information that even intimates to employees that if they vote in favor of unionization, they may endanger their job security. Individuals who depend on their employers for their continued economic existence are unlikely to ignore suggestions that their continued employment security is in jeopardy. The NLRB should require that company representations regarding possible adverse effects of collectivization be based upon objective factual circumstances and be limited to assessments concerning demonstrably probable consequences beyond the control of the firm.[98]

Intentional misrepresentations should be similarly proscribed. The *Midland National Life Insurance Co.*[99] doctrine that permits the dissemination of pre-election misrepresentations is based upon the naive premise that employees are not meaningfully influenced by such factors. Employers would not use these techniques if they did not believe they could influence the election outcome. The Labor Board should return to the *Hollywood Ceramics*[100] approach and refuse to allow representation election outcomes to be determined by the ability of either business or labor entities to distort the truth.

If workers are to vote intelligently in representation elections, they must have the opportunity to become familiar with the arguments for and against unionization. Employers presently enjoy a clear advantage in this regard. They may promulgate rules preventing employees from proselytizing during work time, while their supervisors inform employees about the negative aspects of unionization during the same work time.[101] Employers can lawfully address the issue of unionization at captive audience sessions that workers are required to attend, read anti-union statements over intercom systems, post election propaganda on company bulletin boards, include negative information about unionization in employee pay envelopes, and mail campaign material to worker homes. Labor organizations are generally unable to employ any of these forms of communication to provide employees with a balanced perspective.

Proposals that this communication imbalance be reduced by providing union organizers with limited access to company premises during election drives[102] have been countered by understandable employer concerns with theft, sabotage, and drug usage. A less drastic means of lessening the communication advantage enjoyed by employers would be to provide union organizers with access to prominently displayed bulletin boards. Unions should also be permitted to include information in employee pay envelopes and to mail campaign material to worker homes if employers utilize these communication channels. When company officials give captive audience speeches in person or through public address systems, employees who support the union organizing drive should be provided with the opportunity to respond to the employer's anti-union message. If these channels of communication are available to union supporters, the likelihood of informed voting would increase.

Union officials should be given the names and addresses of employees in the unit being organized at a reasonably early date. Although unions are currently provided with this information *after* a Labor Board election has been directed,[103] the names and addresses of unit personnel should be made available in a more timely manner. This approach would enable organizers to make home visits and to mail campaign literature to worker homes. To ensure that employee privacy would only be compromised during serious organizing drives, the Labor Board could limit the disclosure of this information to cases in which union agents can demonstrate that they have obtained signed authorization cards from 20 or 30 percent of the workers in the proposed unit.

To increase the probability of fair balloting, the Labor Board should mandate that elections be held within two weeks after representation petitions have been filed. NLRB notices could be immediately posted to apprise affected employees of their rights under the NLRA, and Regional Offices could swiftly determine voter eligibility. In most cases in which the employer contests the appropriateness of the bargaining unit proposed by the petitioning union, Regional Directors could decide the possible combinations and direct immediate elections. The votes of different employee groups could be segregated until the Regional Directors resolve the unit questions, and the Labor Board would then aggregate the votes of the relevant groups and certify the results. Because employers are generally aware of union organizing drives well before any election petition is filed from supervisors who inform managers of incipient campaign efforts, company officials would have ample time to disseminate their anti-union message before the election.

The statutory right of employees to organize for collective bargaining purposes is meaningless if workers lack the economic power to support their negotiating demands. Without some degree of meaningful empowerment, unionized personnel are forced to engage in collective begging, rather than collective bargaining. The Supreme Court decision in *NLRB v. Mackay Radio & Telegraph Co.*[104] severely undermined the statutorily protected right of employees to strike.[105] The *Mackay Radio* permanent replacement doctrine is being employed with greater frequency since President Reagan decided in 1981 to terminate 11,000 air traffic controllers who illegally struck against the federal government. A recent AFL-CIO study found that approximately 11 percent of the 243,300 workers who participated in major strikes during 1990 were permanently replaced.[106] Most were forced to seek other employment, and their representative labor organizations ceased to function as viable bargaining agents for the new personnel.

The *Mackay Radio* holding ignored two crucial propositions embodied in the NLRA—"that the law should protect the individual worker as the weaker party, and that the best protection against individual weakness [is] collective action."[107] By permitting employers to hire permanent replacements for striking employees, the Court effectively destroyed the economic balance that Congress established in the NLRA.

The Strike Weapon. Some commentators argue that struck employers should not be permitted to hire temporary or permanent replacements for striking employees, because the retention of such replacements would impermissibly interfere with the unfettered right of workers to resort to work stoppages.[108] A complete prohibition against the employment of any replacement personnel, however, would unduly prevent companies from protecting themselves against truly excessive union demands. A policy that would balance the interests of both struck employers and striking employees is necessary to resolve these competing issues. For example, the NLRA could be amended to bar the hiring of any replacements during the first one, two, or three months of an economic strike. The affected employer could continue to function with regular managerial employees, but could not employ replacement workers during the specified period. After the designated interval elapsed, the struck firm would be permitted to employ temporary or permanent replacements. This type of restriction would preclude the displacement of striking employees during the initial period of a job action, but it could create major problems for business entities unable to maintain minimal operations through the use of managerial personnel.

A more reasonable alternative would involve the balancing approach frequently utilized to determine the degree to which employers may curtail protected employee rights due to business exigencies.[109] Struck employers could be allowed to continue to operate through the hiring of temporary replacement workers who would be laid off as soon as the striking employees terminated their job actions. In most situations, struck companies desiring to maintain operations would be able to locate a sufficient number of qualified temporary replacements to reduce the economic impact of the work stoppages. Struck employers would only be permitted to hire permanent replacements when they could demonstrate by clear and convincing evidence that local labor market conditions preclude the employment of qualified temporary workers. To prevent the Labor Board or courts from permitting the premature hiring of permanent replacements, Congress could enact a statutory provision proscribing the employment of permanent replacements during the first month or two of any work stoppage.

A rule preventing or restricting the hiring of permanent replacements would prevent struck businesses from using employee job actions as an excuse to eliminate the jobs of individuals who engage in concerted activity or to decertify incumbent bargaining representatives through the employment of permanent replacement personnel. Such a rule would also deprive firms countering union organizing campaigns of the ability to caution employees that if their selected bargaining agent calls a work stoppage, workers who participate can be permanently replaced.[110] Disallowing permanent strike replacements would simultaneously prevent "crossover" employees of the existing bargaining unit—who refuse to strike with their fellow workers or who return to work during an ongoing job action—from retaining the positions they obtained ahead of more senior strikers whom they replaced. A rule prohibiting permanent replacements would enable all of the individuals who engaged in a strike to displace temporary replacements, including crossover personnel, who momentarily occupied their positions.

In 1991, bills were introduced in Congress that would have either prohibited the hiring of permanent replacement workers or limited the employment of such persons to circumstances in which temporary replacements could not be retained. Although the House of Representatives voted to adopt H.R. 5, which would have barred the employment of permanent replacements,[111] congressional supporters were unable to overcome business and White House opposition to the proposed legislation.

Secondary Labor Activities. In enacting the NLRA, Congress recognized that workers could only effectively counter the economic power of corporate entities through concerted action. At the present time, employees involved in a labor dispute against an employer are only permitted to direct economic pressure toward that firm. Section 8(b)(4)(B) prohibits workers from inducing employees of secondary business entities to cease handling products going to or coming from the struck company, or from threatening or coercing secondary parties to convince them to cease doing business with the primary company.[112] Employees may engage in consumer picketing at retail stores that request customers not to purchase goods produced by the struck business,[113] so long as the struck goods do not constitute the principal items carried by the secondary retail establishment.[114] They may also distribute handbills asking prospective customers to refrain from patronizing those shops if they continue to carry the struck goods during the labor dispute,[115] but they may not precipitate any cessation of work by the individuals employed by secondary retail establishments. These restrictions on the use of secondary actions by employees in labor disputes severely curtail the economic weapons available to unionized personnel.

The NLRA should be amended to permit some forms of secondary activity. Congress must acknowledge the significant imbalance in bargaining power that has developed over the past two decades as a result of industrial and technological changes that have diminished the efficacy of conventional work stoppages and the ability of struck business enterprises to hire temporary and permanent replacements. Congress must also recognize that a strike at one firm generally has an impact on other unrelated entities.

A successful work stoppage shuts down the operations of the target company. As a result, the business may be forced to suspend its purchases of raw materials and to reduce its shipment of finished goods. When striking employees are unable to generate a complete cessation of primary operations through a strike, they should be able to expand their concerted activities to reach secondary companies that deal directly with the struck employer as suppliers or customers. Workers engaged in a work stoppage should be able to induce the employees of secondary firms to refuse to handle the raw materials destined for the struck firm or the finished goods coming from that establishment during the controversy. If an employer attempts to limit primary employee picketing of suppliers or customers by creating an artificial middle enterprise through which it funnels raw materials or finished goods, the firms dealing directly with that enterprise should be susceptible to primary employee picketing. Congress should also amend Section 8(e)[116] of the NLRA to permit primary employees and their union to ask secondary parties having direct relationships with the primary employer to enter into agreements in which they promise to cease doing business with the primary company during lawful work stoppages.

Congress should amend Section 8(b)(4)(B) to permit striking individuals to appeal to customers of secondary retail stores. If a struck firm is unable to produce during an industrial dispute, retail stores are unable to obtain the products normally manufactured by that company. Strikers should be able to use placards or handbills to induce prospective customers to cease shopping at retail stores that continue to carry the products of the struck firm during the existing labor controversy. No distinction should be drawn between peaceful consumer picketing and peaceful consumer handbilling. Nor should the amount of revenue derived from sales of the struck goods affect the legality of such consumer appeals, since a complete shutdown of the struck company would force the retail establishment to explore the availability of products from alternative firms regardless of the profits lost due to the unavailability of the goods at issue. If the secondary retail store is a direct customer of the primary employer, the striking employees should be permitted to ask the retail workers to cease handling the primary party's goods. If there is no immediate relationship between the two entities, the consumer picketing and handbilling would lose its statutory protection if the participants cause secondary retail employees to stop work.

Were corporate leaders concerned about production losses caused by more effective work stoppages, they could support other innovative alternatives. For example, an NLRA amendment could prohibit economic strikes, but mandate the resolution of collective bargaining impasses through binding interest arbitration procedures. Tri-partite arbitral panels could be empowered to select the more reasonable final offer made by the employer or the union, either on an "issue-by-issue" or a "total package" basis. Various state public sector bargaining laws have successfully employed interest arbitration procedures as a substitute for proscribed strike activity.[117]

Employers could alternatively support an amendment to the NLRA that would permit only "statutory strikes" that would not involve actual work stoppages.[118] After a bargaining impasse was reached, the employer or the labor organization could declare a "strike." Production and services would continue as usual, but employee wages would be reduced by a specific amount (e.g., 25 percent) and company revenues would be reduced by the same percentage. If the parties resolved their dispute promptly, the withheld compensation and revenues would be returned to the workers and the firm. If the controversy were not settled quickly, however, the withheld funds would be permanently transferred to the public treasury. The financial incentives associated with "statutory strikes" would encourage labor and management representatives to resolve their bargaining impasses expeditiously without disrupting production or depriving workers of their livelihood.

Protections for Nonunion Personnel under the NLRA.   Individuals who question safety conditions or file complaints with state or federal regulatory agencies are not insulated from retaliatory employer discipline under the NLRA unless they either act in direct concert with other workers or assert rights codified in existing bargaining agreements.[119] Congress should amend the NLRA to clearly provide that unorganized individuals who raise issues of obvious interest to other employees with their employer or with regulatory bodies shall be considered engaged in "constructive concerted activity" and be entitled to protection under Section 7.[120]

The distinction between union and nonunion personnel established by the Labor Board in *Sears, Roebuck & Co.*,[121] with respect to employees who request the assistance of fellow employees during investigative interviews they reasonably fear may result in discipline, has no foundation in the language of Section 7. Congress should amend that provision to indicate that both organized and unorganized employees have the right to ask for the support of other persons during such investigatory interviews.

The Scope of Bargaining.   The Supreme Court and the Labor Board have unduly restricted the scope of bargaining available to representative labor organizations. The NLRA was designed to enable represented personnel to deprive corporate officials of their ability to make unilateral determinations with respect to issues of direct relevance to bargaining unit members.[122] Congress should amend Section 8(d)[123] to make it clear that designated bargaining agents possess the statutory prerogative to expect negotiations over all company decisions that will meaningfully impact employee "wages, hours, and other terms and conditions of employment." Proposed decisions pertaining to such topics as subcontracting, production transfers, partial closures, and the introduction of new technology should all be subject to mandatory bargaining.

The inconvenience of such negotiations to employers is irrelevant, because the relatively slight infringement of managerial authority associated with mandatory bargaining is outweighed by the need for unionized employees to participate in the decision-making process that bears directly on their continued economic well-being. This expanded scope of bargaining would not enable labor organizations to prevent management decisions that simply displease bargaining unit personnel, but would merely obligate employers to notify representative unions of proposed changes and provide them with the opportunity to discuss the pertinent issues. Businesses would not be required to make any concessions or to agree to any proposals.[124] Management would be free to implement the position rejected by union leaders at the bargaining table, if employee representatives refused to accommodate employer needs and a good-faith impasse were reached.[125]

The ability of representative labor organizations to obtain beneficial contract terms is directly related to their capacity to preserve bargaining unit solidarity. Congress should recognize that labor organizations are democratic institutions and that while members may oppose proposed concerted activity, they should not be able to ignore the affirmative vote of a majority of their fellow members. Unions should be permitted to impose reasonable restrictions upon the right of members to resign during ongoing job actions, to preserve the concerted strength of those organizations. Congress can achieve this end by amending the proviso to Section 8(b)(1)(A)[126] to provide that member resignations would not take effect until thirty days after their submission to the union. Such a rule would preserve the worker solidarity that is essential during the early stages of economic strikes, and would reasonably allow dissenters to escape the disciplinary authority of their labor entities after thirty days.

Labor organization solidarity has been similarly undermined by Supreme Court decisions restricting the right of such entities to expend dues money received from nonmember employees covered by lawful union security agreements. Even though private sector labor organizations derive their representational status from the NLRA, they are not governmental entities. The NLRA should thus be amended to permit unions to expend dues money for nonpolitical and nonideological purposes that advance worker rights, such as union organizing, litigation not related to the immediate bargaining unit, or lobbying efforts, even if these purposes do not immediately concern the negotiation and administration of the collective contract covering the instant unit of employees.

Representative unions should certainly be able to use the dues money received from objecting members to organize new groups of workers. The job security, compensation levels, and employment terms enjoyed by unionized personnel are directly threatened by the ability of unorganized companies to obtain a competitive advantage through the availability of reduced labor costs. To the extent labor organizations are able to organize most or all members of an industry, they greatly protect the job security and working conditions provided to employees covered by collective contracts.

Litigation involving external bargaining units may similarly inure to the benefit of individuals in the immediate unit. Test cases involving wage and hour laws, health and safety regulations, civil rights statutes, and other employment-related enactments generate judicial precedents that will assist all workers. This indirect benefit makes it appropriate to permit representative labor unions to expend dues money received from one bargaining unit to finance litigation involving the employment rights of other groups of workers. In most, if not all, such cases, the labor union would merely attempt to obtain through litigation benefits and protections it would otherwise have to achieve through the collective bargaining process.

Unions should also be allowed to spend dues money to support lobbying efforts designed to advance the employment rights of all workers. While it would be improper under the First Amendment to permit labor entities to expend the dues money of objecting employees to finance political parties or particular candidates, or to proselytize for or against such ideological issues as abortion or aid to parochial schools, unions should be able to utilize dues revenues to support lobbying intended to enhance the employment interests of all workers. Efforts to increase the minimum wage, to improve health and safety protections, to extend unemployment compensation coverage, to proscribe discrimination, or to protect employees displaced by new technology or job relocations are germane to collective bargaining. To the extent labor organizations can obtain legislation to cover these employment-related topics, representative unions will be able to focus on the advancement of other worker objectives through the bargaining process.

Remedial Changes

The Need for More Balanced NLRA Remedies. The remedial scheme of the NLRA favors employers. The primary reason for this statutory imbalance is that the most potent unfair labor practice remedies were added to the NLRA in 1947 by an extremely pro-business Congress. Most of the new remedial provisions added by the LMRA pertained to violations committed by labor organizations, not employers. For example, the new Section 10(1)[127] specified that charges involving secondary union activity under Section 8(b)(4) or 8(e) or regarding organizational or recognitional picketing under Section 8(b)(7) shall be handled on a priority basis. Whenever a charge alleging a violation of one of those provisions is filed, the Labor Board is directed to seek an immediate injunctive order against the offending union, to protect the employer's interests while the subsequent unfair labor practice proceedings are conducted. If the NLRB fails to seek a restraining order against the proscribed union activity, the affected business firm may petition a district court for a writ of mandate ordering the Board to do so.[128] Section 303 of the LMRA[129] provided employers with additional protection against secondary conduct by authorizing federal courts to award damages to parties injured by Section 8(b)(4) violations.

Employers that commit unfair labor practices are not subject to mandatory injunctive orders. If a union files a charge alleging a violation of Section 8(a) by a business entity and the NLRB decides to issue a complaint, the Board may seek a preliminary injunction against the offending conduct under Section 10(j).[130] The Board is not statutorily obligated, however, to seek injunctive relief, and if the NLRB declines to pursue an injunction, the adversely affected employees or labor organization cannot compel that agency to do so. The Labor Board rarely seeks injunctive relief against employer unfair labor practices under Section 10(j).

The number of employer unfair labor practices has increased dramatically over the past ten to fifteen years.[131] It has become relatively common for companies counteracting union organizing drives to discharge the employees leading the collectivization efforts. If firms terminate such individuals publicly and flagrantly, they may be able to provoke an unprotected response from the fired employees and avoid the obligation to reinstate them,[132] thus dampening union support among the remaining workers. If the labor entity is thus prevented from attaining majority status, the company does not have to worry about any remedial bargaining order, no matter how outrageous its violations.[133]

Corporations that ignore the rights of their employees under the NLRA are generally motivated by the fact that the relatively minimal costs associated with unfair labor practice liability are outweighed by the overall costs associated with worker unionization. These corporations ignore the moral and systemic ramifications of their unlawful conduct, and take advantage of the fact that Labor Board remedies with respect to discriminatory terminations are wholly inadequate. The sole monetary remedy available to unlawfully discharged employees is a Board order requiring the offending party to make whole those who have been discriminated against for the compensation they have lost. Unlawfully fired individuals are even required to seek interim employment to mitigate their economic losses during the pendency of the NLRB proceedings.[134] Furthermore, Labor Board reinstatement orders are not particularly effective. Only about 40 percent of those discriminated against actually accept offers of reemployment, and, of those who do, approximately 80 percent leave their employer within two years.[135]

Companies that commit serious unfair labor practices during organizing drives may find themselves encumbered by remedial bargaining orders, if the adversely affected labor organizations can demonstrate that they obtained majority support from the workers despite the employer violations. Even these remedial directives are often ineffectual. Only about 35 to 40 percent of unions that obtain remedial bargaining orders ever achieve collective contracts.[136] The more vigorously employers oppose such remedial orders through judicial appeals, the less likely the chance that the labor union will be able to achieve an initial bargaining agreement.[137]

Even when companies do not employ coercive tactics and unions successfully obtain Labor Board certification, fruitful negotiations do not always result. Recalcitrant employers can simply refuse to accede to worker demands. A good faith bargaining impasse is unactionable under the NLRA. Even if employers refuse to agree to union demands in bad faith, the most they need fear from the NLRB is a cease-and-desist order that will take several years for the petitioning labor organization to obtain and have judicially enforced.[138] By the time meaningful relief is provided, crucial organizing momentum is lost and union effectiveness is irretrievably diluted.

If the proliferating negation of NLRA rights by business entities is to be reversed, Congress must provide more efficacious remedies. To deter the crippling impact of Section 8(a)(3) discharges, Congress should adopt a liquidated damages provision similar to Section 16(b) of the Fair Labor Standards Act[139] that authorizes double backpay awards to employees whose rights have been violated. If the Labor Board were empowered to award double or triple backpay to individuals terminated unlawfully during organizing campaigns, this would increase the cost of employer noncompliance.

To minimize the loss of organizing momentum associated with the illegal termination of key union supporters, Congress should amend Section 10(1) to make mandatory injunctions applicable to Section 8(a)(3) discharges that occur during organizing campaigns. As soon as a meritorious charge is filed, the NLRB should be statutorily obligated to seek an immediate injunctive order directing the offending employer to reinstate the adversely affected individuals. If such persons were promptly returned to their former positions, the negative impact of the employer's violations would be minimized.

Congress should amend the NLRA to authorize the Labor Board to issue remedial bargaining orders in favor of labor organizations that were unlawfully prevented from obtaining majority support because of extreme employer unfair labor practices. To avoid imposing an exclusive bargaining agent on employees who do not desire such representation, remedial bargaining orders should only be employed in extraordinary situations. Nonetheless, when the Board is satisfied that majority status would almost certainly have been achieved in the absence of the company's egregious violations of the NLRA, it should be empowered to protect the rights of the discouraged union supporters through the issuance of a bargaining directive.[140]

When employers indefensibly refuse to bargain in good faith with newly certified unions or labor organizations that will clearly become the recipients of remedial bargaining orders precipitated by flagrant company unfair labor practices, the Labor Board should be similarly directed under Section 10(1) to seek preliminary injunctive orders. These would force the recalcitrant business firms to bargain with the designated labor organizations during the unfair labor practice proceedings. Business enterprises would thus be denied the opportunity to disregard the collective rights of their employees during the several years it takes under current law to obtain a judicially enforced Labor Board order.

When employers unjustifiably refuse to bargain, make-whole relief should be available to place the unlawfully disenfranchised workers in the economic position they would have attained in the absence of the company's outrageous disregard for their NLRA rights. Because the NLRB has decided that it lacks the statutory authority to provide such relief,[141] Congress should amend Section 10(c) of the NLRA[142] to empower the Board to require compensatory relief. Petitioning labor organizations could present Bureau of Labor Statistics data to support their requests for make-whole compensation.

Limiting Labor Board Deferral to Arbitral Procedures.   Although the NLRB is empowered in Section 10(a) of the NLRA[143] to resolve unfair labor practice disputes, and that provision states that its power in this regard "shall not be affected by any other means of adjustment or prevention that has been or may be established by agreement, law, or otherwise," the Labor Board has increasingly declined to perform this function. In *Spielberg Manufacturing,*[144] the Labor Board decided that in unfair labor practice cases it would defer to previously issued arbitral determinations that involved the same factual circumstances and effectively resolved the issues raised in the unfair labor practice case. The NLRB would accept the prior arbitral results where the proceedings were "fair and regular, all parties had agreed to be bound, and the decision of the arbitration panel [was] not clearly repugnant to the purposes and policies of the [NLRA]."[145] The party that sought NLRB deferral to a prior arbitral decision was obliged to demonstrate that the *Spielberg* prerequisites were satisfied.

The *Spielberg* deferral policy was significantly expanded in *Olin*

Corp.,[146] wherein the Labor Board enunciated new standards to be applied when deciding whether to accept a previous arbitral determination in a current unfair labor practice proceeding:

We would find that an arbitrator has adequately considered the unfair labor practice if (1) the contractual issue is factually parallel to the unfair labor practice issue, and (2) the arbitrator was presented generally with the facts relevant to resolving the unfair labor practice. . . . [W]ith regard to the inquiry into the "clearly repugnant" standard, we would not require an arbitrator's award to be totally consistent with Board precedent. Unless the award is "palpably wrong," i.e., unless the arbitrator's decision is not susceptible to an interpretation consistent with the Act, we will defer.

Finally, we would require that the party seeking to have the Board reject deferral and consider the merits of a given case show that the above standards for deferral have not been met. Thus, the party seeking to have the Board ignore the determination of an arbitrator has the burden of affirmatively demonstrating the defects in the arbitral process or award.[147]

The *Olin* formulation makes it exceedingly difficult for parties to challenge prior arbitration decisions that are not entirely compatible with NLRA policies. The burden of proof has been inexplicably transferred from the party seeking acceptance of the previous arbitral findings to the party opposing such acceptance. So long as the arbitral determination was not "palpably wrong," it is entitled to NLRB affirmation. In addition, courts reviewing arbitral decisions are obligated to enforce such awards so long as they "draw their essence" from the bargaining agreement and are not clearly repugnant to law or public policy.[148] Such judicial deference is far greater than that accorded to the review of Labor Board unfair labor practice determinations.[149] The expansive Labor Board deference to arbitral decisions has caused the development of inconsistent legal principles that do not provide individual employees with protection as broad as that envisioned by Congress when it enacted the NLRA.

Spielberg deferral is appropriate where purely factual issues are in dispute, because it reasonably enhances the federal labor policy favoring the private resolution of labor controversies[150] and prevents unnecessarily duplicative litigation. To ensure that the prior arbitral proceedings were truly "fair and regular" and that the award is not "repugnant to the purposes and policies of the [NLRA]," however, deferral should only be employed where the party seeking deferral can demonstrate that the traditional *Spielberg* prerequisites have been satisfied. Congress should amend Section 10(a) to codify the original *Spielberg* standards, and to reject the overly expansive *Olin*

Corp. approach, making it clear that the Labor Board should not accept a prior arbitral award if there is any reason to believe that the *Spielberg* criteria have not been completely met.

The NLRB frequently refuses to consider unfair labor practice claims where no previous arbitral determinations have been issued, if the charges raise issues that might be resolved through available contractual grievance-arbitration procedures. Under the *Collyer Insulated Wire*[151] doctrine, if the respondent is willing to have the controversy submitted to the arbitral process, the Board usually withholds its statutory authority and directs the parties to utilize that means of adjudication. In *General American Transportation Corp.*,[152] the NLRB appropriately acknowledged that such a pre–unfair labor practice hearing deferral is proper where Section 8(a)(5) or 8(b)(3) refusal to bargain charges are involved. In these cases, the rights of the representative labor organization as an institution are to be determined, and the resolution of the underlying contractual question, which will simultaneously dispose of the unfair labor practice issue, will be made in the forum that the parties specifically established to hear such controversies. Where individual rights are raised under provisions such as Section 8(a)(1), 8(a)(3), 8(b)(1)(A), or 8(b)(2), however, the interests of the aggrieved employee may not coincide with those of either the employer or the representative union which control the arbitral process. Application of the *Collyer* deferral policy to such cases effectively deprives allegedly coerced individuals of access to the administrative agency that Congress created to resolve unfair labor practice cases. Congress should amend Section 10(a) to codify the *General American Transportation* approach and limit pre-arbitration deferral to cases involving refusal-to-bargain allegations. Such an amendment would guarantee individual employees the right to have their claims presented by independent Labor Board attorneys before the tribunal that possesses substantial NLRA expertise and whose members have not been selected by the employer and the labor organization involved.

EPILOGUE

Over the past two centuries, the American labor movement has demonstrated remarkable resiliency. Throughout the late eighteenth and nineteenth centuries, craft guilds flourished despite the absence of legislative support. During the second half of the nineteenth century, social and political institutions like the National Labor Union and the Knights of Labor advanced the employment rights of all workers. After those groups declined, the American Federation of Labor created the business union movement. Although AFL affiliates encountered vehement employer and judicial opposition, they were able to organize millions of skilled craft personnel.

Once the federal government established the statutory right of workers to organize for collective bargaining purposes in the NLRA, union membership expanded rapidly. The creation of the industrial union movement through the formation of the Congress of Industrial Organizations in the late 1930s led to the organization of mass production industries. Competition between AFL and CIO affiliates generated significant union growth throughout the 1940s and 1950s. By the time of the AFL-CIO merger in the mid–1950s, unions represented approximately 35 percent of the nonagricultural labor force. Even though the private sector union participation rate has declined over the past three decades, public sector labor organizations have convinced 35 percent of government personnel that they will benefit from collectivization.

As the American labor movement continues to lose membership and conservative presidents appoint more pro-business judges, the likelihood of a private sector union renaissance seems remote. Nonetheless, there is reason for hope. Changing demographics will provide creative union organizers with new sources for membership. In addition, more and more white-collar and professional employees are becoming disenchanted with their routine job tasks, their diminished employment security, and the increasingly rigid hierarchical structures of their corporate employers. If the dissatisfaction of such individuals continues to grow, many will contemplate the possible benefits of unionization. Labor leaders must devise innovative organizing techniques and develop insightful collective bargaining objectives that will appeal to such people.

Even if labor leaders do not make the changes necessary to precipitate increased worker interest in unions, over-confident management officials will probably do so. As American executives decide that labor organizations are moribund entities that will become insignificant factors by the end of the current decade, many will fail to heed Lord Acton's admonition that "power tends to corrupt and absolute power corrupts absolutely." Managers will ignore industrial history and themselves create the circumstances that originally precipitated concerted worker action by abusing their unilateral authority to the detriment of subordinate employees. They will recreate the environments most indigenous to union growth. Their workers will rediscover the reason collective strength is required to counter the excessive economic power possessed by corporate firms.

Public opinion surveys demonstrate that most American workers continue to believe that employment interests can be advanced through unionization, and numerous nonunion personnel have indicated that they would be inclined to collectivize under appropriate circumstances. Despite the disadvantageous industrial and global trends, there continues to be a need for worker representation. If American labor organizations can offer dissatisfied employees representational services that will enhance their employment situations and their personal dignity, they should be able to generate sustained union growth.

NOTES

I. OVERVIEW

1. John Galbraith, *The New Industrial State* (Boston: Houghton Mifflin, 1971), 275.

2. Jeremy Rifkin & Randy Barber, *The North Will Rise Again* (Boston: Beacon Press, 1978), 26.

3. B.N.A., *Daily Labor Report* 172 (Sept. 5, 1991): A–3.

4. Pub. L. No. 93–406, 88 Stat. 829 (1974) ("ERISA").

5. B.N.A., *Daily Labor Report* 165 (Aug. 26, 1991): A–2.

6. Michael Goldfield, *The Decline of Organized Labor in the United States* (Chicago: University of Chicago Press, 1987), 10 Table 1.

7. B.N.A., *Daily Labor Report* 28 (Feb. 11, 1992): B–1.

8. Michael Goldfield, *The Decline of Organized Labor in the United States*, 90.

9. B.N.A., *Daily Labor Report* 46 (Mar. 9, 1992): A–10.

10. B.N.A., *Daily Labor Report* 241 (Dec. 18, 1989): A–1.

11. Thomas Edsall, *The New Politics of Inequality* (New York: W. W. Norton, 1984), 173.

12. Labor organizations indirectly affect working conditions in nonunion shops because many employers provide benefits and working conditions comparable to those of organized business entities in an effort to prevent unionization by their own employees.

13. Paul Jacobs, *Old Before Its Time: Collective Bargaining at 28* (Santa Barbara, Calif.: Center for the Study of Democratic Institutions, 1963), 14; Albert Rees, *The Economics of Trade Unions* (Chicago: University of Chicago Press, 1977), 190.

14. See generally Thomas Geoghegan, *Which Side Are You On?* (New York: Farrar, Straus & Giroux, 1991).

15. Interview with George Meany in *U.S. News & World Report* (Feb. 21, 1972), 28.

16. Howard Fullerton, "The 1995 Labor Force: A First Look," *Monthly Labor Review* 103 (Dec. 1980): 11.

17. James Jordan, "Trends in the Work Force: Individualism, Inflation, and Productivity," *Working in the Twenty-First Century* (C. Stewart Shepard & Donald Carroll eds.) (New York: John Wiley & Sons, 1980), 71.

18. Sanford Cohen, *Labor in the United States* (Columbus, Ohio: Merrill Publishing, 5th ed. 1979), 97.

19. Charles Heckscher, *The New Unionism: Employee Involvement in the Changing Corporation* (New York: Basic Books, 1988), 60–61; Gil Green, *What's Happening to Labor* (New York: International Publishers, 1976), 92.

20. Paul Weiler, "Milestone or Millstone: The Wagner Act at Fifty," *Arbitration 1985: Law and Practice* (Walter Gershenfeld ed.) (Washington, D.C.: Bureau of National Affairs, 1986), 40.

21. *Ibid.*, 43.

22. AFL-CIO Committee on the Evolution of Work, *The Changing Situation of Workers and Their Unions* (Washington, D.C.: AFL-CIO, 1985), 10.

23. Paul Weiler, *Governing the Workplace* (Cambridge: Harvard University Press, 1990), 238–39.

24. B.N.A., *Unions Today: New Tactics to Tackle Tough Times* (Washington, D.C.: Bureau of National Affairs, 1985), 12.

25. E.g., Robert Schrank, "Are Unions an Anachronism?", *Harvard Business Review* 57 (Sept.–Oct. 1970): 107–8.

26. E.g., Eugene Forsey, "Trade Unions in 2020?", *Visions 2020* (Stephen Clarkson ed.) (Edmonton: M. G. Hurtig, 1970), 94.

27. Richard Freeman & James Medoff, *What Do Unions Do?* (New York: Basic Books, 1984), 43–77.

28. *Ibid.*, 150–53.

29. *Ibid.*, 94–110.

30. Charles Craver, "The Inquisitorial Process in Private Employment," *Cornell Law Review* 63 (1977): 6.

31. Daniel Fischel, "Labor Markets and Labor Law Compared with Capital Markets and Corporate Law," *University of Chicago Law Review* 51 (1984): 1062.

32. Richard Freeman & James Medoff, *What Do Unions Do?*, 7.

33. Marion Crain, "Building Solidarity Through Expansion of NLRA Coverage: A Blueprint for Worker Empowerment," *Minnesota Law Review* 74 (1990): 968–69.

2. THE HISTORICAL FOUNDATION OF AMERICAN LABOR

1. The general information discussed in this chapter is taken from various sources: John Commons & Associates, *History of Labor in the United States* (New York: Macmillan, 1918); Albert Blum, *A History of the American Labor Movement* (Washington, D.C.: American Historical Association, 1972); Foster Dulles & Melvyn Dubofsky, *Labor in America* (Arlington Heights, Ill.: Harlan Davidson, 4th ed. 1984); Philip Foner, *Women and the American Labor Movement* (New York: Free Press, 1982); William Forbath, "The Shaping of the American Labor Movement," *Harvard Law Review* 102 (1989): 1109; Samuel Gompers, *Seventy Years of Life and Labor* (New York: E. P. Dutton, 1925); Richard Morris, *Government and Labor in Early America* (New York: Columbia University Press, 1946); Selig Perlman, *A History of Trade Unionism in the United States* (New York: Macmillan, 1935); Selig Perlman & Philip Taft, *History of Labor in the United States, 1896–1932* (New York: Macmillan, 1935); Philip Taft, *Organized Labor in American History* (New York: Harper & Row, 1964); Lloyd Ulman, *The Rise of the National Trade Union* (Cambridge: Harvard University Press, 1955).

2. 45 Mass. (4 Met.) 111, 38 Am. Dec. 346 (1842). This landmark decision is extensively explored in Walter Nelles, "Commonwealth v. Hunt," *Columbia Law Review* 32 (1932): 1128.

3. Philip Foner, *Women and the American Labor Movement* (New York: Free Press, 1982), 61.

4. *Ibid.*, 87.

5. Selig Perlman, *A History of Trade Unionism in the United States* (New York: Macmillan, 1935), 95.

6. *Ibid.*, 111.

7. Philip Taft, *Organized Labor in American History* (New York: Harper & Row, 1964), 117.

8. Samuel Gompers, "Judicial Vindication of Labor's Claims," *American Federationist* 7 (1901): 284.

9. *Ibid.*, 1136.

10. 39 Stat. 721 (1916).

11. 243 U.S. 332 (1917).

12. 47 Stat. 70 (1932).

13. 313 U.S. 177, 187 (1941).

14. 208 U.S. 161 (1908).

15. David Montgomery, *The Fall of the House of Labor* (New York: Cambridge University Press, 1987), 270.

16. *Ibid.*

17. *Ibid.*, 271.

18. *Ibid.*

19. 38 Stat. 730 (1914).

20. Samuel Gompers, "The Charter of Industrial Freedom," *American Federationist* 21 (1914): 971.

21. 38 Stat. 731 (1914), codified at 15 U.S.C. § 17.

22. 254 U.S. 443 (1921).

23. Philip Taft, *Organized Labor in American History*, 290.

24. Barbara Ehrenreich, *Fear of Falling* (New York: Harper Perennial, 1990), 134.

25. Philip Taft, *Organized Labor in American History*, 336.

26. Donna Van Raaphorst, *Union Maids Not Wanted: Organizing Domestic Workers 1870–1940* (New York: Praeger, 1988), 165.

27. *Ibid.*

28. *Ibid.*, 166.

29. Philip Foner, *Women and the American Labor Movement*, 247.

30. Alice Kessler-Harris, *Out to Work* (New York: Oxford University Press, 1982), 157.

31. Philip Taft, *Organized Labor in American History*, 668.

32. Barbara Ehrenreich, *Fear of Falling*, 134.

33. *Ibid.*, 135.

34. David Montgomery, *The Fall of the House of Labor*, 416.

35. *Ibid.*, 419–20.

36. Donna Van Raaphorst, *Union Maids Not Wanted: Organizing Domestic Workers 1870–1940*, 177.

37. George Barnett, "American Trade Unionism and Social Insurance," *American Economic Review* 23 (Mar. 1933): 6.

38. 25 Stat. 501 (1888).

39. 30 Stat. 424 (1898).

40. 38 Stat. 103 (1913).

41. 41 Stat. 456 (1920).

42. 44 Stat. 577 (1926).

43. 49 Stat. 1189 (1936).

44. 48 Stat. 198 (1933).

45. 295 U.S. 495 (1935).

46. 49 Stat. 449 (1935). The NLRA is codified at 29 U.S.C. §§ 151–69.

47. 301 U.S. 1 (1937).

48. The industrial unions generally ignored the female clerical personnel working in these industries.

49. Philip Taft, *Organized Labor in American History*, 472.

50. Paul Weiler, *Governing the Workplace* (Cambridge: Harvard University Press, 1990), 9.

51. Business experts have estimated that the enactment of the NLRA caused a 15.9 percent decline in shareholder wealth. Craig Olson & Brian Becker, "The Effects of the NLRA on Stockholder Wealth in the 1930s," *Industrial & Labor Relations Review* 44 (Oct. 1990): 116.

52. 306 U.S. 240 (1939).

53. *NLRB v. Montgomery Ward & Co.*, 157 F.2d 486 (8th Cir. 1946); *Elk Lumber Co.*, 91 N.L.R.B. 333 (1950).

54. *C. G. Conn, Ltd. v. NLRB*, 108 F.2d 390 (7th Cir. 1939).

55. *UAW Local 232 v. Wisconsin Employment Relations Board*, 336 U.S. 245 (1949).

56. *NLRB v. Mackay Radio & Telegraph Co.*, 304 U.S. 333 (1938).

57. 346 U.S. 464 (1953).

58. *Patterson Sargent Co.*, 115 N.L.R.B. 1627 (1956).

59. 351 U.S. 105 (1956).

60. 61 Stat. 136 (1947).

61. 330 U.S. 485 (1947).

62. 73 Stat. 519 (1959).

63. Philip Taft, *Organized Labor in American History*, 658.

64. *Ibid.*, 661.

65. 77 Stat. 56 (1963).

66. 78 Stat. 253 (1964).

67. 81 Stat. 602 (1967).

68. 84 Stat. 1590 (1970).

69. 88 Stat. 832 (1974).

70. 104 Stat. 327 (1990).

71. Thomas Edsall, *The New Politics of Inequality* (New York: W. W. Norton, 1984), 107–8.

72. Charles Morris, *The Developing Labor Law* (Washington, D.C.: Bureau of National Affairs, 2d ed. 1983), 66–67.

73. Thomas Edsall, *The New Politics of Inequality*, 156.

3. THE EXTENT AND CAUSES OF THE DECLINE

1. Philip Taft, *Organized Labor in American History* (New York: Harper & Row, 1964), 162.

2. Michael Goldfield, *The Decline of Organized Labor in the United States* (Chicago: University of Chicago Press, 1987), 8.

3. *Ibid.*, 10 Table 1.

4. George Barnett, "American Trade Unionism and Social Insurance," *American*

Economic Review 23 (March 1933): 6; Lyle Cooper, "The American Labor Movement in Prosperity and Depression," *American Economic Review* 22 (Dec. 1932), 653–54.

5. Michael Goldfield, *The Decline of Organized Labor in the United States*, 10 Table 1.

6. *Ibid.*

7. *Ibid.*, 11 Table 2.

8. *Ibid.*

9. *Ibid.*, 23 Figure 4.

10. *Ibid.*, 16 Table 3.

11. Michael Curme, Barry Hirsch & David MacPherson, "Union Membership and Contract Coverage in the United States, 1983–1988," *Industrial & Labor Relations Review* 44 (Oct. 1990): 8.

12. B.N.A., *Daily Labor Report* 26 (Feb. 7, 1991): B–8.

13. *Ibid.*

14. *Ibid.*, B–10 Table 2.

15. *Ibid.*, B–8.

16. B.N.A., *Daily Labor Report* 69 (Apr. 10, 1991): A–1.

17. *Ibid.*, D–1.

18. *Ibid.*, A–2.

19. *Ibid.*, D–2.

20. Richard Freeman & James Medoff, *What Do Unions Do?* (New York: Basic Books, 1984), 202–3.

21. Thomas Kochan, Harry Katz & Robert McKersie, *The Transformation of American Industrial Relations* (New York: Basic Books, 1986), 128–29.

22. Barbara Ehrenreich, *The Worst Years of Our Lives* (New York: Pantheon Books, 1990), 203.

23. Sheena McConnell, "Cyclical Fluctuations in Strike Activity," *Industrial & Labor Relations Review* 44 (Oct. 1990): 130.

24. Marion Crain, "Building Solidarity Through Expansion of NLRA Coverage: A Blueprint for Worker Empowerment," *Minnesota Law Review* 74 (1990): 956.

25. Charles Heckscher, *The New Unionism: Employee Involvement in the Changing Corporation* (New York: Basic Books, 1988), 30.

26. United States Department of Labor, *Employment in Perspective: Women in the Labor Force* (First Quarter 1990).

27. Peter Morrison, "Beyond the Baby Boom," *The Futurist* 13 (Apr. 1979): 133.

28. *Ibid.*

29. Commission on Workforce Quality and Labor Market Efficiency, *Investing in People* (Washington, D.C.: U.S. Department of Labor, 1989), 26.

30. William Johnston & Arnold Packer, *Workforce 2000* (Indianapolis: Hudson Institute, 1987), xx.

31. Diane Balser, *Sisterhood and Solidarity* (Boston: South End Press, 1987), 21.

32. Daniel Hamermesh & Albert Rees, *The Economics of Work and Pay* (New York: Harper & Row, 4th ed. 1988), 367–76.

33. William Johnston & Arnold Packer, *Workforce 2000*, 89.

34. Daniel Hamermesh & Albert Rees, *The Economics of Work and Pay*, 347–59.

35. Staff of Senate Special Committee on Aging, 101st Congress, 1st Session, *Aging America: Trends and Projections* (Committee Print, 1988), 8.

36. B.N.A., *Older Americans in the Workforce: Challenges and Solutions* (Washington, D.C.: Bureau of National Affairs, 1987), 5.

37. *Ibid.*, 15.

38. Staff of Senate Special Committee on Aging, 101st Congress, 1st Session, *Aging America: Trends and Projections,* 39 Table 2–1.

39. *Ibid.,* 47–48 Table 2–5.

40. Diane Herz, "Employment Characteristics of Older Women," *Monthly Labor Review* 111 (Sept. 1988): 4.

41. 100 Stat. 3342 (1986), codified at 29 U.S.C. § 631(a).

42. Jeremy Rifkin & Randy Barber, *The North Will Rise Again* (Boston: Beacon Press, 1978), 59–68.

43. Thomas Kochan, Harry Katz & Robert McKersie, *The Transformation of American Industrial Relations,* 67–68.

44. Sanford Cohen, *Labor in the United States* (Columbus, Ohio: Merrill Publishing, 5th ed. 1979), 97.

45. Alvin Toffler, *The Third Wave* (New York: William Morrow, 1980), 139.

46. *Ibid.*

47. Giles Radice, *The Industrial Democrats* (Boston: Allen & Unwin, 1978), 34.

48. Richard Barnet & Ronald Müller, *Global Reach: The Power of the Multinational Corporations* (New York: Simon & Schuster, 1974), 323.

49. William Johnston & Arnold Packer, *Workforce 2000,* 96–97; Viktor Kosolapov, *Mankind and the Year 2000* (Moscow: Progress, 1976), 156.

50. Ronald Kutscher & Valerie Personick, "Deindustrialization and the Shift to Services," *Monthly Labor Review* 109 (June 1986): 4.

51. "Careers for the Long Haul," *Newsweek on Campus* (Sept. 1986), 17.

52. William Johnston & Arnold Packer, *Workforce 2000,* 61; Burnham Beckwith, *The Next 500 Years* (New York: Exposition Press, 1967), 86–87.

53. Alvin Toffler, *The Third Wave,* 181–83, 190–92.

54. Swasti Mitter, *Common Fate, Common Bond* (Oxford: Pluto Press, 1986), 136.

55. George Hildebrand, *American Unionism: An Historical and Analytical Survey* (Reading, Mass.: Addison Wesley, 1979), 118–19.

56. Gary Gappert, "Post-Affluence: The Turbulent Transition to a Post-Industrial Society," *Futurist* 8 (Oct. 1974): 214.

57. G. B. J. Bomers, *Multinational Corporations and Industrial Relations* (Assen, Netherlands: Van Gorcum, 1976), 9–10.

58. Robert Cox, "Labor and the Multinationals," *Foreign Affairs* 54 (Jan. 1976): 345–47.

59. Giles Radice, *The Industrial Democrats,* 40.

60. Louis Turner, *Invisible Empires: Multinational Companies and the Modern World* (New York: Harcourt Brace Jovanovich, 1970), 191.

61. Terrence Collingsworth, "American Labor Policy and the International Economy: Clarifying Policies and Interests," *Boston College Law Review* 31 (1989): 91.

62. *Ibid.*

63. Richard Barnet & Ronald Müller, *Global Reach: The Power of the Multinational Corporations,* 304; Jeremy Rifkin & Randy Barber, *The North Will Rise Again,* 31.

64. International Labour Office, *Multinational Enterprises and Social Policy* (Geneva: International Labour Office, 1973), 77.

65. Robert Reich, *The Work of Nations* (New York: Alfred Knopf, 1991), 113.

66. Swasti Mitter, *Common Fate, Common Bond,* 38–40; Annette Fuentes & Barbara Ehrenreich, *Women in the Global Factory* (Boston: South End Press, 1983), 16–17.

67. Swasti Mitter, *Common Fate, Common Bond,* 38–39.

68. United States International Trade Commission, *Tariff Schedules of the United*

States Annotated (1986), Item 800.00; Terrence Collingsworth, "American Labor Policy and the International Economy: Clarifying Policies and Interests," Boston College Law Review 31 (1989): 80–81.

69. Swasti Mitter, Common Fate, Common Bond, 23; Annette Fuentes & Barbara Ehrenreich, Women in the Global Factory, 12–13.

70. Swasti Mitter, Common Fate, Common Bond, 54.

71. Annette Fuentes & Barbara Ehrenreich, Women in the Global Factory, 27–29.

72. Sandy Tolan, "Hope and Heartbreak," New York Times Magazine (July 1, 1990), 19.

73. Lawrence Rothstein, Plant Closings (Dover, Mass.: Auburn House Publishing, 1986), 14.

74. Robert Reich, The Work of Nations, 120.

75. Ibid., 122.

76. Ibid.

77. Nathaniel Goldfinger, "An American Trade Union View of International Trade and Investment," in American Labor and the Multinational Corporation (Duane Kujawa ed.) (New York: Praeger, 1973), 34.

78. Robert Reich, "Who Is Us?", Harvard Business Review 68 (Jan.–Feb. 1990), 59.

79. Ibid., 61–62.

80. Swasti Mitter, Common Fate, Common Bond, 8–9.

81. Robert Reich, "Who Is Us?", Harvard Business Review 68 (Jan.–Feb. 1990), 58.

82. Charles Levinson, International Trade Unionism (London: Allen & Unwin, 1972), 222.

83. James Atleson, "Reflections on Labor, Power & Society," Maryland Law Review 44 (1985): 845.

84. Ibid., 842–45.

85. Terrence Collingsworth, "American Labor Policy and the International Economy: Clarifying Policies and Interests," Boston College Law Review 31 (1989): 62.

86. Bruno Amoroso, "A Danish Perspective: The Impact of the Internal Market on the Labour Unions and the Welfare State," Comparative Labor Law Journal 11 (1990): 485.

87. E.g., In re Jacobs, 98 N.Y. 98 (1885) (striking down New York law prohibiting cigar manufacturing in tenement dwellings); Ritchie v. People, 155 Ill. 98, 40 N.E. 454 (1895) (invalidating Illinois eight-hour law); Adair v. United States, 208 U.S. 161 (1908) (voiding federal law proscribing yellow-dog contracts).

88. 49 Stat. 449 (1935).

89. The constitutionality of the NLRA was sustained in NLRB v. Jones & Laughlin Steel Corp., 301 U.S. 1 (1937).

90. Philip Taft, Organized Labor in American History, 452–55.

91. 29 U.S.C. § 158(a)(1).

92. Paul Weiler, Governing the Workplace (Cambridge: Harvard University Press, 1990), 238.

93. Ibid., 238 n. 18.

94. 29 U.S.C. § 158(a)(3) prohibits employer discrimination intended to encourage or discourage support for labor organizations.

95. Paul Weiler, "Promises to Keep: Securing Workers' Rights to Self-Organization Under the NLRA," Harvard Law Review 96 (1983): 1780–81.

96. Paul Weiler, Governing the Workplace, 238–39.

97. Robert LaLonde & Bernard Meltzer, "Hard Times for Unions: Another Look at the Significance of Employer Illegalities," *University of Chicago Law Review* 58 (1991): 994 Table 7.

98. Paul Weiler, *Governing the Workplace*, 239 n. 19.

99. Richard Freeman & James Medoff, *What Do Unions Do?*, 233.

100. *Midland National Life Insurance Co.*, 263 N.L.R.B. 127 (1982).

101. Michael Goldfield, *The Decline of Organized Labor in the United States*, 52 Table 10.

102. *Ibid.*

103. Thomas Kochan, Harry Katz & Robert McKersie, *The Transformation of American Industrial Relations*, 66–73.

104. *Ibid.*, 69–75.

105. Jonathan Axelrod, "Common Obstacles to Organizing Under the NLRA: Combatting the Southern Strategy," *North Carolina Law Review* 59 (1980): 147.

106. Michael Goldfield, *The Decline of Organized Labor in the United States*, 190–91.

107. *Ibid.*, 190.

108. David Blanchflower & Richard Freeman, *Going Different Ways: Unionism in the U.S. and Other Advanced O.E.C.D. Countries* (Cambridge, Mass.: National Bureau of Economic Research Working Paper 3342, Apr. 1990), 9–10.

109. Richard Freeman & James Medoff, *What Do Unions Do?*, 43–54.

110. B.N.A., *Daily Labor Report* 161 (Aug. 20, 1990): A–4.

111. Anil Verma & Thomas Kochan, "The Growth and Nature of the Nonunion Sector Within a Firm," *Challenges and Choices Facing American Labor* (Thomas Kochan, ed.) (Cambridge: MIT Press, 1985), 101.

112. Richard Freeman & James Medoff, *What Do Unions Do?*, 162–69.

113. C. Wright Mills, *White Collar* (New York: Oxford University Press, 1951), 294; Benjamin DeMott, *The Imperial Middle* (New York: William Morrow, 1990), 41–42, 130–31.

114. Stanley Aronowitz, *False Promises* (New York: McGraw-Hill, 1973), 141; Lyle Cooper, "The American Labor Movement in Prosperity and Depression," *American Economic Review* 22 (Dec. 1932): 646.

115. Michael Mann, *Consciousness and Action Among the Western Working Class* (Atlantic Highlands, N.J.: Humanities Press, 1973), 30–31.

116. See generally William Ryan, *Blaming the Victim* (New York: Vintage Books, 1976).

117. *Ibid.*, 10–11.

118. Barbara Ehrenreich, *Fear of Falling* (New York: Harper Perennial, 1990), 108–9.

119. *Ibid.*, 140–41.

120. Richard Freeman & James Medoff, *What Do Unions Do?*, 214–17.

121. C. Wright Mills, *White Collar*, 319; Stanley Aronowitz, *False Promises*, 292–93.

122. C. Wright Mills, *White Collar*, 297; Elizabeth Jelin, "The Concept of Working-Class Embourgeoisement," *The American Working Class* (Irving Horowitz, John Leggett & Martin Oppenheimer, eds.) (New Brunswick, N.J.: Transaction Books, 1979), 247–51.

123. Barbara Ehrenreich, *The Worst Years of Our Lives*, 196–97.

124. C. Wright Mills, *White Collar*, 63.

125. Michael Goldfield, *The Decline of Organized Labor in the United States,* 50.

126. Edna Bonacich, "A Theory of Ethnic Antagonism: The Split Labor Market," *The American Working Class* (Irving Horowitz, John Leggett & Martin Oppenheimer, eds.), 82.

127. Robert Bibb, "Blue-Collar Women in Low-Wage Industries: A Dual Labor Market Interpretation," *The American Working Class* (Irving Horowitz, John Leggett & Martin Oppenheimer, eds.), 132–33.

4. THE NEED FOR LABOR UNIONS

1. Jeremy Rifkin & Randy Barber, *The North Will Rise Again* (Boston: Beacon Press, 1978), 20.

2. John Dunlop, "Past and Future Tendencies of American Labor Organizations," *Daedalus* (Winter 1978): 84.

3. George Hardbeck, "Unionism Again at a Crossroads," *Critical Issues in Labor* (Max Wortman, Jr., ed.) (New York: Macmillan, 1969), 67–68; Julius Shister, "The Outlook for Union Growth," *The Annals* 350 (1963): 56–57.

4. Michael Goldfield, *The Decline of Organized Labor in the United States* (Chicago: University of Chicago Press, 1987), 35.

5. B.N.A., *Labor Relations Reporter* 130 (Feb. 27, 1989): 244.

6. Annette Fuentes & Barbara Ehrenreich, *Women in the Global Factory* (Boston: South End Press, 1983), 48–53.

7. Thomas Karier, "Unions and the U.S. Comparative Advantage," *Industrial Relations* 30 (Winter 1991): 1. See generally Lawrence Mishel & Paula Voos, *Unions and Economic Competitiveness* (Armonk, N.Y.: M. E. Sharpe, 1992).

8. Richard Freeman & James Medoff, *What Do Unions Do?* (New York: Basic Books, 1984), 214–15.

9. See 29 U.S.C. § 504(a).

10. B.N.A., *Daily Labor Report* 124 (June 27, 1991): A–12.

11. B.N.A., *Daily Labor Report* 101 (May 26, 1992): A–1; B.N.A., *Daily Labor Report* 240 (Dec. 13, 1991): A–11.

12. Robert Reich, *The Work of Nations* (New York: Alfred Knopf, 1991), 7.

13. *Ibid.*

14. Richard Freeman & James Medoff, *What Do Unions Do?*, 145.

15. *Ibid.*

16. B.N.A., *Unions Today: New Tactics to Tackle Tough Times* (Washington, D.C.: Bureau of National Affairs, 1985), 11.

17. Thomas Kochan, Harry Katz & Robert McKersie, *The Transformation of American Industrial Relations* (New York: Basic Books, 1986), 216.

18. *Ibid.,* 217.

19. Richard Barnet, "A Reporter at Large," *New Yorker* (Apr. 7, 1980), 78.

20. Solomon Barkin, "A New Agenda for Labor," *Fortune* (Nov. 1960), 250–52.

21. Worker Adjustment and Retraining Notification Act, Pub. L. 100–379, 102 Stat. 890 (1988).

22. See generally Paul Osterman, "Elements of a National Training Policy," *New Developments in Worker Training: A Legacy for the 1990s* (Louis Ferman, Michele Hoyman, Joel Cutcher-Gershenfeld & Ernest Savoie, eds.) (Madison, Wis.: Industrial Relations Research Association, 1990), 257.

23. Pub. L. 100–690, 102 Stat. 4304 (1988).

24. See generally Mark Rothstein, "Workplace Drug Testing: A Case Study in the Misapplication of Technology," *Harvard Journal of Law & Technology* 5 (1991): 65.

25. The Drug Free Workplace Act currently indicates that rehabilitation may constitute a "sanction" for workers found to be abusing drugs or alcohol. 41 U.S.C. § 702(a)(1)(F). This provision could be modified to require rehabilitation for all first time abusers.

26. Commission on Workforce Quality and Labor Market Efficiency, *Investing in People* (Washington, D.C.: U.S. Department of Labor, 1989), 2.

27. Sar Levitan & Frank Gallo, "Uncle Sam's Helping Hand: Educating, Training, and Employing the Disadvantaged," *New Developments in Worker Training: A Legacy for the 1990s* (Louis Ferman, Michele Hoyman, Joel Cutcher-Gershenfeld & Ernest Savoie, eds.), 226.

28. *Ibid.*

29. Frank Elkouri & Edna Elkouri, *How Arbitration Works* (Washington, D.C.: Bureau of National Affairs, 1985), 650–53.

30. Howard Specter & Matthew Finkin, *Individual Employment Law and Litigation* (Charlottesville, Va.: Michie Co., 1989), 1: 188–89.

31. See generally Cornelius Peck, "Unjust Discharges From Employment: A Necessary Change in the Law," *Ohio State Law Journal* 40 (1979): 1.

32. Jack Stieber, "Recent Developments in Employment-at-Will," *Labor Law Journal* 36 (1985): 558.

33. See generally Theodore St. Antoine, "A Seed Germinates: Unjust Discharge Reform Heads Toward Full Flower," *Nebraska Law Review* 67 (1988): 56. The National Conference of Commissioners on Uniform State Laws recently adopted a Model Uniform Employment Termination Act that should encourage states to act in this area. B.N.A., *Daily Labor Report* 156 (Aug. 13, 1991): D–1.

34. Robert Rabin, "The Role of Unions in the Rights-Based Workplace," *University of San Francisco Law Review* 25 (1991): 171.

35. Karl Klare, "Workplace Democracy & Market Reconstruction: An Agenda for Legal Reform," *Catholic University Law Review* 38 (1988): 58.

36. *Ibid.*, 206–7.

37. B.N.A., *Daily Labor Report* 39 (Feb. 28, 1984): A–5.

38. Jeffrey Keefe, "Do Unions Influence the Diffusion of Technology?" *Industrial & Labor Relations Review* 44 (1991): 261.

39. Joseph Coates, Jennifer Jarratt & John Mahaffie, "Future Work," *The Futurist* 25 (May–June 1991): 15.

40. Gus Tyler, *The Labor Revolution* (New York: Viking Press, 1967), 126–27.

41. "Where You Can't Get Fired," *U.S. News & World Report* 110 (Jan. 14, 1991): 46.

42. Lawrence Rothstein, *Plant Closings* (Dover, Mass.: Auburn Publishing, 1986), 16.

43. Lloyd Ulman, "Multinational Unionism: Incentives, Barriers, and Alternatives," *Industrial Relations* 14 (1975): 27.

44. Louis Ferman, Michele Hoyman & Joel Cutcher-Gershenfeld, "Joint Union-Management Training Programs: A Synthesis in the Evolution of Jointism and Training," *New Developments in Worker Training: A Legacy for the 1990s* (Louis Ferman, Michele Hoyman, Joel Cutcher-Gershenfeld & Ernest Savoie, eds.), 157; Thomas Pascoe & Richard Collins, "UAW-Ford Employee Development and Training Program: Overview of Operations and Structure," *Labor Law Journal* 36 (1985): 519.

45. Commission of Workforce Quality and Labor Market Efficiency, *Investing in People* (Washington, D.C.: U.S. Department of Labor, 1989), 16.

46. Margaret Hilton, "Shared Training: Learning from Germany," *Monthly Labor Review* 114 (March 1991): 34.

47. Anthony Carnevale & Harold Goldstein, "Schooling and Training for Work in America: An Overview," *New Developments in Worker Training: A Legacy for the 1990s* (Louis Ferman, Michele Hoyman, Joel Cutcher-Gershenfeld & Ernest Savoie, eds.), 30.

48. Richard Freeman & James Medoff, *What Do Unions Do?*, 228–29; Michael Goldfield, *The Decline of Organized Labor in the United States*, 206.

49. *American Hospital Assn. v. NLRB*, 111 S. Ct. 1539 (1991).

50. B.N.A., *Labor Relations Reporter* 136 (April 29, 1991): 497.

51. *Ibid.*

52. 444 U.S. 672 (1980).

53. *College of Osteopathic Medicine & Surgery*, 265 N.L.R.B. 295 (1982).

54. The inappropriateness of the *Yeshiva* decision is discussed in Chapter 6, below.

55. See generally Jules Bernstein, "Union-Busting: From Benign Neglect to Malignant Growth," *University of California, Davis Law Review* 14 (1980): 1.

56. Julius Getman, "Ruminations on Union Organizing in the Private Sector," *University of Chicago Law Review* 53 (1986): 50.

57. Solomon Barkin, *The Decline of the Labor Movement* (Santa Barbara, Cal.: Center for the Study of Democratic Institutions, 1961), 58.

58. Derek Bok & John Dunlop, *Labor and the American Community* (New York: Simon & Schuster, 1970), 469.

59. Gus Tyler, *The Labor Revolution* (New York: Viking Press, 1967), 9.

60. Everett Kassalow, "White-Collar Unionism in the United States," *White-Collar Trade Unions* (Adolph Sturmthal, ed.) (Urbana, Ill.: University of Illinois Press, 1966), 362.

61. Lois Gray & Joyce Kornbluh, "New Directions in Labor Education," *New Developments in Worker Training: A Legacy for the 1990s* (Louis Ferman, Michele Hoyman, Joel Cutcher-Gershenfeld & Ernest Savoie, eds.), 95.

62. *Ibid.*, 112.

63. Julius Getman, "Ruminations on Union Organizing in the Private Sector," *University of Chicago Law Review* 53 (1986): 60.

64. Hoyt Wheeler & John McClendon, "The Individual Decision to Unionize," *The State of the Unions* (George Strauss, Daniel Gallagher & Jack Fiorito, eds.) (Madison, Wis.: Industrial Relations Research Association, 1991), 66.

65. *Ibid.*

66. B.N.A., *Labor Relations Reporter* 138 (Dec. 9, 1991): 475, citing the unpublished work of Professor Kate Bronfenbrenner.

67. Philip Foner, *Women and the American Labor Movement* (New York: Free Press, 1982), 265.

68. *Ibid.*, 270–72.

69. *Ibid.*, 260, quoting Yuri Kuwahara.

70. AFL-CIO Committee on the Evolution of Work, *The Changing Situation of Workers and Their Unions* (1985), 28.

71. B.N.A., *Unions Today: New Tactics to Tackle Tough Times*, 100–101.

72. William Johnston & Arnold Packer, *Workforce 2000* (Indianapolis: Hudson Institute, 1987), 59.

73. Richard Freeman, "Why Are Unions Faring Poorly in NLRB Representation Elections?" *Challenges and Choices Facing American Labor* (Thomas Kochan, ed.) (Cambridge: MIT Press, 1985), 51.

74. Article XX of the AFL-CIO Constitution. See generally Lea Vaughn, "Article XX of the AFL-CIO Constitution: Managing and Resolving Inter-Union Disputes," *Wayne Law Review* 37 (1990): 1.

75. Many employers have intentionally transferred production to southern states or have opened new facilities in that region because of the limited degree of unionization among southern workers. Jonathan Axelrod, "Common Obstacles to Organizing Under the NLRA: Combatting the Southern Strategy," *North Carolina Law Review* 59 (1980): 148.

76. Calvin Beale, "Renewed Growth in Rural Communities," *Futurist* 9 (Aug. 1975): 196.

77. "Unions Still Find the South a Tough Row to Hoe," *U.S. News & World Report* (June 21, 1982): 62.

78. Michael Goldfield, *The Decline of Organized Labor in the United States*, 140–42.

79. B.N.A., *Labor Relations Reporter* 129 (Nov. 7, 1988): 302.

80. *Ibid.*, 303–4.

81. William Johnston & Arnold Packer, *Workforce 2000*, xx.

82. B.N.A., *Older Americans in the Workforce: Challenges and Solutions* (Washington, D.C.: Bureau of National Affairs, 1987), 5.

83. B.N.A., *Labor Relations Reporter* 138 (Dec. 9, 1991): 476, citing the unpublished work of Professor Kate Bronfenbrenner.

84. U.S. Department of Labor, *Time of Change: 1983 Handbook on Women Workers* (Washington, D.C.: U.S. Government Printing Office, 1983): 50.

85. *Ibid.*

86. *Ibid.*, 48.

87. James Medoff, "AFL-CIO Study on Public Image of Unions," B.N.A., *Daily Labor Report* 247 (Dec. 24, 1984): D–2.

88. Philip Foner, *Women and the American Labor Movement*, 492–93.

89. See generally Diane Balser, *Sisterhood and Solidarity* (Boston: South End Press, 1987), 151–61.

90. *Ibid.*, 43–51; Arthur Shostak, *Robust Unionism* (Ithaca, N.Y.: ILR Press, 1991): 85–87.

91. Edna Raphael, "Working Women and Their Membership in Labor Unions," *The American Working Class* (Irving Horowitz, John Leggett & Martin Oppenheimer, eds.) (New Brunswick, N.J.: Transaction Books, 1979), 114; Roberta Goldberg, *Organizing Women Office Workers* (New York: Praeger, 1983), 22–25.

92. William Johnston & Arnold Packer, *Workforce 2000*, 112–13.

93. U.S. Department of Labor, *Time of Change: 1983 Handbook on Women Workers*, 54.

94. See generally Daniel Hamermesh & Albert Rees, *The Economics of Work and Pay* (New York: Harper & Row, 1988): 367–76.

95. Note, "Finding a Voice Through the Union: The Harvard Union of Clerical and Technical Workers and Women Workers," *Harvard Women's Law Journal* 12 (1989): 274–75.

96. *Ibid.,* 275; Marion Crain, "Feminizing Unions: Challenging the Gendered Structure of Wage Labor," *Michigan Law Review* 89 (1991): 1155; Diane Balser, *Sisterhood and Solidarity,* 16–17.

97. Solomon Barkin, "A New Agenda for Labor," *Fortune* (Nov. 1960): 255. See generally William Gould, *Black Workers in White Unions: Job Discrimination in the United States* (Ithaca: Cornell University Press, 1977); F. Ray Marshall, *The Negro and Organized Labor* (New York: John Wiley & Sons, 1965).

98. Pub. L. 88–352, 78 Stat. 253 (1964).

99. James Medoff, "AFL-CIO Study on Public Image of Unions," B.N.A., *Daily Labor Report* 247 (Dec. 24, 1984): D–2.

100. Steve Askin, "Turmoil in the Ranks," *Black Enterprise* (Sept. 1982): 59–60.

101. Under the Age Discrimination in Employment Act, as amended, companies may no longer require the involuntary retirement of employees. See 29 U.S.C. § 631(a). See generally Charles Craver, "The Application of the Age Discrimination in Employment Act to Persons Over Seventy," *George Washington Law Review* 58 (1989): 52.

102. B.N.A., *Unions Today: New Tactics to Tackle Tough Times,* 124.

103. David Rabban, "Distinguishing Excluded Managers From Covered Professionals Under the NLRA," *Columbia Law Review* 89 (1989): 1777.

104. See generally Harry Edwards, R. Theodore Clark & Charles Craver, *Labor Relations Law in the Public Sector* (Charlottesville, Va.: Michie Co., 1991), 1–32.

105. Michael Piore, "The Future of Unions," *The State of the Unions* (George Strauss, Daniel Gallagher & Jack Fiorito, eds.), 406.

106. Seymour Lipset, "White Collar Workers and Professionals—Their Attitudes and Behavior Towards Unions," *Readings in Industrial Sociology* (William Faunce, ed.) (New York: Appleton-Century-Crofts, 1967), 530–31.

107. *Ibid.,* 525, 534–35.

108. David Rabban, "Distinguishing Excluded Managers From Covered Professionals Under the NLRA," *Columbia Law Review* 89 (1989): 1832.

109. Alice Kessler-Harris, "Education in Working-Class Solidarity: The Summer School for Office Workers," *Sisterhood and Solidarity* (Joyce Kornbluh & Mary Frederickson, eds.) (Philadelphia: Temple University Press, 1984), 225–26; C. Wright Mills, *White Collar* (New York: Oxford University Press, 1951), 204–5.

110. Alvin Toffler, *Power Shift* (New York: Bantam Books, 1990), 209.

111. Robert Reich, *The Work of Nations,* 177–78.

112. *Ibid.,* 204.

113. *Ibid.,* 214.

114. Donna Sockell, "The Future of Labor Law: A Mismatch Between Statutory Interpretation and Industrial Reality," *Boston College Law Review* 30 (1989): 997.

115. Michael Goldfield, *The Decline of Organized Labor in the United States,* 147.

116. Charles Heckscher, *The New Unionism: Employee Involvement in the Changing Corporation* (New York: Basic Books, 1988), 240.

117. Michael Mann, *Consciousness and Action Among the Western Working Class* (Atlantic Highlands, N.J.: Humanities Press, 1981), 66.

118. Everett Kassalow, "White-Collar Unionism in the United States," *White-Collar Trade Unions* (Adolph Sturmthal, ed.), 317–30, 351–55; Ronald Miller, "Collective Bargaining in Financial Institutions," *Employee Relations Law Journal* 7 (1981–82): 389.

119. Anthony Giddens, *The Class Structure of the Advanced Societies* (New York:

Barnes & Noble, 1973), 188–92; Everett Kassalow, *Trade Unions and Industrial Relations: An International Comparison* (New York: Random House, 1969), 208–16. Regarding the unionization of white-collar workers in specific countries, see K. F. Walker, "White-Collar Unionism in Australia," *White-Collar Trade Unions* (Adolph Sturmthal, ed.), 1; Guy Routh, "White-Collar Unions in the United Kingdom," *White-Collar Trade Unions* (Adolph Sturmthal, ed.), 165; Günter Hartfiel, "Germany," *White-Collar Trade Unions* (Adolph Sturmthal, ed.), 127; Arne Nilstein, "White-Collar Unionism in Sweden," *White-Collar Trade Unions* (Adolph Sturmthal, ed.), 261; Solomon Levine, "Unionization of White-Collar Employees in Japan," *White-Collar Trade Unions* (Adolph Sturmthal, ed.), 205.

120. David Rabban, "Can American Labor Law Accommodate Collective Bargaining by Professional Employees?" *Yale Law Journal* 99 (1990): 691; Paul Jarley & Jack Fiorito, "Unionism and Changing Employee Views Toward Work," *Journal of Labor Research* 12 (1991): 226. See generally David Rabban, "Is Unionism Compatible with Professionalism?" *Industrial & Labor Relations Review* 45 (Oct. 1991): 97.

121. Marion Crain, "Building Solidarity Through Expansion of NLRA Coverage: A Blueprint for Worker Empowerment," *Minnesota Law Review* 74 (1990): 994.

122. Sar Levitan & Frank Gallo, "Collective Bargaining and Private Sector Professionals," *Monthly Labor Review* 112 (Sept. 1989): 24.

123. Marina Angel, "Professionals and Unionization," *Minnesota Law Review* 66 (1982): 383.

124. Daniel Gallagher & George Strauss, "Union Membership Attitudes and Participation," *The State of the Unions* (George Strauss, Daniel Gallagher & Jack Fiorito, eds.), 143; Michael Mann, *Consciousness and Action Among the Western Working Class*, 25.

125. C. Wright Mills, *White Collar*, 301–2, 312.

126. Stanley Aronowitz, *False Promises* (New York: McGraw-Hill, 1973), 312–13.

127. 29 U.S.C. § 159(a) provides that "[r]epresentatives designated or selected . . . by the majority of the employees in a unit . . . shall be the exclusive representatives of all the employees in such unit for the purposes of collective bargaining. . . . "

128. See, e.g., *International Ladies Garment Workers Union v. NLRB*, 366 U.S. 731 (1961); *J.I. Case Co. v. NLRB*, 321 U.S. 332 (1944).

129. Stanley Aronowitz, *False Promises* (New York: McGraw-Hill, 1973), 151–52.

130. C. Wright Mills, *White Collar*, 139.

131. AFL-CIO Committee on the Evolution of Work, *The Changing Situation of Workers and Their Unions*, 18–20.

132. Robert Rabin, "The Role of Unions in the Rights-Based Workplace," *University of San Francisco Law Review* 25 (1991): 208–9.

133. Jack Fiorito, Cynthia Gramm & Wallace Hendricks, "Union Structural Choices," *The State of the Unions* (George Strauss, Daniel Gallagher & Jack Fiorito, eds.), 126–27.

134. B.N.A., *Daily Labor Report* 123 (June 26, 1991): A–15.

135. Charles Heckscher, *The New Unionism: Employee Involvement in the Changing Corporation* (New York: Basic Books, 1988), 188.

136. B.N.A., *Labor Relations Reporter* 124 (Jan. 19, 1987): 40.

137. See generally Sar Levitan & Frank Gallo, "Can Employee Associations Negotiate New Growth?" *Monthly Labor Review* 112 (July 1989): 5.

138. 925 F.2d 480 (D.C. Cir. 1991).

139. 26 U.S.C. § 511(a)(1).

140. 925 F.2d at 481.

5. ENHANCING ORGANIZED LABOR'S POWER

1. Section 8(d), 29 U.S.C. § 158(d).

2. NLRB v. Katz, 369 U.S. 736, 741–43 (1962). See generally Florian Bartosic & Roger Hartley, Labor Relations Law in the Private Sector (Philadelphia: American Law Institute, 1986), 301–6.

3. NLRB v. American National Insurance Co., 343 U.S. 395, 402–9 (1952). See generally Archibald Cox, "The Duty to Bargain in Good Faith," Harvard Law Review 71 (1958): 1418–28.

4. H. K. Porter Co. v. NLRB, 397 U.S. 99, 108 (1970).

5. NLRB v. International Van Lines, 409 U.S. 48, 52–53 (1972).

6. NLRB v. Mackay Radio & Telegraph Co., 304 U.S. 333, 345–46 (1938). Unfair labor practice strikers, who walk out in protest against unlawful conduct by their employer, may not be permanently replaced and are entitled to reinstatement when they apply for reemployment. Mastro Plastics Corp. v. NLRB, 350 U.S. 270, 278 (1956).

7. Laidlaw Corp., 171 N.L.R.B. 1366, 1368 (1968), enforced, 414 F.2d 99 (7th Cir. 1969), cert. denied, 397 U.S. 920 (1970).

8. B.N.A., Daily Labor Report 114 (June 13, 1991): A–3.

9. Stephen Smith, "National Labor Unions v. Multinational Companies: The Dilemma of Unequal Bargaining Power," Columbia Journal of Transnational Law 11 (1972): 148–53.

10. Hans Gunter, "Erosion of Trade Union Power Through Multinational Enterprises?" Vanderbilt Journal of Transnational Law 9 (1976): 778.

11. Arthur Shostak, Robust Unionism (Ithaca, N.Y.: ILR Press, 1991): 8–11.

12. NLRB v. International Rice Milling Co., 341 U.S. 665, 672–73 (1951). This aspect of the International Rice Milling decision is now codified in Section 8(b)(4)(B) of the NLRA, 29 U.S.C. § 158(b)(4)(B).

13. Edward J. DeBartolo Corp. v. Florida Gulf Coast Building Trades Council, 485 U.S. 568, 578–88 (1988).

14. Thomas Kochan, Harry Katz & Robert McKersie, The Transformation of American Industrial Relations (New York: Basic Books, 1986), 195–97.

15. See generally James Pope, "Labor-Community Coalitions and Boycotts: The Old Labor Law, the New Unionism, and the Living Constitution," Texas Law Review 69 (1991): 889.

16. Ibid., 891–94.

17. Michael Poole, Workers' Participation in Industry (Boston: Routledge & Kegan Paul, 1975), 24–25.

18. John Schmidman, Unions in Postindustrial Society (University Park, Pa.: Pennsylvania State University Press, 1979), 118.

19. George Strauss, "Quality of Worklife and Participation as Bargaining Issues," The Shrinking Perimeter (Hervey Juris & Myron Roomkin, eds.) (Lexington, Mass.: Lexington Books, 1980), 122.

20. Solomon Barkin, The Decline of the Labor Movement (Santa Barbara, Calif.: Center for the Study of Democratic Institutions, 1961), 17.

21. Michael Poole, Workers' Participation in Industry, 26.

22. O.E.C.D., *Workers Participation* (Paris: Organization for Economic Cooperation and Development, 1975), 57–58.

23. Clyde Summers, "Worker Participation in the U.S. and West Germany: A Comparative Study from an American Perspective," *American Journal of Comparative Law* 28 (1980): 371, 384.

24. Robert Simison, "UAW Struggles With a New Idea: Cooperation," *Wall Street Journal* (Apr. 14, 1981): p. 30, col. 3, quoting UAW Vice President Donald Ephlin.

25. Robert McCormick, "Union Representatives as Corporate Directors: The Challenge to the Adversarial Model of Labor Relations," *University of Michigan Journal of Law Reform* 15 (1982): 222–24.

26. John Dunlop, "Past and Future Tendencies of American Labor Organizations," *Daedalus* (Winter 1978): 84.

27. Peter Drucker, *The Unseen Revolution* (New York: Harper & Row, 1976), 140; Giles Radice, *The Industrial Democrats* (Boston: Allen & Unwin, 1978), 124.

28. Daniel Zwerdling, *Workplace Democracy* (New York: Harper & Row, 1980), 168.

29. Sar Levitan & Clifford Johnson, "Labor and Management: The Illusion of Cooperation," *Harvard Business Review* 61 (Sept.–Oct. 1983): 3.

30. Daniel Zwerdling, *Workplace Democracy*, 180.

31. James Furlong, *Labor in the Boardroom* (Princeton, N.J.: Dow Jones Books, 1977), 108–11.

32. Daniel Zwerdling, *Workplace Democracy*, 171.

33. *Ibid.*, 181; Sar Levitan & Diane Werneke, "Worker Participation and Productivity Change," *Monthly Labor Review* 107 (Sept. 1984): 32.

34. B.N.A., *Labor Relations Reporter* 127 (Apr. 18, 1988): 493.

35. F. Ray Marshall, "The Future of the American Labor Movement: The Role of Federal Law," *Chicago-Kent Law Review* 57 (1981): 530.

36. Katherine Stone, "Labor and the Corporate Structure: Changing Conceptions and Emerging Possibilities," *University of Chicago Law Review* 55 (1988): 171.

37. Daniel Zwerdling, *Workplace Democracy*, 176, quoting researcher Paul Blumberg.

38. B.N.A., *Labor Relations Reporter* 119 (July 8, 1985): 188–91; Thomas Kochan, Harry Katz & Robert McKersie, *The Transformation of American Industrial Relations* (New York: Basic Books, 1986), 162–71.

39. Comment, "The Saturnization of American Plants: Infringement or Expansion of Workers' Rights?" *Minnesota Law Review* 72 (1987): 173; U.S. Department of Labor, *U.S. Labor Law and the Future of Labor-Management Cooperation* (Bureau of Labor-Management Relations Report 104, 1986), 3–6.

40. Daniel Zwerdling, *Workplace Democracy*, 175; James Furlong, *Labor in the Boardroom*, 30.

41. Thomas Kochan, Harry Katz & Nancy Mower, "Worker Participation and American Unions," *Challenges and Choices Facing American Labor* (Thomas Kochan, ed.) (Cambridge: MIT Press, 1985), 277–78.

42. Giles Radice, *The Industrial Democrats*, 123.

43. Daniel Zwerdling, *Workplace Democracy*, 2–3.

44. Hem Jain, *Worker Participation* (New York: Praeger, 1980), 324–25.

45. John Schmidman, *Unions in Postindustrial Society*, 143.

46. Hem Jain, *Worker Participation*, 3.

47. *Ibid.*, 8; Bennett Abramowitz, "Broadening the Board: Labor Participation in Corporate Governance," *Southwestern Law Journal* 34 (1980): 981.

48. Note, "Alternatives to the United States System of Labor Relations: A Comparative Analysis of the Labor Relations Systems in the Federal Republic of Germany, Japan, and Sweden," *Vanderbilt Law Review* 41 (1988): 644–46; Shin-ichi Takezawa, "The Quality of Working Life: The Japanese Experience," *Worker Participation* (Hem Jain, ed.), 233.

49. Christopher Byron, "An Attractive Japanese Export," *Time* (Mar. 2, 1981): 74.

50. See generally Hem Jain, *Worker Participation.*

51. Richard Richardi, "Worker Participation in Decisions Within Undertakings in the Federal Republic of Germany," *Comparative Labor Law* 5 (1982): 25.

52. *Ibid.*

53. Note, "Alternatives to the United States System of Labor Relations: A Comparative Analysis of the Labor Relations Systems in the Federal Republic of Germany, Japan, and Sweden," *Vanderbilt Law Review* 41 (1988): 631.

54. Herbert Wiedemann, "Codetermination by Workers in German Enterprises," *American Journal of Comparative Law* 28 (1980): 81.

55. Laurence Zakson, "Worker Participation: Industrial Democracy and Managerial Prerogative in the Federal Republic of Germany, Sweden and the United States," *Hastings International & Comparative Law Review* 8 (1984): 115–16; Manfred Weiss, "Labor Law and Industrial Relations in Europe 1992: A German Perspective," *Comparative Labor Law Journal* 11 (1990): 418–21.

56. Tom Ottervanger & Ralph Pais, "Employee Participation in Corporate Decision Making: The Dutch Model," *International Law* 15 (1981): 395–405.

57. *Ibid.*, 400–401.

58. Joseph Mire, "Trade Unions and Worker Participation in Management," *The Quality of Working Life, Volume One: Problems, Prospects and the State of the Art* (Louis Davis, Albert Cherms & Associates, eds.) (New York: Free Press, 1975), 418–33.

59. Sigvard Rabenowitz, "Experiences of Autonomous Working Groups in a Swedish Car Factory," *Worker Participation* (Hem Jain, ed.), 224.

60. William Batt & Edgar Weinberg, "Labor-Management Cooperation Today," *Harvard Business Review* 56 (Jan.–Feb. 1978): 102.

61. See generally National Center for Productivity & Quality of Working Life, *Recent Initiatives in Labor-Management Cooperation* (Washington, D.C.: National Center for Productivity and Quality of Working Life, 1976).

62. Daniel Zwerdling, *Workplace Democracy*, 19–30.

63. *Ibid.*, 41–51.

64. *Ibid.*, 31–40.

65. B.N.A., *Labor Relations Reporter* 110 (1982): 14–16.

66. Hem Jain, *Worker Participation*, 191; William Batt & Edgar Weinberg, "Labor-Management Cooperation Today," *Harvard Business Review* 56 (Jan.–Feb. 1978): 103.

67. William Whyte, "Organizations for the Future," *The Next Twenty-Five Years of Industrial Relations* (Gerald Somers, ed.) (Madison, Wis.: Industrial Relations Research Association, 1973): 132.

68. B.N.A., *Labor Relations Reporter* 110 (1982): 15.

69. James Furlong, *Labor in the Boardroom*, 91; A. H. Raskin, "Toward a More Participative Work Force," *Working in the Twenty-First Century* (Stewart Shepard & Donald Carroll, eds.) (New York: John Wiley, 1980), 97.

70. Michael Poole, *Workers' Participation in Industry*, 58; Stephen Doyle, "Improving Productivity and Quality of Working Life: The U.S. Experience," *Worker Participation* (Hem Jain, ed.), 255–56.

71. Hem Jain, *Worker Participation*, 190.

72. *Ibid.*, 34.

73. Daniel Zwerdling, *Workplace Democracy*, 176–77; William Batt & Edgar Weinberg, "Labor-Management Cooperation Today," *Harvard Business Review* 56 (Jan.–Feb. 1978): 98.

74. John Blackburn, "Worker Participation on Corporate Directorates: Is America Ready for Industrial Democracy?" *Houston Law Review* 18 (1981): 358.

75. James Furlong, *Labor in the Boardroom*, 29.

76. Comment, "An Economic and Legal Analysis of Union Representation on Corporate Boards of Directors," *University of Pennsylvania Law Review* 130 (1982): 928.

77. Paul Davies, "Employee Representation on Company Boards and Participation in Corporate Planning," *Modern Law Review* 38 (1975): 254.

78. *Ibid.*, 269; Robert McCormick, "Union Representatives as Corporate Directors: The Challenge to the Adversarial Model of Labor Relations," *University of Michigan Journal of Law Reform* 15 (1982): 226–27, 233.

79. Katherine Stone, "The Post-War Paradigm in American Labor Law," *Yale Law Journal* 90 (1981): 1558.

80. Bennett Abramowitz, "Broadening the Board: Labor Participation in Corporate Governance," *Southwestern Law Journal* 34 (1980): 982–86; John Blackburn, "Worker Participation on Corporate Directorates: Is America Ready for Industrial Democracy?" *Houston Law Review* 18 (1981): 359–61.

81. Act on Codetermination by Jobholders of May 4, 1976, I BGBL 1153 (W. Ger.).

82. See generally Note, "Alternatives to the United States System of Labor Relations: A Comparative Analysis of the Labor Relations Systems in the Federal Republic of Germany, Japan, and Sweden," *Vanderbilt Law Review* 41 (1988): 627.

83. Bennett Abramowitz, "Broadening the Board: Labor Participation in Corporate Governance," *Southwestern Law Journal* 34 (1980): 987–90.

84. Robert McCormick, "Union Representatives as Corporate Directors: The Challenge to the Adversarial Model of Labor Relations," *University of Michigan Journal of Law Reform* 15 (1982): 219 n. 4.

85. James Furlong, *Labor in the Boardroom*, 97.

86. Comment, "An Economic and Legal Analysis of Union Representation on Corporate Boards of Directors," *University of Pennsylvania Law Review* 130 (1982): 940–41.

87. Tony Eccles, "Control in the Democratized Enterprise: The Case of KME," *The Control of Work* (John Purcell & Robin Smith, eds.) (New York: Holmes & Meier, 1979), 159.

88. Daniel Zwerdling, *Workplace Democracy*, 172.

89. Robert McCormick, "Union Representatives as Corporate Directors: The Challenge to the Adversarial Model of Labor Relations," *University of Michigan Journal of Law Reform* 15 (1982): 259.

90. Bennett Abramowitz, "Broadening the Board: Labor Participation in Corporate Governance," *Southwestern Law Journal* 34 (1980): 978.

91. 29 U.S.C. § 158(b)(1)(B).

92. Compare *NLRB v. Drivers, Chauffeurs, Helpers, Local 639*, 362 U.S. 274 (1960) (peaceful organizational picketing not coercive under Section 8(b)(1)); *Edward J. DeBartolo Corp. v. Florida Gulf Coast Building Trades Council*, 485 U.S. 568 (1988) and *NLRB v. Fruit & Vegetable Packers & Warehousemen, Local 760*, 377 U.S. 58 (1964) (peaceful consumer picketing not coercive under Section 8(b)(4)(ii), 29 U.S.C. § 158(b)(4)(ii)).

93. *American Broadcasting Cos. v. Writers Guild of America, West, Inc.*, 437 U.S. 411 (1978).

94. 29 U.S.C. § 158(a)(2).

95. 29 U.S.C. § 152(5).

96. 29 U.S.C. § 164(a).

97. *NLRB v. General Steel Erectors*, 933 F.2d 568 (7th Cir. 1991); *Nassau & Suffolk Contractors' Assn.*, 118 N.L.R.B. 174, 187 (1957).

98. Shaun Clarke, "Rethinking the Adversarial Model in Labor Relations: An Argument for Repeal of Section 8(a)(2)," *Yale Law Journal* 96 (1987): 2023–25; Thomas Kohler, "Models of Worker Participation: The Uncertain Significance of Section 8(a)(2)," *Boston College Law Review* 27 (1986): 518–30; Philip Taft, *Organized Labor in American History* (New York: Harper & Row, 1964), 452–55.

99. 308 U.S. 241 (1939).

100. 308 U.S. at 251.

101. 360 U.S. 203 (1959).

102. 360 U.S. at 204.

103. 360 U.S. at 211–14.

104. 503 F.2d 625 (9th Cir. 1974).

105. 503 F.2d at 630.

106. 503 F.2d at 631.

107. 691 F.2d 288 (6th Cir. 1982).

108. 691 F.2d at 289.

109. 691 F.2d at 295.

110. 231 N.L.R.B. 1108 (1977).

111. 231 N.L.R.B. at 1121.

112. 231 N.L.R.B. 1232 (1977).

113. 231 N.L.R.B. at 1234.

114. 231 N.L.R.B. at 1235.

115. 284 N.L.R.B. 621 (1987).

116. 284 N.L.R.B. at 622–23.

117. 29 U.S.C. § 432(a)(5).

118. B.N.A., *Labor Relations Reporter* 106 (1981): 147.

119. *Ibid.*, 147–48.

120. 29 U.S.C. § 186(b)(1).

121. 29 U.S.C. § 501(a).

122. Section 501(a) also obliges union officers and agents to account to their respective labor organizations for any profits received in connection with transactions conducted on behalf of their respective unions. See generally Comment, "Serving Two Masters: Union Representation on Corporate Boards of Directors," *Columbia Law Review* 81 (1981): 642–44.

123. 29 U.S.C. § 186(c)(3).

124. U.S. Department of Labor, *U.S. Labor Law and the Future of Labor-*

Management Cooperation (Bureau of Labor-Management Relations Report 113, 1987), 70–72, quoting letter from George Salem to unidentified addressee (dated September 12, 1986).

125. E.g., Bennett Abramowitz, "Broadening the Board: Labor Participation in Corporate Governance," *Southwestern Law Journal* 34 (1980): 970–75.

126. 15 U.S.C. § 1. E.g., *American Federation of Musicians v. Carroll*, 391 U.S. 99 (1968); *Amalgamated Meat Cutters & Butcher Workmen v. Jewel Tea Co.*, 381 U.S. 676 (1965). See generally Archibald Cox, "Labor and the Antitrust Laws: Pennington and Jewel Tea," *Boston University Law Review* 46 (1966): 317; Bernard Meltzer, "Labor Unions, Collective Bargaining, and the Antitrust Laws," *University of Chicago Law Review* 32 (1965): 659.

127. E.g., *United Mine Workers v. Pennington*, 381 U.S. 657 (1965); *Local 626, Meat & Provision Drivers v. United States*, 371 U.S. 94 (1962).

128. E.g., *H. A. Artists & Associates, Inc. v. Actors' Equity Assn.*, 451 U.S. 704 (1981); *Amalgamated Meat Cutters & Butcher Workmen v. Jewel Tea Co.*, 381 U.S. 676 (1965).

129. 15 U.S.C. § 19.

130. See generally Richard Steuer, "Employee Representation on the Board: Industrial Democracy or Interlocking Directorate?" *Columbia Journal on Transnational Law* 16 (1977): 255.

131. U.S. Department of Labor, *U.S. Labor Law and the Future of Labor-Management Cooperation* (Bureau of Labor-Management Relations Report 104, 1986), 28, quoting letter from Federal Trade Commission to UAW General Counsel John Fillion (dated May 1, 1981).

132. *Ibid.*, quoting letter from Assistant Attorney General Sanford Litvack to UAW General Counsel John Fillion (dated February 26, 1981).

133. Richard Steuer, "Employee Representation on the Board: Industrial Democracy or Interlocking Directorate?" *Columbia Journal on Transnational Law* 16 (1977): 277–79.

134. Comment, "An Economic and Legal Analysis of Union Representation of Corporate Boards of Directors," *University of Pennsylvania Law Review* 130 (1982): 920–22; Comment, "Serving Two Masters: Union Representation on Corporate Boards of Directors," *Columbia Law Review* 81 (1981): 652–60.

135. Comment, "Serving Two Masters: Union Representation on Corporate Boards of Directors," *Columbia Law Review* 81 (1981): 652–60.

136. Comment, "An Economic and Legal Analysis of Union Representation on Corporate Boards of Directors," *University of Pennsylvania Law Review* 130 (1982): 921–22, 948–49.

137. *Ibid.*, 948–49.

138. E.g., *Air Line Pilots Assn. v. O'Neill*, 111 S. Ct. 1127 (1991).

139. *Ford Motor Co. v. Huffman*, 345 U.S. 330, 338 (1953).

140. Comment, "An Economic and Legal Analysis of Union Representation on Corporate Boards of Directors," *University of Pennsylvania Law Review* 130 (1982): 954.

141. Robert McCormick, "Union Representatives as Corporate Directors: The Challenge to the Adversarial Model of Labor Relations," *University of Michigan Journal of Law Reform* 15 (1982): 247, 252–53.

142. Michael Murphy, "Workers on the Board: Borrowing a European Idea," *Labor Law Journal* 27 (1976): 760–61.

143. *NLRB v. Truitt Manufacturing Co.*, 351 U.S. 149 (1956).

144. John Blackburn, "Worker Participation on Corporate Directorates: Is America Ready for Industrial Democracy?" *Houston Law Review* 18 (1981): 366.

145. Giles Radice, *The Industrial Democrats*, 131.

146. James Furlong, *Labor in the Boardroom*, 45, 131.

147. Jeremy Rifkin & Randy Barber, *The North Will Rise Again* (Boston: Beacon Press, 1978), 10–11; W. Michael Kaiser, "Labor's New Weapon: Pension Fund Leverage—Can Labor Legally Beat Its Plowshares into Swords?" *Rutgers Law Review* 34 (1982): 409.

148. George Borhas, *Union Control of Pension Funds: Will the North Rise Again?* (San Francisco: Institute for Contemporary Studies, 1979), 19–20; W. Michael Kaiser, "Labor's New Weapon: Pension Fund Leverage—Can Labor Legally Beat Its Plowshares into Swords?" *Rutgers Law Review* 34 (1982): 409–10; "Unions Bid for Bigger Voice in Pension Funds," *U.S. News & World Report* (June 8, 1981): 85.

149. Jeremy Rifkin & Randy Barber, *The North Will Rise Again*, 81.

150. *Ibid.*, 84.

151. *Ibid.*, 147.

152. *Ibid.*, 149.

153. W. Michael Kaiser, "Labor's New Weapon: Pension Fund Leverage—Can Labor Legally Beat Its Plowshares into Swords?" *Rutgers Law Review* 34 (1982): 412.

154. Jeremy Rifkin & Randy Barber, *The North Will Rise Again*, 179.

155. B.N.A., *Labor Relations Reporter* 109 (1982): 192; B.N.A., *Labor Relations Reporter* 109 (1982): 150.

156. B.N.A., *Daily Labor Report* 63 (Apr. 2, 1991): A–11. By 1991, the Union's initial $12 million investment had grown to over $305 million in assets.

157. Jayne Zanglein, "Pensions, Proxies and Power: Recent Developments in the Use of Proxy Voting to Influence Corporate Governance," *Labor Lawyer* 7 (1991): 771–76.

158. Jeremy Rifkin & Randy Barber, *The North Will Rise Again*, 150–51.

159. 29 U.S.C. § 186(c)(5).

160. W. Michael Kaiser, "Labor's New Weapon: Pension Fund Leverage—Can Labor Legally Beat Its Plowshares into Swords?" *Rutgers Law Review* 34 (1982): 415.

161. Pub. L. No. 93–406, 88 Stat. 829 (1974), codified in various sections of 5, 18, 26, 29, 31 & 42 U.S.C.

162. 29 U.S.C. § 1104(a)(1).

163. W. Michael Kaiser, "Labor's New Weapon: Pension Fund Leverage—Can Labor Legally Beat Its Plowshares into Swords?" *Rutgers Law Review* 34 (1982): 421–24, 429.

164. Jeremy Rifkin & Randy Barber, *The North Will Rise Again*, 186.

165. 29 U.S.C. § 158(e).

166. Michael Gurdon, "An American Approach to Self-Management," *Worker Participation* (Hem Jain, ed.) 295.

167. Daniel Zwerdling, *Workplace Democracy*, 95–96; Deborah Olson, "Union Experiences with Worker Ownership: Legal and Practical Issues Raised by ESOPS, TRASOPS, Stock Purchases and Co-Operatives," *Wisconsin Law Review* 1982 (1982): 769–72.

168. Daniel Zwerdling, *Workplace Democracy*, 53–63.

169. *Ibid.*, 71–74.

170. *Ibid.*, 66–71.

171. Deborah Olson, "Union Experiences with Worker Ownership: Legal and Practical Issues Raised by ESOPS, TRASOPS, Stock Purchases and Co-Operatives," *Wisconsin Law Review* 1982 (1982): 753–60.

172. *Ibid.*, 739–42.

173. *Ibid.*, 775–77.

174. *Ibid.*, 778–80.

175. B.N.A., *Daily Labor Report* 64 (Apr. 3, 1991): A–4.

176. B.N.A., *Daily Labor Report* (Sept. 26, 1983): A–3.

177. Thomas Kochan, Harry Katz & Robert McKersie, *The Transformation of American Industrial Relations* (New York: Basic Books, 1986), 191–93.

178. *Ibid.*, 193–94.

179. 29 U.S.C. § 1107(d)(6).

180. 29 U.S.C. § 1104(a)(1)(B).

181. 29 U.S.C. § 1104(a)(1)(C).

182. 29 U.S.C. § 1104(a)(2).

183. Regarding the legal regulations applicable to the creation and operation of ESOPs, see generally Note, "Employee Stock Ownership Plans: A Step Toward Democratic Capitalism," *Boston University Law Review* 55 (1975): 195; Deborah Olson, "Union Experiences with Worker Ownership: Legal and Practical Issues Raised by ESOPS, TRASOPS, Stock Purchases and Co-Operatives," *Wisconsin Law Review* 1982 (1982): 732–37. See also *ibid.* at 733 n. 2, for a description of TRASOPs, a type of ESOP created by the Tax Reduction Act of 1975, Pub. L. No. 94–12, § 301(d), 89 Stat. 26 (1975), 26 U.S.C. §§ 46, 48, and the Tax Reform Act of 1976, Pub. L. No. 94–455, 90 Stat. 1525 (1976).

184. *Richfield Oil Corp.*, 110 N.L.R.B. 356 (1954), *enforced*, 231 F.2d 717 (D.C. Cir.), *cert. denied*, 351 U.S. 909 (1956).

185. *Brookings Plywood Corp.*, 98 N.L.R.B. 794, 798 (1952).

186. *Coastal Plywood*, 102 N.L.R.B. 300 (1953); *Mutual Rough Hat Co.*, 86 N.L.R.B. 440 (1949); *Muskogee Dairy Products Co.*, 85 N.L.R.B. 520 (1949).

187. 29 U.S.C. § 158(a)(2).

188. 29 U.S.C. § 152(5).

189. Note, "Worker Ownership and Section 8(a)(2) of the National Labor Relations Act," *Yale Law Journal* 91 (1982): 615.

190. 29 U.S.C. § 501(a).

191. Deborah Olson, "Union Experiences with Worker Ownership: Legal and Practical Issues Raised by ESOPS, TRASOPS, Stock Purchases and Co-Operatives," *Wisconsin Law Review* 1982 (1982): 801–2. If representative labor organizations and worker-owned enterprises act in good faith to further the legitimate interests of the employees and do not enter into collective bargaining arrangements designed to restrain trade, their cooperative conduct should be exempt from antitrust liability. *Ibid.*, 803–8.

192. Daniel Zwerdling, *Workplace Democracy*, 100.

193. *Ibid.*, 101.

194. Richard Long, "The Effects of Employee Ownership on Organizational Identification, Employee Job Attitudes, and Organizational Performance: A Tentative Framework and Empirical Findings," *Human Relations* 31 (1978): 39–40.

195. *Ibid.*, 47; Michael Conte & Arnold Tannenbaum, "Employee-Owned Companies: Is the Difference Measurable?" *Monthly Labor Review* 101 (July 1978): 25–26.

196. James O'Toole, "The Uneven Record of Employee Ownership," *Harvard Business Review* 57 (Nov.–Dec. 1979): 194.

197. Michael Conte & Arnold Tannenbaum, "Employee-Owned Companies: Is the Difference Measurable?" *Monthly Labor Review* 101 (July 1978): 24.

198. Daniel Zwerdling, *Workplace Democracy*, 167–68, quoting William Burns, Assistant Research Director for the Amalgamated Meat Cutters.

199. *Ibid.*, 98.

200. Deborah Olson, "Union Experiences with Worker Ownership: Legal and Practical Issues Raised by ESOPS, TRASOPS, Stock Purchases and Co-Operatives," *Wisconsin Law Review* 1982 (1982): 753.

201. Daniel Zwerdling, *Workplace Democracy*, 103.

202. Deborah Olson, "Union Experiences with Worker Ownership: Legal and Practical Issues Raised by ESOPS, TRASOPS, Stock Purchases and Co-Operatives," *Wisconsin Law Review* 1982 (1982): 744–46.

203. Peter Drucker, *The Unseen Revolution*, 146–47.

204. James O'Toole, "The Uneven Record of Employee Ownership," *Harvard Business Review* 57 (Nov.–Dec. 1979): 193.

205. Roger McElrath & Richard Rowan, "The American Labor Movement and Employee Ownership: Objections to and Uses of Employee Stock Ownership Plans," *Journal of Labor Research* 13 (Winter 1992): 106.

206. 42 U.S.C. § 2000e et seq.

207. 42 U.S.C. § 1981, which guarantees all persons the same right to make and enforce contracts, including contracts of employment, as is enjoyed by white citizens.

208. *Wards Cove Packing Co. v. Atonio*, 490 U.S. 642 (1989).

209. *Patterson v. McLean Credit Union*, 491 U.S. 164 (1989). Fortunately for the victims of employment discrimination, organized labor and other groups were able to induce Congress to statutorily reverse this conservative group of Supreme Court decisions through the enactment of the Civil Rights Act of 1991. Pub. Law No. 102–166, 105 Stat. 1071 (1991).

210. Thomas Kochan & Kirsten Wever, "American Unions and the Future of Worker Representation," *The State of the Unions* (George Strauss, Daniel Gallagher & Jack Fiorito, eds.) (Madison, Wis.: Industrial Relations Research Association, 1991), 381.

211. B.N.A., *Daily Labor Report* 26 (Feb. 7, 1991): B–9.

212. John Delaney & Marick Masters, "Unions and Political Action," *The State of the Unions* (George Strauss, Daniel Gallagher & Jack Fiorito, eds.) (Madison, Wis.: Industrial Relations Research Association, 1991), 318.

213. John Delaney, "The Future of Unions as Political Organizations," *Journal of Labor Research* 12 (Fall 1991): 374.

214. Thomas Edsall, *The New Politics of Inequality* (New York: W. W. Norton, 1984), 167.

215. James Bennett, "Private Sector Unions: The Myth of Decline," *Journal of Labor Research* 12 (Winter 1991): 6.

216. *Ibid.*, 7.

217. *Ibid.*, 3.

218. *Ibid.*

219. Lloyd Ulman, "Multinational Unionism: Incentives, Barriers, and Alternatives," *Industrial Relations* 14 (1975): 4–5.

220. International Labour Office, *Employment Effects of Multinational Enterprises in Industrial Countries* (Geneva: International Labour Office, 1981), 17.

221. Stanley Ruttenberg, "The Union View of Multinationals: An Interpretation," *Bargaining Without Boundaries* (Robert Flanagan & Arnold Weber, eds.) (Chicago: University of Chicago Press, 1974): 181–84.

222. B.N.A., *Daily Labor Report* (Dec. 16, 1982): A–4.

223. Herbert Northrup & Richard Rowan, *Multinational Collective Bargaining Attempts* (Philadelphia: Industrial Research Unit, Wharton School, University of Pennsylvania, 1979), 540.

224. International Labour Office, *Multinational Enterprises and Social Policy* (Geneva: International Labour Office, 1973), 95.

225. *Ibid.*, 67, quoting Walter Reuther, "World-Wide Labor Solidarity—Essential for Developing International Co-operation," *International Metalworkers Federation Bulletin* (Nov. 1964): 12.

226. William Curtin, "The Multinational Corporation and Transnational Collective Bargaining," *American Labor and the Multinational Corporation* (Duane Kujawa, ed.) (New York: Praeger, 1973), 212.

227. Jerome Rosow, "International Relations and the Multinational Corporation: The Management Approach, *Bargaining Without Boundaries* (Robert Flanagan & Arnold Weber, eds.), 152–53.

228. Herbert Northrup & Richard Rowan, *Multinational Collective Bargaining Attempts*, 544.

229. Richard Barnet & Ronald Müller, *Global Reach: The Power of the Multinational Corporations* (New York: Simon & Schuster, 1974), 314–18.

230. Charles Levinson, *International Trade Unionism* (London: Allen & Unwin, 1972), 115.

231. Hugh Stephenson, *The Coming Clash* (New York: Saturday Review Press, 1972), 161–65; Louis Turner, *Invisible Empires: Multinational Companies and the Modern World* (New York: Harcourt Brace Jovanovich, 1970), 98–102.

232. Herbert Northrup, "Why Multinational Bargaining Neither Exists Nor is Desirable," *Labor Law Journal* 29 (1978): 330.

233. Lloyd Ulman, "Multinational Unionism: Incentives, Barriers, and Alternatives," *Industrial Relations* 14 (1975): 1.

234. William Curtin, "The Multinational Corporation and Transnational Collective Bargaining," in *American Labor and the Multinational Corporation* (Duane Kujawa, ed.), 203.

235. *Ibid.*, 205–6; G. B. J. Bomers, *Multinational Corporations and Industrial Relations* (Assen, Netherlands: Van Gorcum, 1976), 27.

236. Benjamin Aaron, "Labor Relations in the United States From a Comparative Perspective," *Washington & Lee Law Review* 39 (1982): 1252–53.

237. David Blake, "International Labor and the Regulation of Multinational Corporations: Proposals and Prospects," *San Diego Law Review* 11 (1973): 184–85.

238. Robert Cox, "Labor and Transnational Relations," *International Organization* 25 (1971): 568.

239. *Ibid.*, 560.

240. International Labour Office, *Multinational Enterprises and Social Policy*, 68.

241. John Windmuller, "International Trade Union Organizations: Structure, Functions, Limitations," *International Labor* (Solomon Barkin, ed.) (New York: Harper & Row, 1967), 82–87.

242. Charles Levinson, *International Trade Unionism*, 132–33.

243. G. B. J. Bomers, *Multinational Corporations and Industrial Relations*, 34–36.

244. Roger Blanpain, "1992 and Beyond: The Impact of the European Community on the Labour Law Systems of the Member Countries," *Comparative Labor Law Journal* 11 (1990): 409.

245. Tiziano Treu, "European Unification and Italian Labor Relations," *Comparative Labor Law Journal* 11 (1990): 450–53.

246. B.N.A., *Labor Relations Reporter* 127 (Feb. 1, 1988): 147.

247. Robert Cox, "Labor and the Multinationals," *Foreign Affairs* 54 (Jan. 1976): 362.

248. David Blake, "International Labor and the Regulation of Multinational Corporations: Proposals and Prospects," *San Diego Law Review* 11 (1973): 190.

249. Frank Tannenbaum, "The Survival of the Fittest," *Columbia Journal of World Business* 3 (Mar.–Apr. 1968): 18–19.

250. Robert Cox, "Labor and the Multinationals," *Foreign Affairs* 54 (Jan. 1976): 360.

251. B.N.A., *Daily Labor Report* (Jan. 27, 1983): A–5; B.N.A., *Daily Labor Report* (June 21, 1983): A–1, D–1.

252. B.N.A., *Daily Labor Report* 242 (Dec. 17, 1990): A–5. See generally Note, "The Vredling Directive: The EEC's Failed Attempt to Regulate Multinational Enterprises and Organize Collective Bargaining," *Journal of International Law and Politics* 20 (1988): 967.

253. B.N.A., *Daily Labor Report* 123 (June 26, 1991): A–5. See generally George Kraw, "The Community Charter of the Fundamental Social Rights of Workers," *Hastings International and Comparative Law Review* 13 (1990): 467; Donald Dowling, "Worker Rights in the Post–1992 European Communities: What 'Social Europe' Means to United States–Based Multinational Employers," *Northwestern Journal of International Law and Business* 11 (1991): 564.

6. THE NEED TO REFORM

1. E.g., *Commonwealth v. Pullis*, 3 Doc. Hist. of Am. Ind. Soc. 59 (2d ed. Commons 1910) (Philadelphia Mayor's Court 1806). See generally William Forbath, "The Shaping of the American Labor Movement," *Harvard Law Review* 102 (1989): 1148–53.

2. Felix Frankfurter & Nathan Greene, *The Labor Injunction* (New York: Macmillan, 1930).

3. Philip Taft, *Organized Labor in American History* (New York: Harper & Row, 1964), 136–58.

4. E.g., *Adair v. United States*, 208 U.S. 161 (1908) (yellow-dog contracts); *In re Jacobs*, 98 N.Y. 98 (1885) (voiding New York law precluding production of cigars in tenement dwellings).

5. 38 Stat. 730 (1914).

6. *Duplex Printing Press Co. v. Deering*, 254 U.S. 443 (1921).

7. 47 Stat. 70 (1932).

8. 48 Stat. 198 (1933).

9. *Schechter Poultry Corp. v. United States*, 295 U.S. 495 (1935).

10. 49 Stat. 449 (1935).

11. 49 Stat. 449 (1935). The NLRA, as amended by the Labor-Management Re-

lations Act [Pub. L. No. 101, 61 Stat. 136 (1947)], and the Labor Management Reporting and Disclosure Act [Pub. L. No. 257, 73 Stat. 519 (1959)], is set forth in 29 U.S.C. §§ 151–69.

12. *Ibid.*

13. *Ibid.*

14. *NLRB v. Jones & Laughlin Steel Corp.*, 301 U.S. 1, 33 (1937).

15. N.L.R.B., *NLRB: The First 50 Years* (Washington, D.C.: National Labor Relations Board, 1985), vi.

16. *Ibid.*

17. Section 8(d), 29 U.S.C. § 158(d).

18. 322 U.S. 111 (1944).

19. 330 U.S. 485 (1947).

20. 322 U.S. at 127–28.

21. Robert Gorman, *Labor Law: Basic Text* (St. Paul: West Publishing, 1976), 197–98.

22. E.g., *Dal-Tex Optical Co.*, 137 N.L.R.B. 1782 (1962).

23. 140 N.L.R.B. 221 (1962).

24. *NLRB v. Exchange Parts Co.*, 375 U.S. 405 (1964).

25. *NLRB v. Burnup & Sims, Inc.*, 379 U.S. 21 (1964).

26. E.g., *Joy Silk Mills, Inc.*, 85 N.L.R.B. 1263 (1949), *enforced*, 185 F.2d 732 (D.C. Cir. 1950); *Snow & Sons*, 134 N.L.R.B. 709 (1961), *enforced*, 308 F.2d 687 (9th Cir. 1962).

27. *NLRB v. Gissel Packing Co.*, 395 U.S. 575, 613–14 (1969).

28. E.g., *Conair Corp.*, 261 N.L.R.B. 1189 (1982). The D.C. Circuit Court refused to enforce this portion of the Board's remedial order, since it concluded that any departure from the principle of majority rule should be left to Congress. *Conair Corp. v. NLRB*, 721 F.2d 1355 (D.C. Cir. 1983), *cert. denied*, 467 U.S. 1241 (1984).

29. *Int'l. Ladies Garment Workers Union v. NLRB*, 366 U.S. 731 (1961) (voluntary extension of representation status to minority union per se unfair labor practice regardless of good or bad faith of employer and labor organization).

30. *Interboro Contractors*, 157 N.L.R.B. 1295 (1966), *enforced*, 388 F.2d 495 (2d Cir. 1967). This doctrine was sustained by the Supreme Court in *NLRB v. City Disposal Systems*, 465 U.S. 822 (1984).

31. 221 N.L.R.B. 999 (1975).

32. 420 U.S. 251 (1975).

33. 262 N.L.R.B. 1010 (1982).

34. E.g., *Kohler Co.*, 148 N.L.R.B. 1434 (1964), *affirmed*, 345 F.2d 748 (D.C. Cir.), *cert. denied*, 382 U.S. 836 (1965).

35. 29 U.S.C. § 158(d).

36. *Phelps Dodge Copper Corp.*, 101 N.L.R.B. 360 (1952).

37. *Inland Steel Co. v. NLRB*, 170 F.2d 247 (7th Cir. 1948), *cert. denied*, 336 U.S. 960 (1949).

38. *W. W. Cross & Co. v. NLRB*, 174 F.2d 875 (1st Cir. 1949).

39. *Singer Mfgr. Co.*, 24 N.L.R.B. 444 (1940), *enforced*, 119 F.2d 131 (7th Cir.), *cert. denied*, 313 U.S. 595 (1941).

40. *Central Illinois Public Service Co.*, 139 N.L.R.B. 1407 (1962), *enforced*, 324 F.2d 916 (7th Cir. 1963).

41. *NLRB v. Gulf Power Co.*, 384 F.2d 822 (5th Cir. 1967).

42. *Beacon Piece Dyeing & Finishing Co.*, 121 N.L.R.B. 953 (1958).

43. *NLRB v. Boss Mfgr. Co.*, 118 F.2d 187 (7th Cir. 1941).

44. *United States Gypsum Co.*, 94 N.L.R.B. 112, amended, 97 N.L.R.B. 889 (1951), modified on other grounds, 206 F.2d 410 (5th Cir. 1953), cert. denied, 347 U.S. 912 (1954).

45. *Fibreboard Paper Products Corp. v. NLRB*, 379 U.S. 203 (1964).

46. Comment, "Subjects Included Within Management's Duty to Bargain Collectively," *Louisiana Law Review* 26 (1966): 634.

47. 388 U.S. 175 (1967).

48. 29 U.S.C. § 158(b)(1)(A).

49. 388 U.S. at 181.

50. 412 U.S. 67 (1973).

51. *Union of Electrical Workers, Local 1012*, 187 N.L.R.B. 375 (1970).

52. 351 U.S. 225 (1956).

53. 367 U.S. 740 (1960).

54. 304 U.S. 333 (1938).

55. 304 U.S. at 345–46.

56. *NLRB v. International Van Lines*, 409 U.S. 48 (1972).

57. *Laidlaw Corp.*, 171 N.L.R.B. 1366 (1968), enforced, 414 F.2d 99 (7th Cir. 1969), cert. denied, 397 U.S. 920 (1970).

58. 29 U.S.C. § 159(c)(3).

59. *NLRB v. Erie Resistor Corp.*, 373 U.S. 221 (1963).

60. 675 F.2d 926 (7th Cir. 1982).

61. The *Giddings & Lewis* approach continues to be followed today. *Aqua-Chem, Inc. v. NLRB*, 910 F.2d 1487 (7th Cir. 1990), rehearing denied, 922 F.2d 403 (7th Cir.), cert. denied, 111 S. Ct. 2871 (1991).

62. 489 U.S. 426 (1989).

63. Pub. L. No. 101, 61 Stat. 140 (1947).

64. 29 U.S.C. § 160(1).

65. Section 303 of the LMRA, 29 U.S.C. § 187.

66. Pub. L. No. 86–257, 73 Stat. 525, 542 (1959).

67. Section 8(e) of the NLRA, 29 U.S.C. § 158(e).

68. 29 U.S.C. § 158(b)(7).

69. 61 Stat. 137 (1947), codified at 29 U.S.C. § 152(3).

70. 404 U.S. 157 (1971).

71. *NLRB v. Yeshiva University*, 444 U.S. 672 (1980).

72. *NLRB v. Bell Aerospace Co.*, 416 U.S. 267, 288 (1974).

73. 265 N.L.R.B. 295 (1982).

74. 140 N.L.R.B. 221 (1962).

75. Julius Getman, Stephen Goldberg & Jeanne Herman, *Union Representation Elections: Law and Reality* (New York: Russell Sage Foundation, 1976).

76. 228 N.L.R.B. 1311 (1977).

77. 228 N.L.R.B. at 1313. In *General Knit of California, Inc.*, 239 N.L.R.B. 619 (1978), a new 3–2 Board majority overruled *Shopping Kart* and reinstated the *Hollywood Ceramics* test, but four years later, another 3–2 majority overruled *General Knit* and returned to the "sound rule" that had been enunciated in *Shopping Kart*. *Midland Natl. Life Insurance Co.*, 263 N.L.R.B. 127 (1982).

78. E.g., *Fiber-Lam, Inc.*, 301 N.L.R.B. No. 9, 136 L.R.R.M. 1147 (1991); *Tri-Cast, Inc.*, 274 N.L.R.B. 377 (1985).

79. *Gourmet Foods, Inc.*, 270 N.L.R.B. 578 (1984).

80. 268 N.L.R.B. 493 (1984).

81. *Sears, Roebuck & Co.*, 274 N.L.R.B. 230 (1985).

82. 268 N.L.R.B. 1044 (1984), *affirmed*, 765 F.2d 148 (9th Cir. 1985).

83. 452 U.S. 666 (1981).

84. 452 U.S. at 678–79.

85. 303 N.L.R.B. No. 66, 137 L.R.R.M. 1185 (1991).

86. 409 U.S. 213 (1972).

87. 473 U.S. 95 (1985).

88. 29 U.S.C. § 158(b)(1)(A).

89. 466 U.S. 435 (1984).

90. 111 S. Ct. 1950 (1991). Even though the *Lehnert* case involved a public sector union, the parameters set forth in that decision will undoubtedly be applied to private sector labor organizations.

91. B.N.A., *Daily Labor Report* 72 (Apr. 14, 1992): D–1.

92. B.N.A., *Daily Labor Report* 73 (Apr. 15, 1992): A–9, D–1.

93. 29 U.S.C. § 152(3).

94. E.g., *Yamada Transfer*, 115 N.L.R.B. 1330 (1956); *American Cable & Radio Corp.*, 121 N.L.R.B. 258 (1958).

95. C. Wright Mills, *White Collar* (New York: Oxford University Press, 1951), 86–89.

96. Marion Crain, "Building Solidarity Through Expansion of NLRA Coverage: A Blueprint for Worker Empowerment," *Minnesota Law Review* 74 (1990): 1006–8.

97. Compare *NLRB v. Hendricks County Rural Electric Membership Corp.*, 454 U.S. 170 (1981), wherein the Supreme Court limited the Labor Board's "confidential" employee exclusion to those individuals who actually have access to confidential labor relations information. The Court refused to permit the exclusion to be applied to individuals who have access to other forms of confidential company information.

98. *NLRB v. Gissel Packing Co.*, 395 U.S. 575, 618–19 (1969).

99. 263 N.L.R.B. 127 (1982).

100. 140 N.L.R.B. 221 (1962).

101. *NLRB v. United Steelworkers*, 357 U.S. 357 (1958).

102. Karl Klare, "Workplace Democracy & Market Reconstruction: An Agenda for Legal Reform," *Catholic University Law Review* 38 (1988): 45–51.

103. *Excelsior Underwear, Inc.*, 156 N.L.R.B. 1236 (1966).

104. 304 U.S. 333 (1938).

105. Daniel Pollitt, "*Mackay Radio:* Turn It Off, Tune It Out," *University of San Francisco Law Review* 25 (1991): 296–97.

106. B.N.A., *Daily Labor Report* 114 (June 13, 1991): A–3.

107. Clyde Summers, "Past Premises, Present Failures, and Future Needs in Labor Legislation," *Buffalo Law Review* 31 (1982): 10.

108. Matthew Finkin, "Labor Policy and The Enervation of the Economic Strike," *University of Illinois Law Review* 1990: 569–70.

109. See, e.g., *NLRB v. Great Dane Trailers, Inc.*, 388 U.S. 26 (1967). See generally Thomas Christensen & Andrea Svanoe, "Motive and Intent in the Commission of Unfair Labor Practices," *Yale Law Journal* 77 (1968): 1269; Walter Oberer, "The Scienter Factor in Sections 8(a)(1) and (3) of the Labor Act: Of Balancing Hostile Motive, Dogs and Tails," *Cornell Law Quarterly* 52 (1967): 491.

110. Daniel Pollitt, "*Mackay Radio:* Turn It Off, Tune It Out," *University of San Francisco Law Review* 25 (1991): 306–7.

111. B.N.A., *Daily Labor Report* 138 (July 18, 1991): A–11.

112. 29 U.S.C. § 158(b)(4)(B).

113. *NLRB v. Fruit & Vegetable Packers & Warehousemen, Local 760*, 377 U.S. 58 (1964).

114. *NLRB v. Retail Store Employees Union, Local 1001*, 447 U.S. 607 (1980).

115. *Edward DeBartolo Corp. v. Florida Gulf Coast Building & Construction Trades Council*, 485 U.S. 568 (1988).

116. 29 U.S.C. § 158(e).

117. Charles Craver, "Public Sector Impasse Resolution Procedures," *Chicago-Kent Law Review* 60 (1984): 783–85.

118. See generally George Goble, "The Non-Stoppage Strike," *Labor Law Journal* 2 (1951): 105; Howard Marshall & Natalie Marshall, "Nonstoppage Strike Proposals—A Critique," *Labor Law Journal* 7 (1956): 299. David McCalmont, "The Semi-Strike," *Industrial & Labor Relations Review* 15 (1962): 191.

119. *Meyers Industries*, 268 N.L.R.B. 493 (1984).

120. See generally Richard Fischl, "Self, Others, and Section 7: Mutualism and Protected Protest Activities Under the National Labor Relations Act," *Columbia Law Review* 89 (1989): 789; Charles Morris, "NLRB Protection in the Nonunion Workplace: A Glimpse at a General Theory of Section 7 Conduct," *University of Pennsylvania Law Review* 137 (1989): 1673.

121. 274 N.L.R.B. 230 (1985).

122. Katherine Stone, "The Post-War Paradigm in American Labor Law," *Yale Law Journal* 90 (1981): 1558.

123. 29 U.S.C. § 8(d).

124. Katherine Stone, "Labor and the Corporate Structure: Changing Conceptions and Emerging Possibilities," *University of Chicago Law Review* 55 (1988): 86–87.

125. *NLRB v. Katz*, 369 U.S. 736 (1962).

126. 29 U.S.C. § 158(b)(1)(A).

127. 29 U.S.C. § 160(1).

128. *Terminal Freight Handling Co. v. Solien*, 444 F.2d 699 (8th Cir. 1971), *cert. denied*, 405 U.S. 996 (1972).

129. 29 U.S.C. § 187.

130. 29 U.S.C. § 160(j).

131. Paul Weiler, *Governing the Workplace* (Cambridge: Harvard University Press, 1990), 238–39.

132. *Clear Pine Mouldings*, 268 N.L.R.B. 1044 (1984), *affirmed*, 765 F.2d 148 (9th Cir. 1985).

133. *Gourmet Foods, Inc.*, 270 N.L.R.B. 578 (1984).

134. *Phelps Dodge Corp. v. NLRB*, 313 U.S. 177 (1941).

135. Paul Weiler, "Promises to Keep: Securing Workers' Rights to Self-Organization Under the NLRA," *Harvard Law Review* 96 (1983): 1792.

136. *Ibid.*, 1795 & n. 94.

137. See generally Benjamin Wolkinson, "The Remedial Efficacy of NLRB Remedies in *Joy Silk* Cases," *Cornell Law Review* 55 (1969): 1.

138. Once such Labor Board bargaining orders are judicially enforced, continued contumacy by employers would subject them to contempt liability.

139. 29 U.S.C. § 216(b).

140. See generally Note, "Nonmajority Bargaining Orders: The Only Effective

Remedy for Pervasive Employer Unfair Labor Practices During Union Organizing Campaigns," *Journal of Law Reform* 20 (1987): 617.

141. *Ex-Cell-O Corp.*, 185 N.L.R.B. 107 (1970), *affirmed*, 449 F.2d 1058 (D.C. Cir. 1971).

142. 29 U.S.C. § 160(c) empowers the Labor Board to issue remedial orders that will effectuate the policies of the NLRA.

143. 29 U.S.C. § 160(a).

144. 112 N.L.R.B. 1080 (1955).

145. 112 N.L.R.B. at 1082.

146. 268 N.L.R.B. 573 (1984).

147. 268 N.L.R.B. at 574.

148. *United Steelworkers v. Enterprise Wheel & Car Corp.*, 363 U.S. 593 (1960).

149. *Universal Camera Corp. v. NLRB*, 340 U.S. 474 (1951).

150. Section 203(d) of the LMRA, 29 U.S.C. § 173(d), provides that "[f]inal adjustment by a method agreed upon by the parties is declared to be the desirable method for settlement of grievance disputes arising over the application or interpretation of an existing collective-bargaining agreement."

151. 192 N.L.R.B. 837 (1971).

152. 228 N.L.R.B. 808 (1977).

BIBLIOGRAPHY

Aaron, Benjamin, "Labor Relations in the United States From a Comparative Perspective," *Washington & Lee Law Review* 39 (1982): 1247.

Abramowitz, Bennett, "Broadening the Board: Labor Participation in Corporate Governance," *Southwestern Law Journal* 34 (1980): 963.

AFL-CIO Committee on the Evolution of Work, *The Changing Situation of Workers and Their Unions*. Washington, D.C.: AFL-CIO, 1985.

Amoroso, Bruno, "A Danish Perspective: The Impact of the Internal Market on the Labour Unions and the Welfare State," *Comparative Labor Law Journal* 11 (1990): 483.

Angel, Marina, "Professionals and Unionization," *Minnesota Law Review* 66 (1982): 383.

Aronowitz, Stanley, *False Promises*. New York: McGraw-Hill, 1973.

Askin, Steve, "Turmoil in the Ranks," *Black Enterprise* (Sept. 1982): 59.

Atleson, James, "Reflections on Labor, Power & Society," *Maryland Law Review* 44 (1985): 841.

Atleson, James, *Values and Assumptions in American Labor Law*. Amherst, Mass.: University of Massachusetts Press, 1983.

Axelrod, Jonathan, "Common Obstacles to Organizing Under the NLRA: Combatting the Southern Strategy," *North Carolina Law Review* 59 (1980): 147.

Balser, Diane, *Sisterhood and Solidarity*. Boston: South End Press, 1987.

Barkin, Solomon, *The Decline of the Labor Movement*. Santa Barbara, Calif.: Center for the Study of Democratic Institutions, 1961.

Barkin, Solomon, *International Labor*. New York: Harper & Row, 1967.

Barkin, Solomon, "A New Agenda for Labor," *Fortune* (Nov. 1960): 250.

Barnet, Richard, "A Reporter at Large," *New Yorker* (Apr. 7, 1980): 46.

Barnet, Richard & Ronald Müller, *Global Reach: The Power of the Multinational Corporations*. New York: Simon & Schuster, 1974.

Barnett, George, "American Trade Unionism and Social Insurance," *American Economic Review* 23 (March 1933): 1.

Bartosic, Florian & Roger Hartley, *Labor Relations Law in the Private Sector*. Philadelphia: American Law Institute, 1986.

Batt, William & Edgar Weinberg, "Labor-Management Cooperation Today," *Harvard Business Review* 56 (Jan.–Feb. 1978): 96.

Beale, Calvin, "Renewed Growth in Rural Communities," *Futurist* 9 (Aug. 1975): 196.

Beckwith, Burnham, *The Next 500 Years.* New York: Exposition Press, 1967.

Bennett, James, "Private Sector Unions: The Myth of Decline," *Journal of Labor Research* 12 (Winter 1991): 1.

Bernstein, Jules, "Union-Busting: From Benign Neglect to Malignant Growth," *University of California, Davis Law Review* 14 (1980): 1.

Best, Fred, "Recycling People: Work-Sharing Through Flexible Life Scheduling," *Futurist* 12 (Feb. 1978): 13.

Bibb, Robert, "Blue-Collar Women in Low-Wage Industries: A Dual Labor Market Interpretation," *The American Working Class* (Irving Horowitz, John Leggett & Martin Oppenheimer, eds.) New Brunswick, N.J.: Transaction Books, 1979: 125.

Blackburn, John, "Worker Participation on Corporate Directorates: Is America Ready for Industrial Democracy?" *Houston Law Review* 18 (1981): 349.

Blake, David, "International Labor and the Regulation of Multinational Corporations: Proposals and Prospects," *San Diego Law Review* 11 (1973): 179.

Blanchflower, David & Richard Freeman, *Going Different Ways: Unionism in the U.S. and Other Advanced O.E.C.D. Countries.* Cambridge, Mass.: National Bureau of Economic Research Working Paper 3342, Apr. 1990.

Blanpain, Roger, "1992 and Beyond: The Impact of the European Community on the Labour Law Systems of the Member Countries," *Comparative Labor Law Journal* 11 (1990): 403.

Blum, Albert, *A History of the American Labor Movement.* Washington, D.C.: American Historical Association, 1972.

Bok, Derek & John Dunlop, *Labor and the American Community.* New York: Simon & Schuster, 1970.

Bomers, G. B. J., *Multinational Corporations and Industrial Relations.* Assen, Netherlands: Van Gorcum, 1976.

Bonacich, Edna, "A Theory of Ethnic Antagonism: The Split Labor Market," *The American Working Class* (Irving Horowitz, John Leggett & Martin Oppenheimer, eds.) New Brunswick, N.J.: Transaction Books, 1979: 73.

Borhas, George, *Union Control of Pension Funds: Will the North Rise Again?* San Francisco: Institute for Contemporary Studies, 1979.

Bureau of National Affairs, *The Employment-at-Will Issue.* Washington, D.C.: Bureau of National Affairs, 1982.

Bureau of National Affairs, *Older Americans in the Workforce: Challenges and Solutions.* Washington, D.C.: Bureau of National Affairs, 1987.

Bureau of National Affairs, *Unions Today: New Tactics to Tackle Tough Times.* Washington, D.C.: Bureau of National Affairs, 1985.

Byron, Christopher, "An Attractive Japanese Export," *Time* (Mar. 2, 1981): 74.

Carnevale, Anthony & Harold Goldstein, "Schooling and Training for Work in America: An Overview," *New Developments in Worker Training: A Legacy for the 1990s* (Louis Ferman, Michele Hoyman, Joel Cutcher-Gershenfeld & Ernest Savoie, eds.) Madison, Wis.: Industrial Relations Research Association, 1990: 30.

Chaison, Gary & Joseph Rose, "The Macrodeterminants of Union Growth and Decline," *The State of the Unions* (George Strauss, Daniel Gallagher & Jack Fiorito, eds.) Madison, Wis.: Industrial Relations Research Association, 1991: 3.

Christensen, Thomas & Andrea Svanoe, "Motive and Intent in the Commission of Unfair Labor Practices," *Yale Law Journal* 77 (1968): 1269.

Clarke, Shaun, "Rethinking the Adversarial Model in Labor Relations: An Argument for Repeal of Section 8(a)(2)," *Yale Law Journal* 96 (1987): 2021.

Coates, Joseph, Jennifer Jarratt & John Mahaffie, "Future Work," *The Futurist* 25 (May–June 1991): 9.

Cohen, Sanford, *Labor in the United States*. Columbus, Ohio: Merrill Publishing, 5th ed. 1979.

Collingsworth, Terrence, "American Labor Policy and the International Economy: Clarifying Policies and Interests," *Boston College Law Review* 31 (1989): 31.

Commission on Workforce Quality and Labor Market Efficiency, *Investing In People*. Washington, D.C.: U.S. Department of Labor, 1989.

Comment, "An Economic and Legal Analysis of Union Representation of Corporate Boards of Directors," *University of Pennsylvania Law Review* 130 (1982): 919.

Comment, "The Saturnization of American Plants: Infringement or Expansion of Workers' Rights?" *Minnesota Law Review* 72 (1987): 173.

Comment, "Serving Two Masters: Union Representation on Corporate Boards of Directors," *Columbia Law Review* 81 (1981): 639.

Comment, "Subjects Included Within Management's Duty to Bargain Collectively," *Louisiana Law Review* 26 (1966): 630.

Commons, John & Associates, *History of Labor in the United States*. New York: Macmillan, 1918.

Conte, Michael & Arnold Tannenbaum, "Employee-Owned Companies: Is the Difference Measurable?" *Monthly Labor Review* 101 (July 1978): 23.

Cooper, Lyle, "The American Labor Movement in Prosperity and Depression," *American Economic Review* 22 (Dec. 1932): 641.

Cox, Archibald, "The Duty to Bargain in Good Faith," *Harvard Law Review* 71 (1958): 1401.

Cox, Archibald, "Labor and the Antitrust Laws: Pennington and Jewel Tea," *Boston University Law Review* 46 (1966): 317.

Cox, Robert, "Labor and the Multinationals," *Foreign Affairs* 54 (Jan. 1976): 344.

Cox, Robert, "Labor and Transnational Relations," *International Organization* 25 (1971): 554.

Crain, Marion, "Building Solidarity Through Expansion of NLRA Coverage: A Blueprint for Worker Empowerment," *Minnesota Law Review* 74 (1990): 953.

Crain, Marion, "Feminism, Labor, and Power," *Southern California Law Review* 65 (1992): 1819.

Crain, Marion, "Feminizing Unions: Challenging the Gendered Structure of Wage Labor," *Michigan Law Review* 89 (1991): 1155.

Craver, Charles, "The Application of the Age Discrimination in Employment Act to Persons Over Seventy," *George Washington Law Review* 58 (1989): 52.

Craver, Charles, "The Impact of Financial Crises Upon Collective Bargaining Relationships," *George Washington Law Review* 56 (1988): 465.

Craver, Charles, "The Inquisitorial Process in Private Employment," *Cornell Law Review* 63 (1977): 1.

Craver, Charles, "Public Sector Impasse Resolution Procedures," *Chicago-Kent Law Review* 60 (1984): 779.

Craver, Charles, "The Vitality of the American Labor Movement in the Twenty-First Century," *University of Illinois Law Review* 1983 (1983): 633.

Curme, Michael, Barry Hirsch & David MacPherson, "Union Membership and Contract Coverage in the United States, 1983–1988," *Industrial & Labor Relations Review* 44 (Oct. 1990): 5.

Curtin, William, "The Multinational Corporation and Transnational Collective Bargaining," *American Labor and the Multinational Corporation* (Duane Kujawa, ed.) New York: Praeger, 1973: 192.

Davies, Paul, "Employee Representation on Company Boards and Participation in Corporate Planning," *Modern Law Review* 38 (1975): 254.

Delaney, John, "The Future of Unions as Political Organizations," *Journal of Labor Research* 12 (Fall 1991): 373.

Delaney, John & Marick Masters, "Unions and Political Action," *The State of the Unions* (George Strauss, Daniel Gallagher & Jack Fiorito, eds.) Madison, Wis.: Industrial Relations Research Association, 1991: 313.

DeMott, Benjamin, *The Imperial Middle*. New York: William Morrow & Co., 1990.

Dolan, Brendan, "*Mackay Radio:* If It Isn't Broken, Don't Fix It," *University of San Francisco Law Review* 25 (1991): 313.

Dowling, Donald, "Worker Rights in the Post–1992 European Communities: What 'Social Europe' Means to United States–Based Multinational Employers," *Northwestern Journal of International Law and Business* 11 (1991): 564.

Doyle, Stephen, "Improving Productivity and Quality of Working Life: The U.S. Experience," *Worker Participation* (Hem Jain, ed.) New York: Praeger, 1980: 249.

Drucker, Peter, *The Unseen Revolution*. New York: Harper & Row, 1976.

Dulles, Foster & Melvyn Dubofsky, *Labor in America*. Arlington Heights, Ill.: Harlan Davidson, 1984.

Dunlop, John, "Past and Future Tendencies of American Labor Organizations," *Daedalus* (Winter 1978): 84.

Eccles, Tony, "Control in the Democratized Enterprise: The Case of KME," *The Control of Work* (John Purcell & Robin Smith, eds.) New York: Holmes & Meier, 1979: 156.

Edsall, Thomas, *The New Politics of Inequality*. New York: W. W. Norton, 1984.

Edwards, Harry, R. Theodore Clark & Charles Craver, *Labor Relations Law in the Public Sector*. Charlottesville, Va.: Michie Co., 4th ed. 1991.

Ehrenreich, Barbara, *Fear of Falling*. New York: Harper Perennial, 1990.

Ehrenreich, Barbara, *The Worst Years of Our Lives*. New York: Pantheon Books, 1990.

Elkouri, Frank & Edna Elkouri, *How Arbitration Works*. Washington, D.C.: Bureau of National Affairs, 1985.

Ferman, Louis, Michele Hoyman & Joel Cutcher-Gershenfeld, "Joint Union-Management Training Programs: A Synthesis in the Evolution of Jointism and Training," *New Developments in Worker Training: A Legacy for the 1990s* (Louis Ferman, Michele Hoyman, Joel Cutcher-Gershenfeld & Ernest Savoie, eds.) Madison, Wis.: Industrial Relations Research Association, 1990: 157.

Finkin, Matthew, "Labor Policy and the Enervation of the Economic Strike," *University of Illinois Law Review* 1990: 547.

Fiorito, Jack, Cynthia Gramm & Wallace Hendricks, "Union Structural Choices," *The State of the Unions* (George Strauss, Daniel Gallagher & Jack Fiorito, eds.) Madison, Wis.: Industrial Relations Research Association, 1991: 103.

Fischel, Daniel, "Labor Markets and Labor Law Compared with Capital Markets and Corporate Law," *University of Chicago Law Review* 51 (1984): 1061.

Fischl, Richard, "Self, Others, and Section 7: Mutualism and Protected Protest Activities Under the National Labor Relations Act," *Columbia Law Review* 89 (1989): 789.

Flanagan, Robert & Arnold Weber, *Bargaining Without Boundaries*. Chicago: University of Chicago Press, 1974.

Foner, Philip, *Women and the American Labor Movement*. New York: Free Press, 1982.

Forbath, William, "The Shaping of the American Labor Movement," *Harvard Law Review* 102 (1989): 1109.

Forsey, Eugene, "Trade Unions in 2020?" *Visions 2020* (Stephen Clarkson ed.) Edmonton: M. G. Hurtig, 1970: 94.

Frankfurter, Felix & Nathan Greene, *The Labor Injunction*. New York: Macmillan, 1930.

Freeman, Richard, "Why Are Unions Faring Poorly in NLRB Representation Elections?" *Challenges and Choices Facing American Labor* (Thomas Kochan, ed.) Cambridge: MIT Press, 1985: 45.

Freeman, Richard & James Medoff, *What Do Unions Do?* New York: Basic Books, 1984.

Fried, Charles, "Individual and Collective Rights in Work Relations: Reflections on the Current State of Labor Law and Its Prospects," *University of Chicago Law Review* 51 (1984): 1012.

Fuentes, Annette & Barbara Ehrenreich, *Women in the Global Factory*. Boston: South End Press, 1983.

Fullerton, Howard, "The 1995 Labor Force: A First Look," *Monthly Labor Review* 103 (Dec. 1980): 11.

Furlong, James, *Labor in the Boardroom*. Princeton, N.J.: Dow Jones Books, 1977.

Galbraith, John, *The New Industrial State*. Boston: Houghton Mifflin, 1971.

Gallagher, Daniel & George Strauss, "Union Membership Attitudes and Participation," *The State of the Unions* (George Strauss, Daniel Gallagher & Jack Fiorito, eds.) Madison, Wis.: Industrial Relations Research Association, 1991: 139.

Gappert, Gary, "Post-Affluence: The Turbulent Transition to a Post-Industrial Society," *Futurist* 8 (Oct. 1974): 212.

Gatty, Bob, "Where Unions Are Headed," *Nations Business* (Dec. 1979): 25.

Geoghegan, Thomas, *Which Side Are You On?* New York: Farrar, Straus & Giroux, 1991.

Getman, Julius, "Ruminations on Union Organizing in the Private Sector," *University of Chicago Law Review* 53 (1986): 45.

Getman, Julius, Stephen Goldberg & Jeanne Herman, *Union Representation Elections: Law and Reality*. New York: Russell Sage Foundation, 1976.

Giddens, Anthony, *The Class Structure of the Advanced Societies*. New York: Barnes & Noble, 1973.

Goble, George, "The Non-Stoppage Strike," *Labor Law Journal* 2 (1951): 105.

Goldberg, Roberta, *Organizing Women Office Workers*. New York: Praeger, 1983.

Goldberg, Stephen, "Coordinated Bargaining Tactics of Unions," *Cornell Law Review* 54 (1969): 897.

Goldfield, Michael, *The Decline of Organized Labor in the United States*. Chicago: University of Chicago Press, 1987.

Goldfinger, Nathaniel, "An American Trade Union View of International Trade and Investment," *American Labor and the Multinational Corporation* (Duane Kujawa ed.) New York: Praeger, 1973: 28.

Gompers, Samuel, "The Charter of Industrial Freedom," *American Federationist* 21 (1914): 957.

Gompers, Samuel, "Judicial Vindication of Labor's Claims," *American Federationist* 7 (1901): 284.

Gompers, Samuel, *Seventy Years of Life and Labor.* New York: E. P. Dutton, 1925.

Gorman, Robert, *Labor Law: Basic Text.* St. Paul: West Publishing, 1976.

Gould, William, *Black Workers in White Unions: Job Discrimination in the United States.* Ithaca: Cornell University Press, 1977.

Gray, Lois & Joyce Kornbluh, "New Directions in Labor Education," *New Developments in Worker Training: A Legacy for the 1990s* (Louis Ferman, Michele Hoyman, Joel Cutcher-Gershenfeld & Ernest Savoie, eds.) Madison, Wis.: Industrial Relations Research Association, 1990: 95.

Green, Gil, *What's Happening to Labor.* New York: International Publishers, 1976.

Gunter, Hans, "Erosion of Trade Union Power Through Multinational Enterprises," *Vanderbilt Journal of Transnational Law* 9 (1976): 771.

Gurdon, Michael, "An American Approach to Self-Management," *Worker Participation* (Hem Jain, ed.) New York: Praeger, 1980: 295.

Hamermesh, Daniel & Albert Rees, *The Economics of Work and Pay.* New York: Harper & Row, 4th ed. 1988.

Hardbeck, George, "Unionism Again at a Crossroads," *Critical Issues in Labor* (Max Wortman, Jr., ed.) New York: Macmillan, 1969: 65.

Hartfiel, Günter, "Germany," *White-Collar Trade Unions* (Adolph Sturmthal, ed.) Urbana, Ill.: University of Illinois Press, 1966: 127.

Heckscher, Charles, *The New Unionism: Employee Involvement in the Changing Corporation.* New York: Basic Books, 1988.

Herz, Diane, "Employment Characteristics of Older Women," *Monthly Labor Review* 111 (Sept. 1988): 3.

Hildebrand, George, *American Unionism: An Historical and Analytical Survey.* Reading, Mass.: Addison-Wesley, 1979.

Hilton, Margaret, "Shared Training: Learning from Germany," *Monthly Labor Review* 114 (Mar. 1991): 33.

Horowitz, Irving, John Leggett & Martin Oppenheimer, *The American Working Class.* New Brunswick, N.J.: Transaction Books, 1979.

Hyde, Alan, "Democracy in Collective Bargaining," *Yale Law Journal* 93 (1984): 793.

International Labour Office, *Employment Effects of Multinational Enterprises in Industrial Countries.* Geneva: International Labour Office, 1981.

International Labour Office, *Multinational Enterprises and Social Policy.* Geneva: International Labour Office, 1973.

Jacobs, Antoine, "The Netherlands and the Social Dimension of the Single European Market," *Comparative Labor Law Journal* 11 (1990): 462.

Jacobs, Paul, *Old Before Its Time: Collective Bargaining at 28.* Santa Barbara, Cal.: Center for the Study of Democratic Institutions, 1963.

Jacoby, Robin, "The Women's Trade Union League Training School for Women Organizers, 1914–1926," *Sisterhood and Solidarity* (Joyce Kornbluh & Mary Frederickson, eds.) Philadelphia: Temple University Press, 1984: 1.

Jain, Hem, *Worker Participation.* New York: Praeger, 1980.

Jarley, Paul & Jack Fiorito, "Unionism and Changing Employee Views Toward Work," *Journal of Labor Research* 12 (1991): 223.

Jelin, Elizabeth, "The Concept of Working-Class Embourgeoisement," *The American Working Class* (Irving Horowitz, John Leggett & Martin Oppenheimer, eds.) New Brunswick, N.J.: Transaction Books, 1979: 246.

Johnston, William & Arnold Packer, *Workforce 2000.* Indianapolis: Hudson Institute, 1987.

Jones, Ethel, "Private Sector Union Decline and Structural Employment Change, 1970–1988," *Journal of Labor Research* 13 (1992): 257.

Jordan, James, "Trends in the Work Force: Individualism, Inflation, and Productivity," *Working in the Twenty-First Century.* (C. Stewart Shepard & Donald Carroll, eds.) New York: John Wiley, 1980: 69.

Kaiser, W. Michael, "Labor's New Weapon: Pension Fund Leverage—Can Labor Legally Beat Its Plowshares into Swords?" *Rutgers Law Review* 34 (1982): 409.

Karier, Thomas, "Unions and the U.S. Comparative Advantage," *Industrial Relations* 30 (Winter 1991): 1.

Kassalow, Everett, *Trade Unions and Industrial Relations: An International Comparison.* New York: Random House, 1969.

Kassalow, Everett, "White-Collar Unionism in the United States," *White-Collar Trade Unions* (Adolph Sturmthal, ed.) Urbana, Ill.: University of Illinois Press, 1966: 362.

Keefe, Jeffrey, "Do Unions Influence the Diffusion of Technology?" *Industrial & Labor Relations Review* 44 (1991): 261.

Kessler-Harris, Alice, "Education in Working-Class Solidarity: The Summer School for Office Workers," *Sisterhood and Solidarity* (Joyce Kornbluh & Mary Frederickson, eds.) Philadelphia: Temple University Press, 1984: 223.

Kessler-Harris, Alice, *Out to Work.* New York: Oxford University Press, 1982.

Klare, Karl, "Workplace Democracy & Market Reconstruction: An Agenda for Legal Reform," *Catholic University Law Review* 38 (1988): 1.

Kochan, Thomas, Harry Katz & Nancy Mower, "Worker Participation and American Unions," *Challenges and Choices Facing American Labor* (Thomas Kochan, ed.) Cambridge: MIT Press, 1985: 271.

Kochan, Thomas, Harry Katz & Robert McKersie, *The Transformation of American Industrial Relations.* New York: Basic Books, 1986.

Kochan, Thomas & Kirsten Wever, "American Unions and the Future of Worker Representation," *The State of the Unions* (George Strauss, Daniel Gallagher & Jack Fiorito, eds.) Madison, Wis.: Industrial Relations Research Assn., 1991: 363.

Kohler, Thomas, "Models of Worker Participation: The Uncertain Significance of Section 8(a)(2)," *Boston College Law Review* 27 (1986): 499.

Kornbluh, Joyce & Mary Frederickson, *Sisterhood and Solidarity.* Philadelphia: Temple University Press, 1984.

Kosolapov, Viktor, *Mankind and the Year 2000.* Moscow: Progress, 1976.

Kraw, George, "The Community Charter of the Fundamental Social Rights of Workers," *Hastings International and Comparative Law Review* 13 (1990): 467.

Kujawa, Duane, *American Labor and the Multinational Corporation.* New York: Praeger, 1973.

Kutscher, Ronald & Valerie Personick, "Deindustrialization and the Shift to Services," *Monthly Labor Review* 109 (June 1986): 3.

LaLonde, Robert & Bernard Meltzer, "Hard Times for Unions: Another Look at the Significance of Employer Illegalities," *University of Chicago Law Review* 58 (1991): 953.

LeRoy, Michael, "Multivariate Analysis of Unionized Employees' Propensity to Cross Their Union's Picket Line," *Journal of Labor Research* 13 (1992): 285.

Levine, Solomon, "Unionization of White-Collar Employees in Japan," *White-Collar Trade Unions* (Adolph Sturmthal, ed.) Urbana, Ill.: University of Illinois Press, 1966: 205.

Levinson, Charles, *International Trade Unionism.* London: Allen & Unwin, 1972.

Levitan, Sar & Clifford Johnson, "Labor and Management: The Illusion of Cooperation," *Harvard Business Review* 61 (Sept.–Oct. 1983): 3.

Levitan, Sar & Diane Werneke, "Worker Participation and Productivity Change," *Monthly Labor Review* 107 (Sept. 1984): 28.

Levitan, Sar & Frank Gallo, "Can Employee Associations Negotiate New Growth?" *Monthly Labor Review* 112 (July 1989): 5.

Levitan, Sar & Frank Gallo, "Collective Bargaining and Private Sector Professionals," *Monthly Labor Review* 112 (Sept. 1989): 24.

Levitan, Sar & Frank Gallo, "Uncle Sam's Helping Hand: Educating, Training, and Employing the Disadvantaged," *New Developments in Worker Training: A Legacy for the 1990s* (Louis Ferman, Michele Hoyman, Joel Cutcher-Gershenfeld & Ernest Savoie, eds.) Madison, Wis.: Industrial Relations Research Association, 1990: 226.

Lipset, Seymour, "White Collar Workers and Professionals—Their Attitudes and Behavior Towards Unions," *Readings in Industrial Sociology* (William Faunce, ed.) New York: Appleton-Century-Crofts, 1967: 525.

Long, Richard, "The Effects of Employee Ownership on Organizational Identification, Employee Job Attitudes, and Organizational Performance: A Tentative Framework and Empirical Findings," *Human Relations* 31 (1978): 29.

Mann, Michael, *Consciousness and Action Among the Western Working Class.* Atlantic Highlands, N.J.: Humanities Press, 1973.

Marshall, F. Ray, "The Future of the American Labor Movement: The Role of Federal Law," *Chicago-Kent Law Review* 57 (1981): 521.

Marshall, F. Ray, *The Negro and Organized Labor.* New York: John Wiley, 1965.

Marshall, Howard & Natalie Marshall, "Nonstoppage Strike Proposals—A Critique," *Labor Law Journal* 7 (1956): 299.

McCalmont, David, "The Semi-Strike," *Industrial & Labor Relations Review* 15 (1962): 191.

McConnell, Sheena, "Cyclical Fluctuations in Strike Activity," *Industrial & Labor Relations Review* 44 (Oct. 1990): 130.

McCormick, Robert, "Union Representatives as Corporate Directors: The Challenge to the Adversarial Model of Labor Relations," *University of Michigan Journal of Law Reform* 15 (1982): 219.

McElrath, Roger & Richard Rowan, "The American Labor Movement and Employee Ownership: Objections to and Uses of Employee Stock Ownership Plans," *Journal of Labor Research* 13 (Winter 1992): 99.

Medoff, James, "AFL-CIO Study on Public Image of Unions," *Daily Labor Report* (B.N.A.) 247 (Dec. 24, 1984): D–2.

Meltzer, Bernard, "Labor Unions, Collective Bargaining, and the Antitrust Laws," *University of Chicago Law Review* 32 (1965): 659.

Miller, Ronald, "Collective Bargaining in Financial Institutions," *Employee Relations Law Journal* 7 (1981–82): 389.

Mills, C. Wright, *White Collar.* New York: Oxford University Press, 1951.

Mire, Joseph, "Trade Unions and Worker Participation in Management," *The Quality of Working Life, Volume One: Problems, Prospects and the State of the Art* (Louis Davis, Albert Cherms & Associates, eds.) New York: Free Press, 1975: 416.

Mishel, Lawrence & Paula Voos, *Unions and Economic Competitiveness.* Armonk, N.Y.: M. E. Sharpe, 1992.

Mitter, Swasti, *Common Fate, Common Bond.* Oxford: Pluto Press, 1986.

Montgomery, David, *The Fall of the House of Labor*. New York: Cambridge University Press, 1987.

Morris, Charles, *The Developing Labor Law*. Washington, D.C.: Bureau of National Affairs, 2d ed. 1983.

Morris, Charles, "NLRB Protection in the Nonunion Workplace: A Glimpse at a General Theory of Section 7 Conduct," *University of Pennsylvania Law Review* 137 (1989): 1673.

Morris, Richard, *Government and Labor in Early America*. New York: Columbia University Press, 1946.

Morrison, Peter, "Beyond the Baby Boom," *Futurist* 13 (Apr. 1979): 133.

Murphy, Michael, "Workers on the Board: Borrowing a European Idea," *Labor Law Journal* 27 (1976): 751.

National Center for Productivity & Quality of Working Life, *Recent Initiatives in Labor-Management Cooperation*. Washington, D.C.: National Center for Productivity & Quality of Working Life, 1976.

National Labor Relations Board, *NLRB: The First 50 Years*. Washington, D.C.: National Labor Relations Board, 1985.

Nelles, Walter, "Commonwealth v. Hunt," *Columbia Law Review* 32 (1932): 1128.

Nilstein, Arne, "White-Collar Unionism in Sweden," *White-Collar Trade Unions* (Adolph Sturmthal, ed.) Urbana, Ill.: University of Illinois Press, 1966: 261.

Northrup, Herbert, "Why Multinational Bargaining Neither Exists Nor Is Desirable," *Labor Law Journal* 29 (1978): 330.

Northrup, Herbert & Richard Rowan, *Multinational Collective Bargaining Attempts*. Philadelphia: Industrial Research Unit, Wharton School, University of Pennsylvania, 1979.

Note, "Alternatives to the United States System of Labor Relations: A Comparative Analysis of the Labor Relations Systems in the Federal Republic of Germany, Japan, and Sweden," *Vanderbilt Law Review* 41 (1988): 627.

Note, "Employee Stock Ownership Plans: A Step Toward Democratic Capitalism," *Boston University Law Review* 55 (1975): 195.

Note, "Finding a Voice Through the Union: The Harvard Union of Clerical and Technical Workers and Women Workers," *Harvard Women's Journal* 12 (1989): 260.

Note, "The Future of Labor-Management Cooperative Efforts Under Section 8(a)(2) of the National Labor Relations Act," *Vanderbilt Law Review* 41 (1988): 545.

Note, "Nonmajority Bargaining Orders: The Only Effective Remedy for Pervasive Employer Unfair Labor Practices During Union Organizing Campaigns," *Journal of Law Reform* 20 (1987): 617.

Note, "The Vredling Directive: The EEC's Failed Attempt to Regulate Multinational Enterprises and Organize Collective Bargaining," *Journal of International Law and Politics* 20 (1988): 967.

Note, "Worker Ownership and Section 8(a)(2) of the National Labor Relations Act," *Yale Law Journal* 91 (1982): 615.

Oberer, Walter, "The Scienter Factor in Sections 8(a)(1) and (3) of the Labor Act: Of Balancing Hostile Motive, Dogs, and Tails," *Cornell Law Quarterly* 52 (1967): 491.

Olson, Craig & Brian Becker, "The Effects of the NLRA on Stockholder Wealth in the 1930s," *Industrial & Labor Relations Review* 44 (Oct. 1990): 116.

Olson, Deborah, "Union Experiences with Worker Ownership: Legal and Practical Issues Raised by ESOPS, TRASOPS, Stock Purchases and Co-operatives," *Wisconsin Law Review* 1982 (1982): 729.

O'Neill, Gerard, *2081*. New York: Simon & Schuster, 1981.

Oppenheimer, Martin, "What is the New Working Class?" *The American Working Class* (Irving Horowitz, John Leggett & Martin Oppenheimer, eds.) New Brunswick, N.J.: Transaction Books, 1979: 151.

Organization for Economic Cooperation and Development, *Workers Participation*. Paris: Organization for Economic Cooperation and Development, 1975.

Osterman, Paul, "Elements of a National Training Policy," *New Developments in Worker Training: A Legacy for the 1990s* (Louis Ferman, Michele Hoyman, Joel Cutcher-Gershenfeld & Ernest Savoie, eds.) Madison, Wis.: Industrial Relations Research Association, 1990: 257.

O'Toole, James, "The Uneven Record of Employee Ownership," *Harvard Business Review* 57 (Nov.–Dec. 1979): 185.

O'Toole, James, *Work, Learning, and the American Future*. San Francisco: Jossey-Bass, 1977.

Ottervanger, Tom & Ralph Pais, "Employee Participation in Corporate Decision Making: The Dutch Model," *International Law* 15 (1981): 393.

Pascoe, Thomas & Richard Collins, "UAW-Ford Employee Development and Training Program: Overview of Operations and Structure," *Labor Law Journal* 36 (1985): 519.

Peck, Cornelius, "Unjust Discharges From Employment: A Necessary Change in the Law," *Ohio State Law Journal* 40 (1979): 1.

Perlman, Selig, *A History of Trade Unionism in the United States*. New York: Macmillan, 1935.

Perlman, Selig & Philip Taft, *History of Labor in the United States, 1896–1932*. New York: Macmillan, 1935.

Piore, Michael, "The Future of Unions," *The State of the Unions* (George Strauss, Daniel Gallagher & Jack Fiorito, eds.) Madison, Wis.: Industrial Relations Research Association, 1991: 387.

Pollitt, Daniel, "*Mackay Radio*: Turn It Off, Tune It Out," *University of San Francisco Law Review* 25 (1991): 295.

Poole, Michael, *Workers' Participation in Industry*. Boston: Routledge & K. Paul, 1975.

Pope, James, "Labor-Community Coalitions and Boycotts: The Old Labor Law, the New Unionism, and the Living Constitution," *Texas Law Review* 69 (1991): 889.

Rabban, David, "Can American Labor Law Accommodate Collective Bargaining by Professional Employees?" *Yale Law Journal* 99 (1990): 689.

Rabban, David, "Distinguishing Excluded Managers From Covered Professionals Under the NLRA," *Columbia Law Review* 89 (1989): 1775.

Rabban, David, "Is Unionism Compatible with Professionalism?" *Industrial & Labor Relations Review* 45 (Oct. 1991): 97.

Rabenowitz, Sigvard, "Experiences of Autonomous Working Groups in a Swedish Car Factory," *Worker Participation* (Hem Jain, ed.) New York: Praeger, 1980: 224.

Rabin, Robert, "The Role of Unions in the Rights-Based Workplace," *University of San Francisco Law Review* 25 (1991): 169.

Radice, Giles, *The Industrial Democrats*. Boston: Allen & Unwin, 1978.

Raphael, Edna, "Working Women and Their Membership in Labor Unions," *The American Working Class* (Irving Horowitz, John Leggett & Martin Oppenheimer, eds.) New Brunswick, N.J.: Transaction Books, 1979: 114.

Raskin, A. H., "A Reporter at Large," *New Yorker* (Aug. 25, 1980): 36.

Raskin, A. H., "Toward a More Participative Work Force," *Working in the Twenty-*

First Century (Stewart Shepard & Donald Carroll, eds.) New York: John Wiley, 1980: 97.

Rees, Albert, *The Economics of Trade Unions*. Chicago: University of Chicago Press, 1977.

Rees, Albert, "The Size of Union Membership in Manufacturing in the 1980s," *The Shrinking Perimeter* (Hervey Juris & Myron Roomkin, eds.) Lexington, Mass.: Lexington Books, 1980: 50.

Reich, Robert, "Who Is Us?" *Harvard Business Review* 68 (Jan.–Feb. 1990): 53.

Reich, Robert, *The Work of Nations*. New York: Alfred Knopf, 1991.

Richardi, Richard, "Worker Participation in Decisions Within Undertakings in the Federal Republic of Germany," *Comparative Labor Law* 5 (1982): 23.

Rifkin, Jeremy & Randy Barber, *The North Will Rise Again*. Boston: Beacon Press, 1978.

Roberts, Ernie, *Workers' Control*. London: Allen & Unwin, 1973.

Rosow, Jerome, "International Relations and the Multinational Corporation: The Management Approach," *Bargaining Without Boundaries* (Robert Flanagan & Arnold Weber, eds.) Chicago: University of Chicago Press, 1974: 147.

Rothstein, Lawrence, *Plant Closings*. Dover, Mass.: Auburn House, 1986.

Rothstein, Mark, "Workplace Drug Testing: A Case Study in the Misapplication of Technology," *Harvard Journal of Law & Technology* 5 (1991): 65.

Routh, Guy, "White-Collar Unions in the United Kingdom," *White-Collar Trade Unions* (Adolph Sturmthal, ed.) Urbana, Ill.: University of Illinois Press, 1966, 165.

Ruben, George, "Organized Labor in 1981: A Shifting of Priorities," *Monthly Labor Review* 105 (Jan. 1982): 21.

Ruttenberg, Stanley, "The Union View of Multinationals: An Interpretation," *Bargaining Without Boundaries* (Robert Flanagan & Arnold Weber, eds.) Chicago: University of Chicago Press, 1974: 179.

Ryan, William, *Blaming the Victim*. New York: Vintage Books, 1976.

Schmidman, John, *Unions in Postindustrial Society*. University Park: Pennsylvania State University Press, 1979.

Schrank, Robert, "Are Unions an Anachronism?" *Harvard Business Review* 57 (Sept.– Oct. 1979): 107.

Shister, Julius, "The Outlook for Union Growth," *The Annals* 350 (1963): 56.

Shostak, Arthur, *Robust Unionism*. Ithaca, N.Y.: ILR Press, 1991.

Smith, Stephen, "National Labor Unions v. Multinational Companies: The Dilemma of Unequal Bargaining Power," *Columbia Journal of Transnational Law* 11 (1972): 124.

Sockell, Donna, "The Future of Labor Law: A Mismatch Between Statutory Interpretation and Industrial Reality?" *Boston College Law Review* 30 (1989): 987.

Soldon, Norbert, *The World of Women's Trade Unionism*. Westport, Conn.: Greenwood Press, 1985.

Specter, Howard & Matthew Finkin, *Individual Employment Law and Litigation*. Charlottesville, Va.: Michie Co., 1989.

St. Antoine, Theodore, "A Seed Germinates: Unjust Discharge Reform Heads Toward Full Flower," *Nebraska Law Review* 67 (1988): 56.

Stephenson, Hugh, *The Coming Clash*. New York: Saturday Review Press, 1972.

Steuer, Richard, "Employee Representation on the Board: Industrial Democracy or Interlocking Directorate?" *Columbia Journal on Transnational Law* 16 (1977): 255.

Stieber, Jack, "Recent Developments in Employment-at-Will," *Labor Law Journal* 36 (1985): 558.

Stone, Katherine, "Labor and the Corporate Structure: Changing Conceptions and Emerging Possibilities," *University of Chicago Law Review* 55 (1988): 73.

Stone, Katherine, "The Post-War Paradigm in American Labor Law," *Yale Law Journal* 90 (1981): 1509.

Strauss, George, "Quality of Worklife and Participation as Bargaining Issues," *The Shrinking Perimeter* (Hervey Juris & Myron Roomkin, eds.) Lexington, Mass.: Lexington Books, 1980: 121.

Strauss, George, Daniel Gallagher & Jack Fiorito, *The State of the Unions.* Madison, Wis.: Industrial Relations Research Association, 1991.

Sturmthal, Adolf, *White-Collar Trade Unions.* Urbana, Ill.: University of Illinois Press, 1966.

Summers, Clyde, "Industrial Democracy: America's Unfulfilled Promise," *Cleveland State Law Review* 28 (1979): 29.

Summers, Clyde, "Past Premises, Present Failures, and Future Needs in Labor Legislation," *Buffalo Law Review* 31 (1982): 9.

Summers, Clyde, "Worker Participation in the U.S. and West Germany: A Comparative Study from an American Perspective," *American Journal of Comparative Law* 28 (1980): 367.

Taft, Philip, *Organized Labor in American History.* New York: Harper & Row, 1964.

Takezawa, Shin-ichi, "The Quality of Working Life: The Japanese Experience," *Worker Participation* (Hem Jain, ed.) New York: Praeger, 1980: 233.

Tannenbaum, Frank, "The Survival of the Fittest," *Columbia Journal of World Business* 3 (Mar.–Apr. 1968): 13.

Tocqueville, Alexis de, *Democracy in America.* (Phillips Bradley ed.) New York: Alfred Knopf, 1945.

Toffler, Alvin, *Power Shift.* New York: Bantam Books, 1990.

Toffler, Alvin, *The Third Wave.* New York: William Morrow, 1980.

Tolan, Sandy, "Hope and Heartbreak," *New York Times Magazine* (July 1, 1990): 16.

Treu, Tiziano, "European Unification and Italian Labor Relations," *Comparative Labor Law Journal* 11 (1990): 441.

Turner, Louis, *Invisible Empires: Multinational Companies and the Modern World.* New York: Harcourt Brace Jovanovich, 1970.

Tyler, Gus, *The Labor Revolution.* New York: Viking Press, 1967.

Ulman, Lloyd, "Multinational Unionism: Incentives, Barriers, and Alternatives," *Industrial Relations* 14 (1975): 1.

Ulman, Lloyd, *The Rise of the National Trade Union.* Cambridge: Harvard University Press, 1955.

United States Department of Labor, *Employment in Perspective: Women in the Labor Force* (First Quarter 1990).

United States Department of Labor, *Time and Change: 1983 Handbook on Women Workers.* Washington, D.C.: U.S. Government Printing Office, 1983.

United States Department of Labor, *U.S. Labor Law and the Future of Labor-Management Cooperation* (Bureau of Labor-Management Relations Report 104, 1986).

United States Department of Labor, *U.S. Labor Law and the Future of Labor-Management Cooperation* (Bureau of Labor-Management Relations Report 113, 1987).

Van Raaphorst, Donna, *Union Maids Not Wanted: Organizing Domestic Workers, 1870–1940*. New York: Praeger, 1988.

Vaughn, Lea, "Article XX of the AFL-CIO Constitution: Managing and Resolving Inter-Union Disputes," *Wayne Law Review* 37 (1990): 1.

Verma, Anil & Thomas Kochan, "The Growth and Nature of the Nonunion Sector Within a Firm," *Challenges and Choices Facing American Labor* (Thomas Kochan ed.) Cambridge: MIT Press, 1985: 101.

Walker, K. F., "White-Collar Unionism in Australia," *White-Collar Trade Unions* (Adolph Sturmthal, ed.) Urbana, Ill.: University of Illinois Press, 1966: 1.

Weil, David, "Enforcing OSHA: The Role of Labor Unions," *Industrial Relations* 30 (1991): 20.

Weiler, Paul, *Governing the Workplace*. Cambridge: Harvard University Press, 1990.

Weiler, Paul, "Hard Times for Unions: Challenging Times for Scholars," *University of Chicago Law Review*, 58 (1991): 1015.

Weiler, Paul, "Milestone or Millstone: The Wagner Act at Fifty" *Arbitration 1985: Law and Practice*. (Walter Gershenfeld ed.) Washington, D.C.: Bureau of National Affairs, 1986: 40.

Weiler, Paul, "Promises to Keep: Securing Workers' Rights to Self-Organization Under the NLRA," *Harvard Law Review* 96 (1983): 1769.

Weiler, Paul, "Striking a New Balance: Freedom of Contract and the Prospects for Union Representation," *Harvard Law Review* 98 (1984): 351.

Weiss, Manfred, "Labor Law and Industrial Relations in Europe 1992: A German Perspective," *Comparative Labor Law Journal* 11 (1990): 411.

Wheeler, Hoyt & John McClendon, "The Individual Decision to Unionize," *The State of the Unions* (George Strauss, Daniel Gallagher & Jack Fiorito, eds.) Madison, Wis.: Industrial Relations Research Association, 1991: 47.

Whyte, William, "Organizations for the Future," *The Next Twenty-Five Years of Industrial Relations* (Gerald Somers, ed.) Madison, Wis.: Industrial Relations Research Association, 1973: 132.

Wiedemann, Herbert, "Codetermination by Workers in German Enterprises," *American Journal of Comparative Law* 28 (1980): 79.

Willborn, Steven, "Industrial Democracy and the National Labor Relations Act: A Preliminary Inquiry," *Boston College Law Review* 25 (1984): 725.

Windmuller, John, "International Trade Union Organizations: Structure, Functions, Limitations," *International Labor* (Solomon Barkin, ed.) New York: Harper & Row, 1967: 82.

Wolkinson, Benjamin, "The Remedial Efficacy of NLRB Remedies in *Joy Silk* Cases," *Cornell Law Review* 55 (1969): 1.

Yankelovich, Daniel, *New Rules*. New York: Bantam, 1982.

Zakson, Laurence, "Worker Participation: Industrial Democracy and Managerial Prerogative in the Federal Republic of Germany, Sweden and the United States," *Hastings International & Comparative Law Review* 8 (1984): 93.

Zanglein, Jayne, "Pensions, Proxies and Power: Recent Developments in the Use of Proxy Voting to Influence Corporate Governance," *Labor Lawyer* 7 (1991): 771.

Zwerdling, Daniel, *Workplace Democracy*. New York: Harper & Row, 1980.

TABLE OF CASES

INDEX